The PLO
The Struggle Within

Alain Gresh

To Issam Sartawi and Henri Curiel
who died that the Palestinian and Israeli
peoples might live in peace.

The PLO
The Struggle Within

Towards an Independent Palestinian State

(revised and updated edition)

Alain Gresh

Translated by A.M. Berrett

with a Preface by Maxime Rodinson

Zed Books Ltd.
London and New Jersey

The PLO: The Struggle Within (revised and updated edition) was first
published by Zed Books Ltd, 57 Caledonian Road, London N1 9BU, UK, and
171 First Avenue, Atlantic Highlands, New Jersey 07716, USA, in 1988.
The first edition was published in English by Zed Books Ltd in 1985.
Originally published in French by S.P.A.G./Papyrus, 39 Boulevard
Magenta, 75010 Paris, France, in 1983.

Cover designed by Andrew Corbett.
Typeset by Composer Typesetting, Bath
and Marsh Typesetting, Cornwall.
Printed and bound in the United Kingdom
at The Bath Press, Avon.

British Library Cataloguing in Publication Data

Gresh, Alain
  The PLO: the struggle within: towards an
  independent Palestinian state.
  — Rev. and updated ed.
  1. Palestine Liberation Organization — History
  I. Title   II. OLP *English*
  322.4'2'095694   DS119.7

  ISBN 0-86232-754-7
  ISBN 0-86232-755-5 Pbk

Contents

Chronology

1967
5 June: Israel attacks Egypt and Syria. Six-Day War.
22 November: The UN Security Council adopts Resolution 242.
December: Shukairy resigns from the chairmanship of the PLO.

1968
21 March: Battle of Karameh, in Jordan, between the fedayeen and the Israeli army.
10-17 July: Fourth session of the PNC. Adoption of the new national covenant and rejection of Resolution 242.
November: Ahmed Jibril leaves the PFLP and sets up the PFLP-CG.
    First serious crisis between King Hussein and the Palestinian commandos.
    The commandos begin to establish themselves in Lebanon.
28 December: Israeli raid on Beirut International Airport.

1969
1 January: Fatah statement calling for the creation of a democratic Palestine.
1-4 February: 5th PNC in Cairo. The fedayeen take control of the PLO and Yasser Arafat becomes chairman of the Executive Committee.
February: Serious clashes within the PFLP. Naif Hawatmeh leaves the organization and sets up the PDFLP.
Spring: First clash between the fedayeen and the Lebanese government.
April: The Iraqi Ba'ath sets up the Arab Liberation Front (ALF).
May: First heavy Israeli attacks on the Palestinians in Lebanon.
20 October-6 November: Renewed clashes between the PLO and Lebanese troops. Signing of secret Cairo agreements setting out the conditions for the Palestinian presence in Lebanon.

1970
February: Clashes between the Palestinian Resistance and the Jordanian government.
    Yasser Arafat's first official visit to Moscow.
June: New crisis between the Jordanians and Palestinians.

July: Nasser and Hussein accept the 'Rogers plan'. The PLO rejects it.
August: Suleiman Franjieh elected President of Lebanon.
September: Attempted assassination of King Hussein. PFLP hijacks airplanes to Zarka airport in Jordan.
        Violent clashes between the Resistance and the Jordanian army; the latter gets the upper hand but the clashes cause thousands of victims ("Black September"). On 27 an agreement is signed in Cairo between Hussein, Arafat and Nasser. The Raïs dies the following day.

1971

28 February–5 March: The 8th PNC adopts the slogan of a democratic state.
April: The Fedayeen are expelled from Amman.
July: During the 9th PNC held in Cairo, the PLO is finally expelled from Jordan.
Summer: General Sharon brutally puts down the armed resistance in Gaza.
28 November: The Palestinian organization 'Black September' assassinates the Jordanian Prime Minister and thus launches Fatah into international terrorism.

1972

February: The Tashal occupies several Lebanese villages for a few days.
15 March: King Hussein announces his plan for a United Arab Kingdom, which is rejected by the PLO.
28 March and 2 May: Municipal elections in the West Bank. Heavy turn-out despite PLO calls for a boycott.
July: Soviet military experts expelled from Egypt.
5–6 September: 'Black September' takes several members of the Israeli Olympic team hostage in Munich—11 Israelis and 5 Palestinians killed.
28 September: Sadat's call for the creation of a Palestinian government-in-exile.

1973

6–12 January: 11th session of the PNC. It is decided to set up a National Front in the occupied territories.
10 April: Israeli raid on the centre of Beirut; assassination of 3 major leaders of Fatah and the PLO.
April–May: Clashes in Lebanon between the army and the fedayeen.
15 August: Creation of the Palestine National Front in the West Bank.
September: The non-aligned summit in Algiers recognizes the PLO as the sole representative of the Palestinian people.
6 October: Joint attack by Syrian and Egyptian forces against Israeli troops. Beginning of the 'October War'.
22 October: The Security Council adopts Resolution 338 reaffirming the need to implement Resolution 242.
26–28 November: Arab summit in Algiers, which recognizes the PLO as the sole representative of the Palestinians. The Jordanian delegation expresses

reservations.

21 December: Opening of the Geneva conference under the co-chairmanship of the USSR and the USA. Syria and the PLO are not represented.

31 December: The Labour coalition in Israel loses votes in the Knesset elections, but retains power.

1974

January: First Israeli-Egyptian disengagement agreement on Sinai.

February: The Islamic Conference Organization summit recognizes the PLO as the sole representative of the Palestinians.

31 May: Israeli-Syrian disengagement agreement on the Golan Heights.

1-9 June: 12th PNC in Cairo. For the first time the PLO agrees to intermediate stages.

30 July-3 August: Yasser Arafat visits the USSR at the invitation, for the first time, of the Soviet government. The USSR recognizes the PLO as the sole representative of the Palestinians.

14 October: By 105 votes to 4 the UN General Assembly invites the PLO to take part in its debates.

26-29 October: Arab summit in Algiers. Jordan joins in recognizing the PLO.

13 November: Yasser Arafat addresses the UN General Assembly.

22 November: The UN General Assembly recognizes 'the right of the Palestinian people to sovereignty and national independence' and invites the PLO to take part in its debates as an observer.

1975

13 April: Beginning of the Lebanese civil war.

4 September: Second Israeli-Egyptian disengagement agreement on Sinai, which is criticized by Syria and the PLO.

1976

January: For the first time, the PLO takes part in a Security Council debate.

April: Pro-PLO candidates win the municipal elections in the West Bank. They take control of the large towns (Nablus, Ramallah, Hebron, etc.).

8 May: Elias Sarkis elected president of Lebanon.

1 June: Open and large-scale intervention by Syria in Lebanon against the PLO and the Lebanese left.

21 July: First meeting, in Paris, between Issam Sartawi and General Peled.

6 September: Palestine becomes a full member of the Arab League.

October: End of the first phase of the war in Lebanon, with the defeat of the PLO and its allies. The Syrian presence is endorsed by the Arab states.

1977

February-March: Jordanian-Palestinian reconciliation.

12-20 March: The 13th PNC adopts the 15-point programme. The PLO demands the creation of an independent national state.

3-4 May: First official meeting between the PLO and the Israeli Communist

Party.
17 May: Right-wing coalition wins the Israeli elections. Menachem Begin becomes prime minister.
1 October: American–Soviet statement on the solution of the Middle East conflict. Supported by Yasser Arafat.
19 November: Sadat's visit to Jerusalem.
2-5 December: Creation of the 'Steadfastness Front' in Tripoli including Libya, Algeria, Syria, South Yemen and the PLO.

1978
14 March: Israel invades southern Lebanon.
17 September: Signing of the Camp David agreements.
5 November: End of the Arab Summit in Baghdad which condemns the Camp David agreements.

1979
February: Victory of the 'Islamic Revolution' in Tehran.
26 March: Signing, in Washington, of the peace treaty between Cairo and Tel-Aviv.
27-31 March: The Arab conference in Baghdad confirms sanctions against Egypt whose membership of the Arab League is suspended.
6 July: Arafat–Brandt–Kreisky meeting in Vienna.
19 September: Yasser Arafat visits Amman for the first time since 1971.

1980
2 June: Attacks on the mayors of Ramallah, Nablus and El Bireh.
13 June: 'Venice Declaration' adopted by the EEC.
30 July: The Knesset passes a basic law declaring "reunited" Jerusalem the eternal capital of Israel.
September: Beginning of the Iran–Iraq war.

1981
July: Israeli–Palestinian war on the Lebanese border. Israeli bombardment of Beirut. Israeli attack on the nuclear reactor at Tamuz (Iraq).
7 August: 'Fahd Plan' put forward by the Crown Prince of Saudi Arabia.
6 October: Assassination of President Sadat.
November: Breakdown of the Arab summit in Fez which is suspended *sine die*.
1 December: Establishment of a 'civilian administration' in the occupied territories. Palestinians demonstrate their opposition.

1982
March–April: Palestinian uprising in the occupied territories. The elected mayors are removed from office.
25 April: Israel completes the evacuation of Sinai.
6 June: Beginning of the Israeli invasion of Lebanon. The siege of Beirut

begins a few days later.
21 August: The PLO begins the evacuation of Beirut, protected by the Multinational Force.
1 September: President Reagan outlines his pleace plan in a speech.
9 September: The Arab summit adopts the 'Fez plan'.
14–17 September: Assassination of Bashir Gemayel. The Israelis enter West Beirut. Massacres at Sabra and Chatila.
15 September: President Leonid Brezhnev makes a speech outlining the USSR's proposals for peace in the Middle East.
21 September: Amin Gemayel elected president of Lebanon.

1983
January: Arafat-Avneri-Peled meeting in Tunis.
February: 16th PNC in Algiers. The PLO accepts the Fez plan.
April: Failure of negotiations between Hussein and Arafat.
10 April: Assassination of Issam Sartawi.
May: Beginning of dissidence within Fatah.
August-September: The civil war in Lebanon breaks out again. In Israel, Begin resigns and is replaced by Shamir.
November: Beginning of the siege of Tripoli by Syrian troops allied to the Fatah 'dissidents'.
20 December: Yasser Arafat and 4,000 fighters leave Tripoli.
22 December: Arafat and Mubarak meet in Cairo. The PFLP, DFLP and Palestine Communist Party strongly condemn the PLO leader.

1984
19 January: The Islamic summit in Casablanca readmits Egypt.
6 February: The Amal Shiite militias take control of West Beirut.
5 March: Abrogation of the Israeli-Lebanese agreement.
22 March: Early dissolution of the Knesset.
Late April: Formation of a national unity government in Lebanon after the abrogation of the Israeli–Lebanese agreement.
27 June: Announcement in Aden of a political agreement between Fatah on the one hand and the PFLP, DFLP, PLF and PCP on the other. The talks had lasted 6 months.
24 July: Parliamentary elections in Israel. The very close result forces the Labour Party and Likud to form a national unity government.
22–29 November: 17th PNC in Amman, boycotted by the PFLP, the DFLP, the PCP and the pro-Syrian groups.

1985
January: Transfer of many Ethiopian Jews to Israel.
15 January: Announcement of the staged withdrawal of Israeli troops from Lebanon.
11 February: Signature in Amman of the Jordanian-Palestinian agreement between King Hussein and Yasser Arafat.

Spring: First major Amal attack on the Palestinian camps in Lebanon.

June: Completion of the Israeli withdrawal from Lebanon, with the exception of the so called 'security zone' in the south.

1 October: Israeli Air Force raid on the PLO headquarters in Tunis.

7 October: Seizure of the Italian liner *Achille Lauro* by a Palestinian commando group.

27 December: Terrorist attacks on El Al stands at Rome and Vienna airports.

1986

February: King Hussein announces the termination of 'coordination' with the leadership of the PLO. He calls for changes in the Palestinian resistance.

March: The mayor of Nablus, appointed by the Israelis, is assassinated. His funeral turns into a massive pro-PLO demonstration.

April: Further fighting in the Lebanese camps which drags on intermittently for months.

July: Closure of 25 PLO offices in Jordan.

21 July: Meeting between Shimon Peres and King Hassan II.

6 August: The Knesset adopts the law forbidding contact between Israelis and the PLO.

October: Shamir replaces Peres as Prime Minister.

November–December: The fighting in the Beirut and Sidon camps, between Amal and the now reunited Palestinian forces, intensifies.

1987

February: Palestinian Writers and Journalists' conference in Algiers. For the first time since the break-up, all Palestinian fractions come together.

March: Syrian troops enter Beirut. End of the long siege of the Palestinian camps.

April: 18th PNC in Algiers.

Spring: Several attempts to hasten the calling of an international conference on peace in the Middle East. Major divisions within the Israeli Cabinet.

5 June: 20th anniversary of the occupation of Gaza and the West Bank. Increasingly widespread demonstrations over the previous six months.

Preface

The book that Alain Gresh has asked me to introduce to the public merits attention, reflection and study. All those people (and they are many) who are concerned, even if only occasionally, about the Israeli–Arab conflict, about Israeli and Palestinian problems, who would sincerely like to know and try to understand before pronouncing more or less categorical judgements should read it. For it throws light on a point that is crucial in forming an opinion and taking a stand on these issues.

European public opinion, indeed virtually all non-Arab and non-Muslim opinion, is particularly disoriented by the difficulty of grasping the ideas of the Palestinian Resistance on the future of the former mandated Palestine, the future it wants or plans in the event of victory for the Jews settled there since various dates and for their state structures, currently the state of Israel. The prevailing impression is one of incoherence, irrationality, unrealism, even, at worst, irresponsible word-mongering.

Not all that is real is rational, far from it, whatever Hegel may have said on the subject, or else these two words have to be given special meanings. It is not uncommon for individuals and even groups to exhibit behaviour that is incoherent, illogical, crazy or suicidal. It falls to the psychologist, the psychiatrist and the sociologist to study the reasons. But, while this sort of study is always useful, those who maintain practical relations with such individuals or groups are justified in everyday life in ignoring their assertions, their vision of things and their interpretations.

However, when we are dealing with a political constellation that has endured for over 30 years on the basis of a profound movement which began more than a century ago, if its behaviour manifests constant characteristics that awaken the reactions we have mentioned, then one must presume *a priori* that this behaviour springs from profound causes, and that the surface incoherence is the consequence of permanent external and internal conditions driving it in this direction, and which its statements translate (as best they can). Any political movement that pursues a goal over so many years, draws up plans for the future and defends them and attempts to advance towards their achievement, is normally constrained — under the multiple, permanent and multiform pressure of reality — to adjust itself progressively to that reality, and to give its plans, strategies and tactics some coherence.

The profound causes that condition and explain the statements and actions of the Palestinians lie in the region's total political dynamic. All who seek to understand this dynamic must therefore take them into account. Statements made by actors must not be taken at face value, but an analysis of them helps to understand them. Alain Gresh, who has a thorough and detailed knowledge of the problem, and has followed it day by day over many years, here provides much basic information which enables us to understand the causes and background of these characteristics of the Palestinian movement. He reveals clearly and in detail, for a decade of vital importance, the mechanism underlying the declared options and the public declarations. It is this mechanism, itself the outcome of the fundamental constraints imposed on the movement by the realities prevailing at its birth and development, that alone makes it possible to explain the superficial manifestations and their often astonishing, enigmatic, sometimes even repulsive, characteristics.

I cannot simply tell the reader to study the detailed analyses that Alain Gresh presents in elucidating this point. The reader may not (I do not) always agree with some of Gresh's formulations or perspectives. But he will be obliged to recognize the seriousness and solidity of the approach. At any event, many, it is to be hoped, will be convinced by the overall intentions that guide the author's thinking on these problems.

First — and it is a preliminary problem that Alain Gresh scarcely touches on since he has long since resolved it for himself and it does not form part of his work here — there is the implicit rejection of the very widespread thesis that I shall call the thesis of 'Palestinian sacrilege'. In books, articles, talks by sometimes very sympathetic figures, the prior accusation constantly recurs: How could such people oppose the very existence of the state of Israel? Is this not prima facie a criminal, sacrilegious stand?

The reply was given long ago. But there are none so deaf as those who do not wish to hear. While referring the reader to more detailed discussions of this point (including my own), I shall here do no more than summarize this reply for the sole reason that I am certain that a good many readers will approach this book with this basic question in mind. One ought to be able to reply quite easily if one simply makes the effort to put oneself, for a few moments, mentally, in the place of others. What can be expected in the twentieth century other than an obstinate and initially outright rejection from a people that sees another people come and settle on its land, declare that it is going to turn it into its own homeland, build for its own purposes, needs and aspirations, and force the 'natives' either to adapt to this proposal or get out? Can this be altered by the fact that this invading people claims (not to say declares) that it lived in this territory some two thousand years earlier and that it plays a vital role in its ideology? Can it be altered by the fact that the said people has suffered — elsewhere, at the hands of others — terrible persecution and been the victim of an atrocious massacre?

If one can ask oneself this basic question honestly, without losing sight of it in a plethora of issues that remain secondary, despite the importance that they may assume, one can only reply as do Alain Gresh, myself and many others, not to mention the Palestinians themselves. It might help the imagination, which often finds it difficult to concentrate on problems far removed from everyday life, if one were to imagine what it would be like if the gipsies — a people persecuted for centuries, and exterminated *en masse* by the Nazis — were to demand a state in the *département* of the Bouches-du-Rhône where there is a sanctuary that they venerate, at Les Saintes-Maries-de-le-Mer, and succeed in carrying out their plan with the support of the United States and the Soviet Union, after laying a territorial base through the systematic purchase of land, and after militarily defeating the French forces (from the Bouches-du-Rhône and elsewhere) who attempted to resist. Just think of the reaction of the inhabitants reduced to a subordinate position, forced to learn Zingaro in order to have a place in the gipsy state, or else driven to settle elsewhere (France is big, there are 94 other *départements*, the apologists of the gipsy state would say!).

Lying behind all Alain Gresh's particular options and viewpoints — which one may not accept, or not accept in their entirety — there is a basic viewpoint that comes through clearly in his conclusion. If the reader does not accept it, he will of course be able to profit from numerous details in the analysis, but he will not follow the author entirely. It is a viewpoint that I share, despite all my disagreements with Alain Gresh. It is the viewpoint that may be called, so long as one is careful about the nuances, 'internationalist'.

This term has been misused to justify dubious operations and, in particular, operations inspired by a hidden nationalism. That does not prevent it being a moral stance that is essential, without which it is both idle and dishonest to make value judgements on international politics. And it is a moral stance that has moreover a primordial rational function.

Let me not be misunderstood. It is not a question of denying the right of nations to an independent existence, to the development of an autonomous culture, and to work, strive and struggle for the defence and advancement of the collective rights and aspirations which are peculiar to them. At least, that is, when they are legitimate; and therein lies the whole question. A certain nationalism is legitimate, especially when it is defensive and is struggling to preserve the essential rights of a community, but it becomes hateful and must be fought when it makes itself absolute and trespasses on the legitimate rights of others.

Absolute nationalism secretes a host of ethically condemnable acts but also an ideology that deforms reality, warps judgement, and drives people towards the irrational. The adversary is deemed to be in essence fundamentally evil; it is from this that springs his opposition to the will of the people whose judgement is posited *a priori* as the absolute good. There is no need to seek to know this enemy, it is enough to be aware of this evil essence to fight it on all levels. Such an essence can only have been constituted at some indefinite date in the past and must be destined to endure everlastingly into the future. Beings so made by God or by nature — the question of the causes of this disposition can be ignored and left to the debates of professional hair-splitters — cannot be compared with normal average peoples, in whom good and evil are mixed and fight each other, and far less with the people making the judgements, who obviously represent Good. These must therefore be beings who are outside the human norm, sub-humans, monsters whom a deceitful fate has clothed with a human shape and appearance.

Such is the view of the adversary to which the struggle between peoples leads. Among strategists, politicians, diplomats, and the finer intellectuals, it is of course attenuated by direct and unavoidable contact with the reality of the other side. But it is strengthened by the incidents of war with its painful and barbarous twists and turns. The barbarism inherent in all war can even be improved upon, and lead to atrocities when some elements at least in the enemy camp turn it into a system and a method, and that often happens. Professional propagandists, in their desire to ply their trade and mobilize the masses, reinforce this image of the adversary. Politicians make this reinforcement into an instrument of their attempts to outbid one another in their struggle for power.

We should add that while the Zionist fight for Palestine was not waged militarily (except sporadically) for very long before 1948, it was imbued — in practice, if not always consciously — with a contemptuous view of the 'native', who was seen generally as a non-partner, a minor part of the scenery; in short he was seen as a sub-human. From this usually unspoken, almost instinctive view, grafted onto the European colonial vision of the world, there flowed acts of dispossession committed with a clear conscience; their consequences were often atrocious, even leaving aside the real atrocities (think of Deir Yassin!) deliberately committed by the most extreme elements in the movement, who were following the logic of fundamentalist nationalism to its conclusion.

All this easily explains the view (a negative one in the full sense of the word) that the Palestinian movement, in turn, initially held of Israel and the Israelis. This view could not but be reinforced by the promptings of ancient or contemporary ideologies; every movement of this type needs an ideology and cobbles it together in part with any material lying around the ideological field that can be used for this purpose. Elements of traditional Islamic ideology were readily available in which the sacred texts provided invectives against the Jews and the Jewish religion going back to the time of the Prophet Muhammad's struggle against the Jews of Medina. Similarly, the rivalry between the communities over 14 centuries had provided an abundance of available ammunition in the way of derogatory judgements on the Jews. The nineteenth-century atmosphere in the Middle East (one cannot generalize absolutely to all areas of the Muslim world) had led to all this hostile material being shelved and its being replaced by judgements full of goodwill and toleration, redolent with the mutual friendliness and esteem that the traditions supplied just as amply. Above all, at the end of the nineteenth and beginning of the twentieth century in the same area, experience had pushed in the same direction. But every concrete struggle with the Jews was to drive people to reuse the stock available for anti-Judaism. By way of comparison, one might mention all the ideological clutter of the centuries-long struggle between France and England: it was virtually forgotten in France at the time in question, and had indeed even been replaced by warm demonstrations of friendship; but German propaganda and its fellow-travellers successfully breathed new life into it in the 1930s and 1940s. How easy it was on some occasions (and even in Free France, as I myself witnessed) to summon up the ordeal of Joan of Arc, the removal of Napoleon, the humil-iation of Fashoda, in short all perfidious Albion's treacherous manoeuvres against gentle France and the pure-white sons of the Gauls.

No doubt the main contribution of Alain Gresh's work is to show in detail how, and through what a complex and complicated mechanism, constantly threatened by countless obstacles arising from an inextricable situation, the abysmal lack of understanding of the realities of Israel and the clear determination not to take account of them (which these factors and doubtless others as well explain) gradually gave way to a greater realism and a better understanding of the adversary. Moreover, pure nationalism inevitably led to many a dead end; the contradictions between Palestinian nationalism and overarching Arab nationalism, which were in principle complementary, had to reveal themselves in the starkest light; the theory of the connection between the whole conflict and a Manichaean world mechanism in which Imperialism (with a capital I) acted as the Devil had to begin at least to show its shortcomings. All this had to happen before it became possible to discern clearly the premises of a truly new direction within the struggle on the ideo-logical level, to come to a deeper understanding of the adversary, and his structures and motivations, to begin to draw political, strategic and tactical lessons from them, and for leaders who had long been clear-headed to be widely followed.

It is unfortunate that this clarity should have been able to spread at a time when it could play only a reduced role compared with what it could have played in the past. Moreover, the disasters that brought it to the fore dramatically reduced its effectiveness. Let us hope that this will be only a passing phase. But it is yet another example of the tormented, contradic-tory, disconcerting process of history, full of setbacks and obstacles. It is again Hegel who warned us of this: 'Minerva's owl takes flight only when darkness falls'.

Maxime Rodinson

Acknowledgements

A book is the result of a long labour, a long process; and even if the author alone takes responsibility for the contents, they are the end product of numerous discussions and meetings. I cannot mention them all here but I want to thank all those who have encouraged me in this labour and, in particular, all the Palestinian and Israeli cadres and intellectuals whom it has been my good fortune to meet during these last two years.

I should also like to thank M.O. Carré, M. Rodinson and H. Portelli for their advice.

Finally, I must recognize that, without the attentive re-reading of the manuscript by Geneviève Saller, the assistance of Françoise Cristobal and J. Hazan and the skills of Marianne Ivsic this book would never have seen the light of day.

Alain Gresh

Introduction

The future and status of Palestine and the respective places of the peoples living in it have been open questions since the establishment of the British mandate over the territory at the end of the First World War. For the Palestinian national movement, the first task was to thwart the Balfour Declaration, and to limit and even prevent Jewish immigration, which was broadly encouraged by the mandatory power. It was a defensive struggle: the idea of independence was pushed into the background. But with the advent of Nazism in Germany, and the resulting spread of anti-Semitism, immigration took on new dimensions. It precipitated increasingly violent reactions on the part of the Arabs, culminating in the great uprising of 1936–39, marked by a radicalization of the struggle and a calling into question of the British mandate over Palestine. Although harshly put down, the revolt was one of the factors that led Great Britain to adopt the 1939 White Paper limiting Jewish immigration, and rejecting the idea of a Jewish state in Palestine.

The end of the Second World War marked a turning-point in the history of the Middle East and Palestine. Aspirations to national independence became stronger; Great Britain emerged from the conflict gravely weakened; the Zionist movement was strengthened and could draw on widespread international sympathy following the discovery of the Nazi extermination camps; the Palestinian movement, decimated by the 1939 repression, was completely under the thumb of the Arab regimes. In these circumstances, Britain, despite its reservations, but faced with the development of Zionist terrorism and the instability prevailing in Palestine, laid the problem of the future of the territory before the United Nations. The plan to partition Palestine into two states, one Jewish, the other Arab, was adopted by the General Assembly in November 1947. The Zionist movement accepted it in principle. The Palestinian movement — whose autonomy was limited — rejected it outright: it was unable to grasp the reality constituted by the presence of 600,000 Jewish settlers; it lacked even the means, and doubtless the will, to take charge of the territories assigned to the Arab state; it left the Arab states and the Zionist leaders to share out the remains between them. The absolute rejection of the Partition Plan and the continued insistence on the demand for a united Palestinian state ended in a new catastrophe for the people of

Palestine. The creation of the state of Israel radically altered the fundamentals of the problem. And it was not until the late 1950s, with the renaissance, first cultural and then political, of the Palestinian movement that the new realities resulting from the 1948 war began to be grasped.

What territory are the Palestinians claiming? For which state? What is to happen to the 'Jewish settlers'? These are the questions Palestinians have had to answer, and they have no precedents to guide them. The Algerian and Vietnamese peoples' liberation movements were united on a strategic goal: the total liberation of their occupied homeland, even though stages or compromises could be accepted along the road to the ultimate goal. But the Palestinians are faced with a peculiar problem arising from the very nature of Jewish colonization: not only the presence of 3 million Israelis – as many, or nearly so, as there are Palestinians – but also their existence as a 'national community' living its own autonomous existence, economically, politically and militarily. And to this one should add the fact that the Palestinians have been expelled from their homeland and that, in much of historic Palestine, they have no physical presence whatsoever today.

Faced with this reality, the Palestinian movement adopted, from 1948, a position of total rejection. Apart from some tiny groups, it dreamed only of 'return' and the expulsion of the occupiers. Its total dependence on the Arab regimes did nothing to encourage any evolution. It was not until the Palestinian awakening, the creation of the Palestine Liberation Organization in 1964 and the development of Yasser Arafat's Fatah that there began to be any evolution in Palestinian political thought. From febrile calls for the destruction of the Jewish state, to the idea of a state in part of Palestine by way of the slogan of a democratic state in which Muslims, Christians and Jews could coexist: from total rejection of the 'Zionist entity' to *de facto* acceptance of Israel was a long march – halting and full of contradictions – accomplished by the Palestinian national movement, and in particular by the PLO, which gradually asserted itself as the most authentic representative of the Palestinian people. This long evolution of Palestinian political thought and the profound debate still rocking the PLO is vital not only for the Palestinians; it is also vital – the 1982 war in Lebanon confirms it – for the future of the Middle East.

The long-drawn-out discussion precipitated by the unparalleled situation in which the Palestinians find themselves is further complicated by the fact that the majority of the Palestinian people live in a diaspora, and that the fragmentation following the exodus of 1948 has placed the various fractions of the Palestinian people in different situations. The reactions of a Palestinian will obviously differ according to whether his house is in Haifa or Nablus, whether this or that solution would enable him either to get rid of the occupation or to formalize his exile, and so on. No Palestinian leader can escape this contradictory reality.

The PLO has been placed at the centre of this study – while not forgetting other participants in the discussion – because the organization has imposed itself as the key Palestinian force. But it should be noted that the import of its internal debates varies. Thus all the discussion between 1967 and 1971 about a democratic state had little practical impact: the PLO's authority on the international level was limited and its participation in a solution to the problems of the Middle East seemed illusory. This in no way reduces the political significance of the acceptance of the slogan, however. The situation changed dramatically in 1973, when it became clear that PLO participation in negotiations was a central problem. The discussion which was going on within it then had an obvious practical impact. For this period, it therefore seemed interesting to concentrate on the decision-making process in the PLO.

While trying to bring out some of the general features of the functioning of the PLO, the questions this study has attempted to answer are: what was the long road that led to acceptance of the slogan of building a national authority on any part of liberated Palestinian territory? What were the factors — especially the internal ones — that weighed on such a decision, and at the price of what ambiguities was agreement reached?

Closely linked with the question of a state is the issue of the 'Jewish settlers' and how the Palestinians perceive them. Here we run up against one of the essential limitations of Palestinian political thought. Despite the rejection — at least by the majority of the PLO — of chauvinistic positions, an outside observer cannot but be struck by the lack of appreciation of the reality of Israel. The causes of this go very deep: the perception of the Israelis as occupiers, but above all a lack of contact with this reality. While the Israeli–Palestinian talks in the 1970s marked a turning-point in this respect, they still only affected a small number of Palestinian cadres; but they did prepare the ground for later developments.

It was not until 1982, with the war in Lebanon and the psychological shock caused by the sight of 400,000 people demonstrating in Tel Aviv against the war while the Arab capitals remained silent, that hopes of greater understanding between the two peoples began to take concrete shape.

This book takes as its starting-point the aftermath of the Six-Day war, for 1967 was a pivotal year in the history of the Middle East and the Palestinian people. On the one hand, the pan-Arab dreams, incarnated in particular by Nasser, collapsed. On the other, for the first time since the great revolt of 1936-39, the Palestinian people emerged as an autonomous actor on the Arab stage. With the occupation of the West Bank and Gaza, Israelis and Palestinians found themselves face to face without Arab intermediaries. The Israeli–Arab conflict was, little by little, turning into an Israeli–Palestinian conflict.

What is known as the Palestinian Resistance, partly freed from external controls, came face to face with its responsibilities. It had to spell out its goals and objectives, in particular the state and territories to which it laid claim.

The present work is based mainly on the study of Palestinian or Arab documents. Most of these have been collected by the Institute for Palestine Studies and the PLO Research Centre, both in Beirut.[1] They cover documents of the PLO and the main Palestinian organizations, and their political and theoretical stands. It should be noted however that this material, while very plentiful, contains gaps that I have endeavoured to fill: for example, the interesting debate launched by the Popular Democratic Front for the Liberation of Palestine (PDFLP) during the summer of 1973 on a 'national authority' was not to be found in these collections of documents. Nor were most of the documents relating to the Israeli-Palestinian talks of 1974-77 — this latter 'oversight' being of course not simply a matter of chance.

To the documents and the study of political texts must be added an examination of the 'political practice' of the PLO. As with every organization, a gap exists between this practice and the texts that inspire it: but for the PLO this gap is even greater, for reasons that will be explained throughout this study. This contradiction raises a problem which, as I see it, cannot be resolved by giving pride of place to one or the other aspect. Both the texts and the political practice must be studied, while asking questions about the gap between the two.

The work would not have been possible without numerous journeys to the region, to Beirut, the West Bank and Gaza, or without discussions with many Palestinians (and Israelis) who provided an 'inside' view of the Palestinian movement. The visible part of this work is to be seen in a series of interviews with a dozen Palestinian leaders and personalities who — despite the limitations of this sort of work (the fact that the interviews took place 10 or 15 years after the events, the tendency to self-justification, and so on) — have helped to clarify and clear up numerous points.

In the course of my research, I have encountered a number of difficulties and problems that I should like to touch on now. First, the recent nature of the events studied sometimes makes it difficult to grasp the main lines of their evolution. To this objection, which is a real one, I would reply as Fontaine did:

> Some people say that history of this sort is too recent for it to be possible to write it rationally . . . To have read widely and travelled extensively, and to have spoken with many of the figures who appear in this book constitutes, perhaps to find one's own bearings, an advantage that is not available to the historian of a more distant past.[2]

When I embarked on this research, I expected to find that there was already an abundance of studies. While there are countless works on the Arab-Israeli conflict, however, and works on the sociology of the Palestinians are beginning to appear in growing numbers,[3] there are very few devoted to the Palestinian Resistance and its ideology, or to the PLO and its functioning as a political organization. The mass of material available — declarations and documents of the various organizations, the Palestinian press, and so on — is far from having been exhaustively analysed. I was thus starting in a field that had been little cleared and this led me to limit my ambitions. I have therefore essentially studied the positions of the 'top' without always being in a position to say how the 'grass-roots' reacted. This would have required more case studies and these have yet to be made.

The varied nature of the Palestinian national reality creates an added difficulty for the researcher. No people in recent history has been placed in such a variety of situations. There are Palestinians in the West Bank, in Gaza, in Lebanon, in Israel, in Jordan, in the Gulf, in Syria, and so on, to mention only the largest communities: and these situations are reflected in diverse political practices. While an attempt has been made to take account of the largest possible number of these components – and of course the most important ones – it must be recognized that some gaps remain. Thus, what was the role of Palestinians in the Gulf – who made a major financial contribution to the Resistance – in the various debates? Did they have a specific impact? Only more localized studies will be able to answer these questions.

Although the PLO is a modern-type political organization, it is far from having succeeded in eliminating the influence of clans and families, of geographical and religious origins, in Palestinian politics. This is especially true of Fatah, the most important of the organizations, and the one whose ideological outlines are the least clear. It has not been possible to study this dimension in the present work thoroughly; but an attempt has been made to take it into account, particularly in discussing the backgrounds of Palestinian leadership groups.

These difficulties and limits lead me to raise a question that is current – the question of a political history of the PLO. It still remains to be written and I see this book as a contribution to that enormous task.

Notes

1. Gresh, Alain, 'Informations sur les centres de recherches palestiniens', *Recherches Internationales*, no. 2, 3rd quarter, 1981.

2. A. Fontaine, *Un seul lit pour deux rêves*, Paris, Fayard, 1982.

3. Gresh, Alain, 'Etat et société palestinienne: une deuxième vague d'études', *La Pensée*, no. 224, July–August 1982.

Part I:
The Palestinian Resistance and the Slogan of a Democratic State (1967-1971)

The slogan of a democratic state was formulated by Fatah in mid-1968. It precipitated a wide-ranging debate among Palestinian organizations and within the PLO. Formulation of this objective raised two questions central to the strategy of the Palestinian Resistance.

1. The question of the relationship between the Arab struggle and the Palestinian struggle. By calling for the formation of what its opponents (both Arab and Palestinian) scornfully called a fourteenth or fifteenth Arab state, Fatah ran counter to an entire strategy that made Arab unity the prerequisite for the liberation of Palestine. The PLO Charter of 1964, for example, makes no reference to a Palestinian state. The very idea of Palestinian sovereignty is absent, whether sovereignty over 'liberated' territory (not to mention the rejection written into the Charter of any action in the West Bank, Gaza and al-Himma, a Palestinian city under Syrian control) or the PLO's sovereignty *vis-à-vis* the Arab states. According to the Charter, the battle of 'liberation' will be an Arab one and Palestine will be included in a great Arab grouping. The very idea of a specifically Palestinian struggle or of a particular role for the Palestinian people is treated as regionalism (*iqlimiya*) and is, as such, suspect. Fatah deserves credit for having taken the first steps, in the late 1950s, towards another strategy, involving an independent struggle by the Palestinian people which would lead after 1967 to the idea of self-determination and a state.

2. The question of the relationship between Palestinians and 'Jewish settlers'. Here too Fatah, by its definition of a democratic state in which Muslims, Christians and Jews would coexist, broke with traditional Palestinian and Arab thought and introduced a highly significant distinction between Jews and Zionists. The organization called on Jews to join the armed struggle and accepted that most Jews would remain in Palestine. This was not accepted without internal contradictions and opposition from the PLO's old guard and Arab nationalist organizations; nevertheless, my opinion is that its acceptance, after a long debate, by the PLO was an essential step in the political evolution of the Palestinian Resistance and prepared the ground for the acceptance, in 1974, of the 'phased stages' strategy and of a Palestinian state in the West Bank and Gaza. It was also the prerequisite for deeper reflection on the reality of Israel, its contradictions and the progressive forces existing within it.

Part 1 covers the period from the June 1967 war and the first formulation by Fatah of the slogan of a democratic state to 1971 and the eighth Palestine National Council (PNC). This latter date has been selected for two reasons: the first is that the eighth PNC, in which all the Palestinian organizations participated (even if the Popular Front for the Liberation of Palestine, PFLP, did so somewhat symbolically), accepted the slogan. It has changed little since then. The second reason is that after the defeat of Black September in 1970, the Palestinian Resistance began its journey through the wilderness: debates on the future of Palestine declined. Virtually all forces were thrown into the struggle against any proposal for the creation of a Palestinian entity (state in the West Bank, proposal for a United Arab Kingdom, and so on). Parts 2 and 3 are devoted to this struggle and its implications.

Before looking at the debate as it unfolded within the PLO, we must briefly look at the circumstances surrounding it — both the balance of power within the PLO and the Resistance organizations and the history of the Resistance during this short period.

1. The Circumstances Surrounding the Discussion within the PLO

The Positions Adopted within the PLO and the Question of 'National Unity'

In the period from June 1967 to the eighth PNC (February-March 1971), the Palestine Liberation Organization was transformed. It had been founded by the Arab states in 1964 and tied to their strategy, and so like them was discredited by the 1967 defeat. It became no more than one Palestinian organization among many; the resignation of its chairman Ahmad Shuqairy in December 1967 gave concrete expression to the profound crisis in which it was involved. Two formulae were then being contemplated: either a front made up of the various existing Palestinian organizations, with the PLO just one among others, or the transformation of the PLO into a 'framework' of national unity.[1] The fourth PNC was held in July 1968, attended by the old leadership of the PLO, Fatah, Sa'iqa [Lightning] and the PFLP, and a new National Charter and a new Basic Constitutional Law were adopted. There was no agreement on the ruling body and the old one was reappointed. At the fifth PNC, in February 1969, Yasser Arafat was elected chairman of the PLO executive committee. Sa'iqa belonged to the executive committee but the PFLP boycotted the meeting. It rejected what it called the hegemony of Fatah over the PLO. A unity agreement was signed on 6 May 1970 between all Palestinian organizations (except the Communist Ansars), in which all the groups recognized the PLO as the umbrella structure of national unity. The PNC, the highest body, has somewhat more than 100 members. It represents all tendencies. It is in principle the sole organ authorized to lay down the broad policy options of the PLO.

But each Palestinian organization still retains a broad measure of autonomy. The period 1968-70 brought out two essential characteristics of the PLO which distinguish it from other national liberation movements:

1. The autonomy of the organizations, which, at times, can take decisions independent of the PLO, sometimes even contrary to its line. This came out during the events of September 1970 in Jordan, when the PFLP and the PDFLP dragged the whole of the Resistance into a confrontation that the majority had been seeking to avoid and into which the Hashemite Kingdom wanted to draw it.

2. The proliferation of small organizations (about a dozen, six of which are recognized by and participate in the PLO, not to mention organizations which issue communiqués but whose influence is difficult to determine). While this diversity can have extremely negative effects, it also makes for wide-ranging theoretical debates. The existence of ideological currents claiming allegiance to Marxism, Ba'thism, and so on, and which are quite free to put forward their views, creates a very special situation (which is very different from that of the FLN in Algeria, for example). It also helps to explain the occasional contradictions between statements by Palestinian leaders.

The reasons for this fragmentation of the Palestinian movement are not accidental. Their roots lie deep in the reality of the Palestinian people and it is worth taking a moment to look at them.[2]

a) The diaspora of 1948, when the Palestinian people were split up. Some now live in Israel, others live under Jordanian rule, others again in Gaza under Egyptian rule, not to mention the hundreds of thousands of refugees in Lebanon, Syria and the Gulf. This physical division has led to divergent political and social experiences. A Palestinian bourgeois living in Kuwait and a peasant living in a refugee camp have nothing in common. Each of these groups often produces its own leadership.

b) The totally different backgrounds of the various leaderships and groups (see Quandt *et al.* for a comparison of the background of the leading groups in Fatah and the Arab Nationalist Movement).

c) The strong dose of individualism that Quandt attributes to Arab-Palestinian cultural values.

d) The ideological divergences that are all the greater because the relatively high level of Palestinian education makes the PLO more sensitive to the controversies and different ideologies flowing through the Arab world.

e) Interference by the Arab states. This occurs on two levels: direct interference, that is, the creation of organizations dependent directly on one or other Arab regime (Sa'iqa on Syria; the Arab Liberation Front, ALF, on Iraq), or indirect interference in the shape of alliances made with this or that Palestinian organization at a particular time making it possible to influence PLO decisions.

Dr Issam Sartawi's experience provides a good illustration of these various points.[3] A member of Fatah and one of the founders of the Palestine Red Crescent, he was influenced by pan-Arab theories and did not always accept Fatah's 'regionalism'. But it was due to an argument arising over a minor issue that he broke with Arafat in the autumn of 1968: during a meeting with the chairman and other members of the PLO, tempers rose and Sartawi left the room shouting to his colleagues: 'I came into this room as a member of Fatah, I'm leaving it as the secretary-general of the Action Organization for the Liberation of Palestine.' He then collected together his supporters in Fatah, a total of just 17! Although he stressed the fact that Fatah did not seek to eliminate him physically, he recalled that he owed the survival of his organization solely to the 'hospitality' of the Iraqi troops stationed in Jordan; the new Ba'thist government — with which he had connections, having lived in Baghdad for several years — promised to protect his training camps. He was thus able to set up a force of several hundred men which was to become one of the ten main Palestinian organizations.

Arafat himself summarized the circumstances of this diversity on 14 January 1970. After mentioning the existence of numerous organizations, he said:

> We have no intention of engaging in armed liquidation for a number of considerations. Firstly because, fundamentally, we do not believe in this method. Secondly, these organizations and their conflicts are part and parcel of the conflict within the Arab nation — and what are we if not part of that nation? Thirdly, because some of these organizations are attached to Arab countries, so that an armed dispute with them would mean an armed dispute with those countries.[4]

On other occasions, he would compare the 'Vietnamese way' (that is, a broad front) with the 'Algerian way' of settling conflicts,[5] strongly preferring the former. In Sartawi's opinion, this position must also be understood as a sign of the real humanism of the Palestinian leaders. It may be added that the shared experience of the 'leading group' of Fatah both in the Palestine Students Union and during the struggle in Gaza in 1955-56[6] probably contributed to this rather exceptional tolerance.

This acceptance of diversity among Palestinian organizations had significant consequences. Unity and consensus became a central goal: first, because the complex situation of the Resistance — whether in the face of reactionary 'plots' or attempts at a peaceful settlement — required the union of all Palestinian forces; and secondly, because it was the best way of securing the widest support among Arab countries and preventing them from being able to manipulate inter-Palestinian contradictions.

This premium placed on unity (which was to be seen in the PNC's agendas and the declarations of each organization, as well as in the numerous 'unitary' proposals, whether implemented or not) and this quest for consensus provide one of the keys to the discussions of 1967-70. They also explain the 'disorganized' character of the Resistance, at least as it appeared to observers, with organizations fighting one another, leaders issuing contradictory statements, and so on. At the same time, however, they were the source of a democratic debate rarely seen in a liberation movement. All the various ideological tendencies were expressed, and there is no other way of understanding the breadth of the debate on the democratic state.

Another important factor that must be taken into account for the period under review is the fact that the PLO did not represent all fractions of the Palestinian people. The main support for the Resistance was in the refugee camps in Jordan and Lebanon. There the strategy of armed struggle and people's war found widespread support,[7] as did the stress placed on the role of the Palestinians and the rejection of political solutions. The base in the camps was aided by the establishment of parallel power structures,[8] which in Jordan were virtually 'liberated zones'. The situation on the West Bank, on the other hand, was altogether different.[9] Attempts to set up a guerrilla movement there in 1967 had failed; the traditional leaderships allied to the Hashemite monarchy managed broadly to retain their hegemony. It was not until early 1973 that the masses on the West Bank became closely involved in the PLO.

In Gaza the situation was less clear-cut, to the extent that Resistance organizations remained active there (despite the absence of rear bases). O'Neill sees two interrelated reasons for this: the high proportion of refugees (half the total number of inhabitants), and their grinding poverty[10] which made them uninterested in any solution that did not give them back 'their lands'.

Here we see the appearance of an important cleavage within the Palestinian people, between the refugees and the rest (we are not thinking here of all those living abroad, but of the poorest among them, those living in the camps), the former being less inclined to 'compromise'. It is thus worth nothing that in the period 1967–71 the former strongly influenced the Resistance organizations, the bulk of whose 'mass' support they made up, whereas the latter did not yet see the PLO as 'their' organization.

The History of the Palestinian Resistance

The history of the Palestinian Resistance is influenced by the defeat of the Arab countries in June 1967. This defeat created a vacuum that enabled the Resistance to win a measure of autonomy and to define its strategy.

Armed Struggle and Relations with Israel

As regards Israel and attempts at a peaceful settlement, there was relative unity: armed struggle was the sole form of confrontation with the 'Zionist enemy'. After the failure of attempts to set up bases in the West Bank in late 1967, the Palestinian Resistance fell back on 'secure bases' first in Jordan and then in Lebanon. The period 1968–69 marked the high point of military operations.

'Incidents' on the border between Jordan and Israel rose from 97 in 1967 (after June) to 916 in 1968, 2,432 in 1969 and 1,887 (up to August) in 1970. They then fell to 45 in 1971. In Gaza the process was rather different: the fedayeen were acting from within and, despite a falling-off in 1971, the number of incidents remained high. The relative success of this struggle, especially after the defeat of the Arab armies, created a feeling of euphoria among the Arab and Palestinian masses, and also in the Resistance organizations. Despite numerous reminders that the struggle would be a long one, there developed a notion that success would come rapidly.

Fatah laid down four phases in the guerrilla struggle: 'hit and run', 'limited confrontation', 'temporary occupation' and finally 'permanent occupation' (that is, of the liberated zones). Numerous statements in the second half of 1969 and early 1970 asserted that the second phase had begun with the battle of Karameh (22 March 1968), the third with the temporary occupation of the village of al-Himma (2 May 1969) and that the Resistance was now entering the final phase of its struggle.[11] Other declarations were more realistic,[12] but the overall impression of quick victory was very widespread.

This assessment was proved wrong not only by the dangerous situation in which the Resistance found itself *vis-à-vis* the Arab countries, but also by the operations in the West Bank and the effectiveness of the Israeli military response which, from the beginning of 1970, reduced its losses and the number of internal support bases through repression and a certain amount of collaboration.[13]

This setback in the armed struggle, which was only partial (in fact, the most striking successes of the PLO in this period were political), does not alter the fact that it is impossible to reconstruct the debate seen during this period without taking into account the fact that the PLO saw armed struggle as the only form of Palestinian struggle and believed that victory was at hand.

For the PLO the role attributed to armed struggle justified the rejection of every political solution, from UN Security Council Resolution 242 to the Rogers Plan. The Rogers Plan was summed up in the proposals made at the end of June 1970, by American Secretary of State William Rogers for the implementation of Resolution 242. These proposals, which were accepted by Jordan, Egypt and Israel, put a final end to the war of attrition between Cairo and Tel Aviv along the Suez Canal. The PLO's rejection of the plan was to have distinctly negative effects by depriving the Palestinian Resistance of possible international alliances; and by leading it into confrontation with a number of Arab governments, and particularly that of Nasser, after the latter had accepted the Rogers Plan.

Relations with Arab countries

The Palestinian Resistance was locked into a contradiction that has marked its entire history right down to the present day. On the one hand, it cannot hope to win without the support of the Arab states (even though, at times, it has done so); on the other, its very development leads to contradictions with these countries, but of two different types. In countries where it had a military presence, in other words in Jordan and Lebanon, it came to resist the authority of the state, establish its own authority over the Palestinians (who in the case of Jordan were a majority of the population) and oblige these states to confront Israeli reprisals. With the other states, such as Egypt and Syria, it tended to oppose their immediate goal (the liberation of the territories occupied in 1967), which it felt to be in contradiction with its own strategy of the total liberation of Palestine.

The number of confrontations grew: Jordan in November 1968, February,

15

June and finally September 1970 and the expulsion of the fedayeen in July 1971; Lebanon in April and October 1969, and March 1970. Two lines confronted each other: Fatah's line of non-interference in the affairs of Arab states — on condition that they did not hinder the activities of the Resistance — and the PFLP and PDFLP's that can be summed up in the formula 'the road to Jerusalem goes through Amman, Damascus and Cairo'.

In short, the period under consideration saw two developments occurring simultaneously:

— with Black September, the liquidation of a large part of the Palestinian armed potential and its capacity to shake, let alone destroy, Israel;
— the emergence of the PLO as the institutional framework which the Palestinian people as a whole and its organizations gradually came to see as their own, and which increasingly asserted itself as an autonomous factor in the politics of the Middle East.

2. The Premises of the Debate

Fatah's Formulation

Fatah first publicly formulated its proposal for a democratic state in mid-1968. In June 1968 it asserted that the end of Israel as a state and the liberation of Palestine did not have as their goal the liquidation of the Jews but aimed rather to give them the possibility of living in an Arab Palestine.[14]

On 1 October 1968 Abu Iyad, an influential member of the Fatah central committee, unveiled at a press conference the goal of turning Palestine into a democratic society in which Muslims, Christians and Jews would live in complete equality.[15] It was after a year of internal debates — and despite opposition — that Fatah finally took the decision to formulate the goal of a democratic state.

On 1 January 1969, the fourth anniversary of the launching of the armed struggle, the central committee of Fatah put out a statement which said, among other things:

> The Fatah Palestinian National Liberation Movement is not fighting the Jews as an ethnic or religious community. It is fighting against Israel, the expression of a colonization based on a racist and expansionist technocratic system, the expression of Zionism and colonialism ... The Fatah Palestinian National Liberation Movement solemnly declares that the ultimate objective of its struggle is the restoration of an independent and democratic Palestinian state in which all citizens, of whatever religion, will enjoy equal rights.[16]

Abu Hatem (Muhammad Abu Mayzar), the Fatah representative in Paris at the time, told me the story of this declaration and its adoption:[17]

> It was after the battle of Karameh that Fatah decided to open an office outside the Arab world, and in particular in Western Europe. The place chosen was Paris. And I came here to live and work. This raised new questions for us. Various forces, Arab and non-Arab, with whom we had developed contacts began questioning us about the nature of the Palestinian revolution, its goals, and so on. In the light of our experience

and contacts, we adopted the resolution of 1 January 1969 which was released in Paris . . . This was done also in continuation of our history. Before 1948 several organizations, notably the National Liberation League,[18] had advocated a democratic state.

At the end of the fifth PNC in February 1969 — during which Fatah took control of the executive committee and Yasser Arafat became chairman of the executive committee — a statement of policy was adopted which said that the objectives of the Palestinian people was 'to set up a free and democratic society in Palestine, for all Palestinians, including Muslims, Christians and Jews, and to liberate Palestine and its people from the domination of international Zionism'.[19] This statement, it should be noted, makes no mention of a Palestinian state. It appears that it was in April 1969 that the PLO first mentioned a democratic state.[20]

At this stage, the debate was already well under way in the Palestinian organizations. The proposal for a democratic state provoked controversy and opposition (even inside Fatah). We shall now see the themes around which the debate was organized; but before doing so, it should be noted that, so far, in none of Fatah's formulations had the idea of a secular state appeared. We shall return to this issue later.

Arab Nationalism and Palestinian Nationalism

The first, and doubtless the most vigorous, opposition that Fatah faced was among the pan-Arabists, those for whom the very idea of an independent Palestinian state in the whole 'land of Palestine' was anathema. The debate on the relations between Palestinian nationalism and Arab nationalism goes back to the very formation of national feeling in Palestine. Before the First World War, some nationalist Arab leaders saw the Zionist question within the pan-Arab, and not simply the Palestinian, framework. This enabled them to see the 'positive aspect' of Jewish immigration for Syria and the Arab provinces without calling Arab unity into question.[21] But the British occupation of Jerusalem, the Balfour Declaration and the end of the war posed the problem in new terms. The tendency to unite with Faisal's Syria in the formation of what was called 'Southern Syria' dominated the Palestinian movement until 1920.[22] This is to be explained less by a feeling of belonging to the same entity than by growing opposition to Zionism and Jewish immigration. Faisal, the son of Sharif Hussein, had established himself in Syria and hoped to set up an independent government: the Anglo–French declaration of 7 November 1918 asserted that the Allies' war aims were to free oppressed peoples and assist in the formation of national governments in Syria and Iraq. The prospect of an independent regime in Damascus inspired the desire among Palestinians to unite with it so as to be able to oppose proposals for Zionist immigration. France, which made no secret of its ambitions in Syria, favoured the advocates of 'Syrian unity', hoping in this way to see unity come about to France's benefit and under its control.

Faisal's negotiations with the Zionist executive in January 1919 (the Faisal–Weizmann agreements), echoes of which reached Palestine a few months later, the stiffening of Allied policy in the face of Arab demands (the San Remo Conference in April 1920), the entry of French troops into Damascus on 25 July 1920 and the fall of Faisal all contributed to turning the Palestinian movement away from its leaning towards a 'Greater Syria', which, it must be admitted, was no more than a tactic.

From this time until 1936 the struggle was centred on Palestine and against Zionism, with no attempt to seek anything but external support from Arab and Muslim countries. The year 1936, with the beginning of the great revolt, marked a new turning-point which gradually resulted in the transformation of the Palestinian question into an Arab question.[23] In fact, various factors were working in this direction. The first was the development of the nationalist movement throughout the Arab world (there were demonstrations in Egypt and Iraq against proposals for a treaty with Great Britain) and a growing public awareness of the Palestinian question. The second was London's willingness, despite some reservations, to play the card of Arab nationalism (to its own benefit, of course; and above all in the perspective of a new world war) and to use the Arab leaders as a moderating factor, which linked up with the anxiety felt by some Palestinian leaders, concerned at the rise of a popular movement that they did not control. The general strike of 1936, which lasted six months, was ended after an appeal from Arab heads of state. The third factor was that in 1938-39, after the second phase of the revolt, a terrible repression was let loose on the Palestinian movement, with arrests, deportations, assassinations, and so on. It took a generation for a new leadership of the Palestinian movement to emerge. The final factor was Britain's adoption of the 1939 White Paper, which restricted Jewish immigration and the purchase of Arab land, and envisaged a unitary state in ten years with a Jewish minority that was not to be allowed to exceed a third of the population. This marked a significant success for the Palestinian movement and was seen above all as the result of pressures by Arab countries. (The White Paper was adopted unilaterally at the end of a conference with representatives of Arab countries and some leading figures in the Palestinian movement.)

Thus the Palestinian movement, deprived of autonomous leadership, and subjected to the slogans put out by Arab countries — whose regimes were on their last legs and were collaborating with Britain — embarked on a path that was to lead to the catastrophe of 1948. The movement was playing no more than a subordinate role: for 20 years the Palestinian question would remain an Arab question, or rather a question for the Arab countries.

The 1947-48 war and the failure to establish a Palestinian state in even part of Palestine deepened the dependence on the Arab countries. This situation led the new generation to question the validity of rejecting an independent state. In his book, Abu Iyad asks himself:

Why had the Palestinian leaders not accepted a transitional solution, as the Zionist leaders had, which consisted in the formation of a state in the portion of the national territory allocated to them by the UN?

When I asked Haj Amin al-Husseini this question three months before his death, the Palestinian leader put forward several reasons to justify what he said was his inability to save at least a portion of the national homeland. The Arab states involved, whether of their own volition or under pressure from the British, who, he maintained, had it in for him particularly, blocked the foundation of a state in the West Bank and Gaza, territories that the Jewish army had been unable to conquer. King Abdullah of Transjordan quite obviously had no interest in favouring the formation of a Palestinian entity since he intended to annex the West Bank to his kingdom, which moreover is what he did shortly after the 1948 war.

King Farouk, for his part, did not seek to absorb Gaza into Egypt; in September 1948 he authorized the meeting in this town of a Palestinian congress, which appointed a government led by Ahmed Hilmi Pasha, whose main aim — according to Haj Amin al-Husseini — was to establish its effective authority over Gaza and the West Bank. However, the Egyptian government prevented it from even establishing itself in Gaza on the grounds that this would constitute a 'provocation' to the Israeli army which might occupy the enclave. The Palestinian government had therefore to establish itself in Cairo, where its president, Ahmed Hilmi Pasha, who was a banker, spent more time on his business affairs than on his shadow cabinet. Betrayed by the Arab states, Haj Amin al-Husseini was abandoned by most of the Palestinian leaders, who split into two groups, one pro-Jordanian and the other Egyptian.

Although plausible, Haj Amin's justifications did not all seem convincing to me. At the time, Egypt and Saudi Arabia were hostile to the reigning family in Amman and thus disapproved of the annexation of the West Bank by King Abdullah. Could he not have relied on these two Arab states against Jordanian expansionism? And if that was not possible, why had he not appealed to the Arab world as a whole, or even to the UN, which had decided on partition, to lay claim to the West Bank and Gaza? In any event, no document in the Palestinian archives, which we have looked at closely, corroborated Haj Amin al-Husseini's argument.[24]

Contrary to what Abu Iyad asserts — and given the balance of power in the Arab world — the Arab Higher Committee never really had any possibility of forming a government and an independent authority in the territories controlled by the Arab armies. The dominant factors at the time were inter-Arab rivalries and the annexationist designs of the Hashemites. Even the creation of an Arab government for the whole of Palestine in September 1948, by the Mufti, appears to have been much more an Egyptian manoeuvre intended to counter Hashemite designs than a desire to nurture an embryo Palestinian government. This government was soon forgotten.

But in the Middle East things began to move, and fast.[25] Within ten years the old order was totally transformed. The rise of Arab nationalism shook every regime. Nasser took power in Cairo in 1952, Qassim in Baghdad in 1958; the Suez expedition of 1956 saw the collapse of British and French dreams of colonial reconquest. The union of Egypt and Syria in 1958 created the belief that 'Arab unity' was just around the corner.

The impact of this advance on the Palestinian masses was enormous. These masses had been traumatized by the events of 1948 and exile, and had won little support from traditional governments such as those of Jordan or Lebanon.[26] They replaced faith in traditional Arab nationalism with whole-hearted faith in its revolutionary version, anti-imperialist and non-aligned, of which Nasserism was to be one of the most significant forms (but not the only one). To these factors were added the various Arab rivalries and the out-bidding over the Palestinian question, which were to be a feature particularly of the struggle between Qassim and Nasser.

It was out of this background that the PLO came into being, marking a major step towards the political renaissance of the Palestinian movement.

We shall now look briefly at the events leading to the birth of the PLO in 1964.[27] After the union of Syria and Egypt in 1958, the Arab Higher Committee launched a campaign for the integration of Palestine into the federation. This was a clever manoeuvre designed to relaunch the Palestinian question and oblige Nasser to take it up. Nasser accepted the idea, but refused to implement it until the Palestinian people had been properly consulted, which amounted to denying any representative status to the Arab Higher Committee and the Gaza assembly. New institutions were set up in Gaza and the Mufti left Egypt to take refuge in Lebanon. Colombe comments: 'Nasser was, in short, concerned not with forming a provisional government destined to be that of a future independent state . . . but only with creating a sort of Palestinian body intended to be the spokesman for Cairo's policy'.

Thus, at this time, the question of the Palestinian people and its self-determination and independent struggle was not an issue either for Nasser or for the Arab Higher Committee. This view was, with some nuances, shared by the Palestinians themselves, and by their cadres who were actively struggling in the various Arab nationalist movements. Only Fatah, after the Suez campaign, began, in Gaza, to sound a discordant note. We shall return to this point later.

On 9 March 1959, under pressure from Haj Amin al-Husseini in Beirut, who was demanding the formation of an independent Palestinian state, the thirty-first session of the Arab League decided to reconstitute the organization of the Palestinian people, to set up its 'entity' (*kiyan*) which would represent it and to form a Palestinian army.[28] But Qassim's Iraq set the argument going again in spectacular fashion. Acting as if Nasser and Hussein of Jordan had no role in the matter, Qassim proposed the formation of a Palestinian government in Gaza and the West Bank, and the proclamation of a Palestinian Republic. In August 1960 he set up a Palestine Liberation Army. This had a considerable impact on the Palestinians and his ideas may have influenced Fatah. By launching the notion that the Palestinians should take control of their own affairs, Qassim cut clean across the Arab national-ism represented by Nasser and encouraged the Palestinian political tendency that favoured autonomy.

Despite Qassim's fall in August 1963, and faced with their inability to prevent the Israeli plan to divert the waters of the Jordan, the Arab states had to move further. In January 1964 Nasser proposed the setting up of a Palestinian 'entity'. Shuqairy, who had been representing Palestine at the Arab League since September 1963 (following the death of Ahmad Hilmi Pasha), was appointed, after the first Arab Sujmmit in Cairo, to carry out consultations on the creation of a 'Palestinian entity'. On 28 May 1964 the first Palestine National Congress met: the Palestine Liberation Organization was born.

The birth of the PLO was not achieved without the participation of the Palestinian people, even if inter-Arab rivalries played a determining role. A new generation of Palestinian leaders was emerging which stressed the Pales-tinian people's own struggle. It was represented in the National Congress.[29] But its ideas were still very much those of a minority, as is clear from the discussions. The Congress was held in Jerusalem from 28 May to 2 June 1964 and was attended by 420 delegates. It adopted two basic texts: the National Charter and the Basic Constitutional Law of the PLO.

The most striking feature of these texts is the absence of all reference to any sovereignty either of the Palestinian people[30] or of the PLO, or to a Palestinian state. Article 24 of the Charter even states specifically that the PLO exercises no 'regional' (*iqlimiya*) sovereignty over the West Bank of the Jordan, the Gaza Strip of the al-Himma area. Articles 24 and 25 make no mention of any military responsibilities falling on the PLO. These two points were the conditions laid down for the presence of King Hussein at the opening of the Congress.[31] But the PLO did not adopt these positions only because of Arab pressures; it did so also because Arab nationalism was still heavily predominant. Thus the stress in the Charter was laid above all on the definition of Palestine as 'an Arab homeland bound by ties of nationalism [*qawmiya*] to the other Arab countries which, together with Palestine, constitute the greater Arab homeland' (Article 1).

It is not until Article 3 that the Charter refers to 'the Palestinian Arab people [which] possesses the legal right to its homeland', but it goes on to add immediately that this homeland 'is an inseparable part of the Arab Nation'.[32]

This brief summary (we shall return to these issues in discussing the modi-fication of the Charter in 1968) enables us to appreciate how original Fatah's positions were at this time.

Fatah's Originality

Fatah came into existence in October 1959, in Kuwait. Its leaders had mostly been educated in Cairo and participated in the struggles of 1955–56 in Gaza and along the Canal. This particular experience gave rise to a distinctive stance within the Palestinian movement; but it was not until 1967 that it won over the bulk of the Palestinian people.

> By the fall of 1959, Fatah was beginning to publish its views, although not openly under its own name. The essential point in Fatah's argument was that the liberation of Palestine was primarily a Palestinian affair and could not be entrusted to the Arab states. At best, the Arab regimes could provide aid and protection, and if the occasion arose they might also contribute their conventional armies. But Palestinians were to take the lead in the battle with Israel. The Algerian war of liberation was cited as an example of what might be done in Palestine.[33]

These themes, propounded in the paper *Filastinuna* [*Our Palestine*] — published by members of Fatah in Beirut between 1959 and 1964 — clearly went against the prevailing pan-Arabism. They were strengthened by the breakdown of the union between Syria and Egypt in 1961 and the victory of the Algerian revolution in 1962. Some formulations were violently against the Arab regimes. Thus one of the editors of *Filastinuna* wrote:

> All we ask is that you [the Arab regimes] surround Palestine with a defensive belt and watch the battle between us and the Zionists. [Or again:] All we want is that you [the Arab regimes] keep your hands off Palestine.[34]

This enabled Ehud Yaari to assert:

> 'Palestinianism' is the cornerstone, both in terms of the date of its appearance and in terms of its theoretical importance, of Fatah's political views . . . It is based on the belief that the conflict is above all a Palestinian-Jewish conflict and that the Arabs have generally only a secondary role in it, as well as on their desire to facilitate a 'national renaissance' of the dispersed Palestinian people. It was only at a later stage that other elements were added to this principle, in particular the People's Liberation War.[35]

One of the historic leaders of the Arab Nationalist Movement — a pan-Arabist organization set up in Beirut in the 1950s which was to be Fatah's great rival (it was the ANM that was to give birth to the PFLP in 1967) — summarized for me the differences between the two organizations at the time:

> In 1964 the ANM did not believe that the Palestinians could liberate Palestine. For us it was only a matter of keeping the Palestinian question alive. We thought that liberation would come from Nasser.

And he told this typical story:

> We first met Yasser Arafat in 1964. At that time he had no mass support, but he asked us to co-ordinate the action of Fatah and the ANM. We agreed, on condition that we could agree on a common political programme. Yasser Arafat then said it was not worth the bother, and that the problem was one of joint armed action, 'blood unity', as he put it. The negotiations failed. From 1965 onwards, Fatah embarked on armed actions whereas we were explaining to our militants that we must wait, that we must train, and so on. Then we saw that our militants were joining Fatah. Because of the rightist leadership of the ANM [i.e. George Habash], we lost a historic opportunity.[36]

Fatah's break with the dominant ideology in the Arab world could not fail to provoke opposition from Arab governments; after the first military operations, the organization was even called an agent of CENTO. Only with Syria, and then only for a short time, did some limited collaboration occur — but the Syrian regime saw this in the context of opposition to the pro-Egyptian PLO. Several Fatah leaders, who already had some influence, participated in the first Palestine National Congress.

After the launching of the first armed operations against Israel in January 1965, Fatah confirmed its stand in a memorandum addressed to the second PNC (May–June 1965).[37] It stated that the Palestinian people was responsible for the liberation of its homeland, adding that the role of the Arab armies was to defend the borders against Israeli reprisals.

These theories had a direct influence on the formulation of Palestinian goals and on the notion of soveriegnty. Instead of leaving the sovereignty of Palestine vague (as had been done in the 1964 Charter), or merging it in an Arab sovereignty, Fatah proclaimed clearly that a Palestinian government had to be set up and Palestinians given a passport. Above all, it proclaimed that there existed parts of Palestine under Arab control and that there had to be movement in these parts towards the proclamation of a governing revolutionary Palestinian national authority acting for Palestine in co-operation with Arab regimes.[38] This is a formulation that was to reappear in 1974, at the time of the twelfth PNC. Moreover this line was confirmed when Fatah denounced the failure of the Palestinian movement to create a state in Gaza and the West Bank in 1948. The argument was frequently made in Fatah's publication that the failure to create such a state had deprived the independent Palestinian struggle against Israel of its 'geographic base'.[39]

As has been pointed out earlier, Fatah's distinctive stand is partly explained by the origins and background of the 'leading group'. A comparative study, which is at present rather sketchy, of the leaders of Fatah and those of the ANM (which was to give birth to the PFLP and the PDFLP) is quite revealing.[40]

In 1969-70 there were ten members of the Fatah central committee. Study of the available biographies leads to a number of conclusions: They were all born in Palestine in the late 1920s and early 1930s and grew up there. Their families were generally solid Sunni Muslim bourgeois. They all studied in Egypt (except Khalid al-Hassan), were active in the Palestine Students Union and took part in the events in Gaza in 1955-56, helping the resistance during the Israeli occupation. They suffered Nasserist repression, either in Cairo (Abu Iyad, Arafat) or Gaza (Abu Jihad, Muhammad al-Najjar).

If we take the leaders of the ANM, they are more difficult to place and for some of them there are no reliable biographies. From the available evidence, however, some conclusions can be drawn. The ANM was a pan-Arabist movement and many of its leaders were not Palestinians. Even among the leaders of the PFLP (and the group which split off from it in 1969, the PDFLP, later to become the DFLP), a sizeable proportion were not Palestinians (Nayef Hawatmeh, Hani al-Hindi) or were born outside Palestine (Abu Leila). They were mostly from the middle bourgeoisie, and several were non-Muslims (Habash, Wadi Haddad). According to Quandt, one-third of the members of the central committee of the PDFLP were non-Palestinians or non-Muslims. Finally, these leaders acquired their political experience in Beirut (often at the American University) or in Amman.

What can we deduce from these observations? While for both groups Palestine was the central issue, this 'centrality' was perceived differently in the light of different experiences. For the leaders of Fatah, it was related to the fact that they were all born in Palestine and to the links they kept up with the last relatively autonomous fraction of the Palestinian people, those in Gaza (five members of the central committee were born in Gaza or had become refugees there in 1948). They had taken a direct part in the many struggles in Gaza, such as the demonstrations of 1 March 1955,[41] for which Muhammad al-Najjar was imprisoned for two years; or in guerrilla operations against Israel (Abu Jihad). In Cairo, where several of them went to pursue their studies, they had organized themselves into the Palestine Students Union and thus had experience of an autonomous organization of Palestinian people. Appreciating the virtues of Arab nationalism of the Nasserist type, they also saw its limits and even suffered repression. The experience of the Gaza campaign and the struggle against the Israeli occupation was the final decisive formative factor;[42] they participated directly or indirectly in the only great confrontation between the Palestinian masses and Israel between 1948 and 1967. They learned several lessons from it, of which the first and most important was that the struggle rested above all on the Palestinian people; the second lesson was that initiatives by Arab states, including Egypt, were, as Abu Iyad put it, dictated 'by reason of state and not by the Palestinians'.

The leaders of the PFLP and the PDFLP, coming through the ANM, had a different experience. In Lebanon, as in Jordan, official policy was to eliminate Palestinian consciousness among the refugees. Repression on a significant scale, and the desire to assimilate in Jordan, prevented the development of the Palestinians' own struggles. The Palestinian masses were part of the overall struggles (against the Baghdad Pact, the 1956–57 struggles in Jordan, the civil war in Lebanon in 1958). The existing regimes were obstacles to the liberation of Palestine; the Jordanian government had been directly responsible for the 'catastrophe' of 1948; in the struggle dividing the Arab world, the Palestinians in Lebanon and Jordan naturally found themselves on Nasser's side. The presence of non-Palestinians, or of Palestinians who were not born in Palestine, made their attachment to Palestine more 'ideological'; they felt its loss more as a catastrophe for the Arab nation than as a direct loss for themselves. And it was this too that created the desire to give priority to finding solutions to the crisis of the Arab homeland.

These few observations enable us to have a better understanding of the 'two lines' in the Palestinian movement. One last observation should be added. It concerns the cohesion of the two groups: Fatah was far more united (of the ten members of the central committee in 1969, six were still members in 1984, while the other four were dead). Herein lies one of the main reasons for the superiority of Fatah over all the other Palestinian groups.[43]

A more detailed study of this theme would be most rewarding. It ought to make possible a comparison with the Palestinian leaderships of 1936–39, in terms of social background, age, level of education, and so on.

The 1967 War and the Changes in the PLO

The 1967 war and its disastrous results for the Arab leaders created a new situation. It contributed to the retreat of Arab nationalism, in particular its Nasserist version. The 'regionalists', those who had banked on the independence and autonomous decision-making of the Palestinian people, saw their position strengthened.[44] The ensuing political, ideological and military situation enabled the groups of the Palestinian armed Resistance, and Fatah above all, to move to the front of the Arab stage.

Shuqairy's PLO, which had symbolized the attitude of submission to the Arab countries, was engulfed in crisis; Shuqairy resigned. The armed organizations had the wind in their sails. Negotiations were held to integrate them into the PLO. Even before it affected the PLO, the debate on Palestine and its future had begun in Cairo among intellectuals in the corridors of power. In October 1967 Ahmad Baha' al-Din, a leading Egyptian personality, launched the debate in the newspaper *al-Ahram* by proposing the formation of a Palestinian state in Jordan (including the West Bank) and Gaza.[45] A long debate followed in which numerous Palestinians participated, such as Ghassan Kanafani, Shafiq al-Hut and Barhan al-Dajani, to name but a few.

Baha' al-Din's argument was that whereas, until then, the Palestinian question had been treated as an Arab question – a situation helped by the fact that the Arabs had taken part in the partition of Palestine in 1948 — there now had to be a Palestine state. This was so, he argued, for a whole series of reasons.

First, a Palestinian state would demand its due, the return of the seized lands; then, it would help the Palestinian people to return to its homeland rather than going into exile. The PLO would thus have both a people and a land for its fight. But there was no question of those who returned to the state giving up their right of return (to the pre-1948 land). Finally, the nature of the regime in the future state would not be a fundamental problem. The homeland was more important than the regime.

In a second article,[46] Baha' al-Din surveyed the initial reactions to the first one. This survey is of particular interest because it dealt with objections that were to re-emerge later in the debate on the democratic state.

The first objection came from those who asserted that there was a contradiction between the creation of a Palestinian state and Arab unity. The problem, they said, was not one of creating a new state but of liberation. Agreed, replied Baha' al-Din; Arab unity is our ultimate goal, but it is difficult to attain. Must we wait for Yemen (then still under British colonial rule) before we can achieve Arab unity? Palestine would be a state like any other Arab state.

The second objection was that the time was not ripe and the first priority was to liquidate the consequences of the aggression of 6 June 1967. Yes, replied Baha' al-Din, we must liquidate the consequences of the aggression, but not so as to return to the *status quo ante*. The proposal for a Palestinian state would also make it possible to create an intermediate stage between the ultimate goal (the liberation of the whole of Palestine) and the existing situation. This idea of stages was important, he concluded.

Another worry, said the author, came from those who saw a similarity between his proposal and Israel's proposal for setting up a Palestinian entity in the West Bank which would enjoy some degree of autonomy. This was misguided, he replied, since his idea presupposed the withdrawal of Israeli forces from the territories occupied in 1967. Nor was there any question of returning to the 1947 Partition Plan, since this plan was intended to put an end to the Palestinian problem. Baha' al-Din added however that, like Ghassan Kanafani, he thought that the proclamation of a Palestinian government — on 15 May 1948 (without accepting the Partition Plan) — would have greatly altered many things.

In a third article,[47] the author asserted that his proposal did not specify the means by which it would be achieved: political means? military means? Similarly, the process of setting up the state, its relations with the Hashemite monarchy and the PLO, and so on, were left somewhat vague.

These then were some of the questions being discussed among Arab intellectuals in the period following the 1967 defeat. The fourth PNC, which met in Cairo in July 1968, continued the debate. The PNC included 100 participants from the Resistance groups: 38 from Fatah, Sa'iqa and several small organizations; 10 from the PFLP; 30 from the old PLO; 20 from the

Palestine Liberation Army (PLA). The National Charter and the PLO Basic Constitutional Law were amended, but there was no agreement on a new executive committee.

What were the key amendments in the area that concerns us, the relationship between Arab and Palestinian nationalism? The fundamental amendment concerned the place of armed struggle; it is worth noting that it is linked in the same article to self-determination and sovereignty. Article 9 reads:

> Armed struggle is the only way to liberate Palestine and is therefore a strategy . . . The Palestinian Arab people affirms . . . its right of self-determination in . . . and sovereignty over [its homeland].

Article 1 defines Palestine as:

> the homeland of the Palestinian Arab people and an integral part of the great Arab homeland and the people of Palestine is part of the Arab nation.

Thus the emphasis is put, from the beginning, on the Palestinian Arab people, whereas the former definition of Palestine made no mention of it.

This insistence is also seen in the Charter's definition of the role of the PLO. Thus Article 26 stipulates:

> The Palestine Liberation Organization, which represents the forces of the Palestinian revolution, is responsible for the movement of the Palestinian Arab people in its struggle to restore its homeland, liberate it, return to it and exercise the right of self-determination in it. This responsibility extends to all military, political and financial matters, and to all else that the Palestine issue requires in the Arab and international spheres.

All the limitations on the role of the PLO that had been listed in the 1964 Charter were thus lifted: the former article concerning the West Bank, Gaza and al-Himma was purely and simply abrogated.

As for the Arab regimes, Article 28 is particularly clear:

> The Palestinian Arab people insists upon the originality and independence of its national (*wataniya*) revolution and rejects every manner of interference, guardianship and subordination.

Finally, according to Hourani,[48] there was a debate on the rights of Palestinians in the West Bank and Gaza. Article 29, which asserted that 'the Palestinian Arab people possesses the prior and original right in liberating and restoring its homeland', was a response to Hashemite designs on the West Bank, as well as to the theories of 'Arab nationalists' for whom the Arabness of the West Bank and Gaza was all that mattered. But the formulation remained vague, and the future of the 'occupied territories' was not yet clear for the PLO.

Thus this fourth PNC saw Fatah's theses triumph; the Arab character of the liberation struggle was certainly not rejected but pride of place was given to its Palestinian aspect.

While no reference was made to a Palestinian state either in the Charter or in the Basic Constitutional Law, or in a long political resolution adopted,[49] this was not the case (in the last-mentioned text only) for a state in the West Bank and Gaza. The PLO bluntly rejected the creation of what it called a 'puppet Palestinian entity'. This view may seem surprising, given that, as we have seen above, Fatah had pronounced itself in favour of a Palestinian authority in the West Bank and Gaza. Abu Iyad himself wrote that:

> In July 1967 F. Kaddoumi submitted a political report to the Fatah central committee in which he put forward proposals for the strategy and tactics of our movement. It was in this document that he was already suggesting that we should come out in favour of a mini-state in the West Bank and Gaza, in the event that these two areas were returned by Israel, which had just conquered them. Such a short- and medium-term goal was, he maintained, not only in conformity with the ownership rights of the Palestinian people over every inch of its homeland, but was also in line with an objective analysis of the situation. For it was obvious that, however extensive and vigorous guerilla activities against the Jewish state might [sic] be, Israel would remain invincible for the foreseeable future. In these circumstances, it would be foolish not to envisage stages leading to the strategic objective, the creation of a democratic state in the whole of Palestine.
>
> Although realistic and well-thought-out, the Kaddoumi report, particularly the part dealing with a mini-state, provoked strong opposition within Fatah leading circles. At the time our implantation among the masses was not sufficiently well established for us to submit the document to intermediate-level cadres of the movement and, still less, to open up a public debate on the subject. We therefore decided to shelve the Kaddoumi report until better days.[50]

What were the reasons for this change? They were, without doubt, varied and not always easy to discern. They are examined in greater detail in Part Three, although they can be summarized here. The first reason lay in the desire not to confront the Hashemite regime directly, especially right after the war, by demanding sovereignty over a territory that it had annexed in 1948.

The second was that the objective itself seemed rather unclear, given that quite sizeable fractions of the Palestinians in the West Bank did not see the PLO as their organization. Who would rule the future state? In any event, not the PLO; it could not decide for such a solution. The total rejection of Resolution 242 must also be traced to this fear. This obstacle could not be removed until the PLO had asserted itself indisputably as the representative of the whole Palestinian people. Moreover, there were the divisions within the PLO itself and the organizations of the Palestinian Resistance. At the fourth PNC, Fatah confronted not only the old guard of the PLO but also the PFLP which was playing an active role, and the Arab nationalist tendencies that were opposed to 'regionalism'.

Finally, in 1967–68 certain rumours, together with some attitudes among Israeli leaders, led to the impression that they were not hostile to a 'Palestinian entity'. This substantially increased Fatah's misgivings.

The Debate on the 'Jewish Settlers'

At this point, it is important to look at the other facet of the definition of the democratic state, the issue of the 'Jewish settlers'. This issue had already been discussed in the period before 1948. Lesch stresses that during the 1936 revolt the aim was not to drive the Jewish community out, but to make it realize that it formed part of a predominantly Arab area.[51] Nabil Sha'ath, a leading figure in Fatah, developed the same idea by referring to the testimony of the Peel Commission in 1937 and that of Count Bernadotte in 1948.[52] He added moreover that after 1948 the idea of coexistence disappeared; it was replaced by that of a 'return' to the lost paradise. The enemy was identified as the Jew who had driven the Palestinian people out; there was no longer any distinction between Jew and Zionist.

On this point, there appears to be wide agreement, in the texts of both Fatah and the ANM;[53] to European ears, they have a distinctly anti-Semitic ring.[54] This consensus was expressed in the 1964 PLO Charter where it is stated: 'Jews who are of Palestinian origin will be considered Palestinians if they will undertake to live loyally and peacefully in Palestine.' Thus all those not 'of Palestinian origin' (that is, those who had been living in Palestine for several generations) were excluded, and they made up 95% of Israeli Jews. It might be noted that in Article 18 Judaism is described as a 'revealed religion' and not as a nationality.

Fatah's positions, such as they were expressed in *Filastinuna*, were the same. There was talk of 'criminal Jews'[55] or the 'destruction of the Jewish presence'.[56] The change of position came about after the 1967 war.

In an interview with the Algerian paper *Moudjahid* in late 1967 a Fatah leader, most probably Arafat, declared:

> We are not the enemies of Judaism as a religion nor are we enemies of the Jewish race. Our battle is with the colonialist, imperialist, Zionist entity which has occupied our homeland. We affirm that the presence of Israel as a state constitutes a bridgehead for imperialistic American colonialism in the Arab world, a gendarmerie which imperialism can spur into action at any time it so desires. The interests of imperialism and of Zionism in our homeland are one and the same.[57]

This position was clarified in Fatah's Press Release No. 1 of January 1968, which specified that its operations were not aimed at:

> the Jewish people as such, with whom they [the Arabs] lived in harmony in the past for so many centuries. Nor does it [Fatah] intend to throw them into the sea. The resistance and the liberation movement that *Fatah* is co-ordinating is aimed solely at the Zionist-military-Fascist regime which has usurped our homeland and expelled and repressed our two million people, condemning them to a life of destitution and misery. [The press release ended:] *Fatah* and the entire Palestinian people believe in their just cause and their ultimate victory. And they also know that on the day the flag of Palestine is hoisted over their freed, democratic, peaceful land, a new era will begin in which the Palestinian Jews will again live in harmony side by side with the original owners of the land, the Arab Palestinians.[58]

This distinction between Judaism and Zionism was first made explicit in the Palestinian Resistance (except for the Communists): it led Fatah to draw a distinction among Israelis themselves, but such a distinction was not easy to make.

The aims as regards the Israelis remained far from clear; thus in a statement made in early 1968 a Fatah leader explained that the aim of Palestinian organizations waging the internal struggle was:

> to prevent immigration and encourage migration . . . To prevent immigrants becoming attached to the land [of Palestine] . . . To create and maintain an atmosphere of strain and anxiety that will force the Zionists to realise that it is impossible for them to live in Israel.[59]

The 'democratic' objective of co-existence among Jews, Muslims and Christians is completely absent from this formulation.

The amendment of the Charter at the fourth PNC, on the question of the 'Jewish settlers', reflected these ambiguities. It should be recalled that this session took place at a time when the central question was that of Palestinian sovereignty *vis-à-vis* the Arab states; and that Fatah was in a minority and in addition divided on the question of a democratic state. Abu Iyad stresses[60] that the internal discussions had already been going on for over a year when, in October 1968, Fatah announced publicly the proposal for a democratic state.

This situation doubtless explains the gap between the text of the Charter and the proposals adopted by Fatah a few months later. Article 6 of the Charter laid down:

> Jews who were living permanently in Palestine until the beginning of the Zionist invasion will be considered Palestinians.

The equivalent article in 1964 stated:

> Jews who are of Palestinian origin will be considered Palestinians if they will undertake to live loyally and peacefully in Palestine.

As can be seen, the new formulation omitted 'undertake to live loyally and peacefully', a restriction that distinguished between Jews and other Palestinians. On the other hand, it remained vague and ambiguous. If the date of the 'Zionist invasion' was 1917 (as laid down in other PNC documents), by 1968 there were no, or very few, Jews living in Israel who met this criterion: no reference being made — contrary to Article 5, which defines the Palestinian Arabs — to their descendants.

The dominant impression prevailing in the outside world was that Article 6 was simply a repetition of Shuqairy's slogan 'drive the Jews into the sea'. Extremely clever Israeli propaganda was to use this argument for all it was worth.[61]

A few months later, the third Fatah Congress defined its conception of the Palestine of the future: 'A democratic, progressive, non-sectarian state in which Jews, Christians and Muslims would live together in peace and enjoy the same rights.'[62]

This did not mean that the ambiguities had been removed, indeed to a degree they were deliberately sought by the leadership of Fatah. This is what Abu Iyad said of them after the press conference at which he had presented these new proposals:

> Journalists attending my press conference asked with which Israelis we intended to coexist: with those born in the country? with the immigrants? with new ones or old ones? I replied evasively, as I did also to questions on the precise content of the democratic state. I did so for two reasons: on the one hand, we felt that we had to await the response of the other party before going into details and negotiating a compromise (and the fact is that up to today neither Israel nor any other power, big or small, has shown the least interest in our proposal, by asking us to spell it out, for example); on the other hand, as had been foreseen, the proposal that I announced, even though in prudently vague terms, caused a wave of protests both in the ranks of the Palestinian movement (and even within Fatah) and among the Arab rulers. The idea that one could coexist with a people that had usurped and colonized our homeland, after half a century of bloody struggles, was still too novel, not to say intolerable, for many. It took much courage, even daring, to go beyond the accumulated traumas and frustrations, and also a political mentality formed over several decades. But we overcame the burden of the past by getting adopted, four months after my press conference, by the fifth Palestine National Council (1–4 February 1969), a resolution confirming our strategic aim.[63]

This ambiguity was reflected in the very diverse proposals that were made, some of which were later condemned by Fatah itself; thus, in a statement to *Tribune Socialiste* on the occasion of the second Solidarity Conference with Arab Peoples (Cairo, 25–27 January 1969), a Fatah leader declared:

> There is a large Jewish population in Palestine and it has grown considerably in the last twenty years. We recognize that it has the right to live there and that it is part of the Palestinian people. We reject the formula that the Jews must be driven into the sea. If we are fighting a Jewish state of a racial kind, which had driven the Arabs out of their lands, it is not so as to replace it with an Arab state which would in turn drive out the Jews. What we want to create in the historical borders of Palestine is a multi-racial democratic state . . . a state without any hegemony in which everyone, Jew, Christian or Muslim, will enjoy full civic rights. *It is possible to imagine many formulae to achieve this, from the Lebanese solution to a confederal type of arrangement. We are ready to look at anything with all our negotiating partners once our right to live in our homeland is recognized.*[64] [author's italics]

Such stands could not fail to evoke widespread opposition from the various camps in the Palestinian Resistance and the Arab countries. At the same time, the appearance in February 1969 of a new organization, the PDFLP, born out of a leftist split in the PFLP and proclaiming allegiance to Marxism–Leninism, helped to make the debate more wide-ranging.

Before examining the debate, we must emphasize the significance that many Palestinian leaders attach to the battle of Karameh as a turning-point for the adoption of the slogan of a democratic state and above all of co-existence with the Jewish settlers. According to Dr Sartawi:

> Until Karameh we were living a dream, the dream of 'return': return to the old Palestine, to our houses, our fields, and so on. We looked to the Palestine of the past. Karameh gave back the dimension of hope to the Palestinian people; after Karameh, victory once again became possible for the Palestinians and then we (I am speaking from a collective point of view, of group psychology) saw the Israelis for the first time. And we asked ourselves, what are we going to do with them?[65]

3. The Debate

Opposition to the Slogan of a Democratic State

The various objections to the slogan were summarized in an internal PDFLP circular[66] drawn up at the end of the sixth PNC (September 1969), which had seen a major confrontation over the question of a democratic state. They can be reduced to two positions: one that maintained that the democratic state was a tactical slogan that was useful to brandish for propaganda reasons; and one that rejected the slogan and saw it as being in contradiction with the Arab nature of Palestine and the principle of self-determination enshrined in the National Charter. This school of thought also refused to envisage a peaceful settlement in which the Jews of Palestine would participate.

It was the latter school that publicly expressed its stand most clearly. The pro-Iraqi Arab Liberation Front (ALF), formed in April 1969, gave a good summary of these views, especially as they related to the links between the Palestinian struggle and the Arab struggle. In a long political statement, released in Amman on 30 August 1969,[67] it spelled out its argument. According to the ALF, the danger threatening the Palestinian revolution after two years was: 'the attempts to contain the revolution within its regional framework and to cut the artery which joins it with its source of strength, ability and competence in the masses of the Arab revolution'. While not questioning the need that had once existed to stress Palestinian identity, it condemned the attempts to: 'provide the Palestinian identity with an image that is distinct from the Arab identity and even, whenever possible, at variance with it'.

After this scarcely veiled attack on Fatah and the warning against 'exaggerating Palestinian capacity', the ALF asserted that what was necessary was 'armed popular struggle characterized by Arabism, socialism and democracy', which would mobilize the entire Arab nation. The ALF added that the concentration of this mobilization on Palestine would:

> both create unity [of the Arab nation] and liberate Palestine, and just as unity will restore to Palestine its freedom, so Palestine will restore to the Arabs their unity. Palestine is the road to unity and unity is the road to Palestine.

On this basis, it was not surprising to see the ALF oppose the proposal for a democratic state[68] as a symbol of 'regionalist'. (*qutria*) thinking which was seeking to build a fifteenth or sixteenth Arab state, and assert that the question of the Jews could only be settled within the framework of the Arab nation. This was specified even more clearly during a debate organized by the review *al-Anwar* in March 1970;[69] criticism of the slogan of a democratic state, said the representative of the ALF:

> is not directed at its democratic aspect, but primarily against the Palestinian state it talks about. We are convinced that no state set up in Palestine can remain democratic — whoever governs it — in conditions of Arab disunity and imperialist influence and designs such as exist in the area today.

This school of thought was also backed by the Nasserist organizations, such as Sartawi's, for example.[70] But it should be noted that this line seems to have had no support from Cairo, which gave its whole-hearted support to Fatah until the Rogers Plan. In an interview, moreover,[71] Sartawi confirmed that the link between his organization and Cairo was purely ideological and that during the period 1968–70 he had had no contact with Nasserist leaders.

Another important tendency adopting this same line of argument, but in a different perspective, was the PFLP. This organization was the heir to the ANM, which had made the question of Arab unity the corner-stone of its strategy. Born of the Arab defeat in Palestine; the ANM was mainly organized around a number of intellectuals at the American University of Beirut.[72] Its theories on the Palestinian question were very clear; they were expressed in the review of *al-Th'r* [Vengeance], which appeared between 1952 and 1958. On 25 March 1954 it wrote:

> So long as a unified state grouping Iraq, Jordan and Syria does not exist (as a first step), our confrontation with the Jews and the Western alliance will be virtually impossible.

And on 22 December of the same year it wrote:

> the regionalist [*iqlimi*] treatment of the question of the Arabs in Palestine is one of the causes of the *nakba* [the catastrophe of 1948]

and added that it

> drives a wedge between the other Arab masses and the Palestinian Arabs.

This publication did not use the words Palestinians or Palestinian people, but spoke of Arabs of Palestine or Arab refugees.[73]

The ANM later converted to Nasserism and adopted the views of the

Egyptian leaders until the 1967 defeat, despite the opposition of a left-wing element that was more and more critical of Nasser, organized around the Lebanese Mohsen Ibrahim, and Nayef Hawatmeh. During this period, and unlike Fatah, the ANM's theories on Palestine (it had set up a Palestinian branch called the Palestine National Liberation Front) were not based on the idea of mobilizing Palestinians but on the idea of intervention by the Arab states; the Palestinians' task was to act as catalysts. Its military operations began even before the 1967 war.

The 1967 war hit the ANM very hard and in July 1967 it published a long manifesto with the significant title, *The Struggle of Destiny between the Arab Revolutionary Movement and Neo-Imperialism*,[74] in which Palestine went almost unmentioned. The reasoning was as follows: since Israel is linked to imperialism and Arab reaction, no victory is possible without a direct confrontation with imperialism and reaction. This total war must not be confined to the single battlefield of the war with Israel, but extended to the whole Arab world. A united front must be formed for the Arab struggle, and that requires embarking on armed struggle. Once again, the Palestinian struggle had been subordinated to the Arab struggle and the victory of Arab unity, but this unity could only be achieved through revolution.

A perceptible change occurred, however, with the foundation of the PFLP as an independent organization; its first policy statement was published in the newspaper *al-Hurriya* on 11 December 1967.[75] The emphasis was placed not only on the Palestinian struggle and armed struggle but also on the Arab character of this struggle and the 'organic link' between the Arab nation's struggle and the Palestinian struggle. The shift very rapidly became even more marked. The revolution in the Arab world became the condition for the liberation of Palestine. 'The road to Jerusalem goes through Amman', the PFLP was to say, taking up an old slogan of Shuqairy's during the PLO-Jordanian crisis of 1966.

Thus George Habash, questioned on the problems of the Jews and Arab refugees, asserted on 10 December 1969 that these problems could not be settled in the framework of a 'democratic state' but only in the Arab framework, and only once that framework had been transformed.[76] In an interview with *al-Ahrar* on 22 May 1970, he disputed the idea that the democratic state could have 'a definite national identity. . . separate from the Arab homeland and the Arab nation, and not forming an integral part of the Arab nation'. He argued that the process of liberating Palestine would be:

> the climax of unification and the radical change that will overtake the whole Arab region and especially the area bordering Israel. Consequently, Palestine liberated from Zionism and imperialism will become, through a natural process, a part of a unified revolutionary Arab entity.

The democratic solution to the Jewish question was an altogether different problem:

all Jewish citizens in liberated Palestine who are organically [*sic*] linked to the Arab homeland and nation will enjoy their rights as citizens.[77]

Thus despite a critique of Arab reaction, the (Iraqi) Ba'thists and the PFLP were taking up, albeit in a modified form, what had been the ANM's theory on Palestine during the previous 20 years. However, neither of the two organizations contemplated 'driving the Jews into the sea'. The right of Jews to remain in Palestine was gradually asserting itself in Palestinian political thought.

The proposal also ran up against the hostility of the traditional leaderships of the Palestinian people, be they the PLO old guard or the Arab Higher Committee. Nabil Sha'ath noted this in the report he made to the Kuwait symposium in early 1971. The generation that had guided the destinies of the Palestinian people between 1945 and 1965 saw, he said, only the 'Palestine of the past, that is a Palestine without three million Jews'.

The Arab Higher Committee expressed this clearly in a long statement on 12 March 1970,[78] in which it denounced the idea of a democratic state, and spoke out against coexistence with Jews as impossible and against the minority status of the Palestinians in such a future state. This statement must also be seen as taking issue with the PLO, whose representatives the Arab Higher Committee had always disputed.

The PLO old guard, which had rallied to Arafat in 1968-69, took a stand that was subtler but all the same very reticent. Thus Shafiq al-Hut, a member of the executive committee of the PLO since before 1967, declared during the *al-Anwar* debate, 'Let us be honest, when we speak of a democratic state, that means a non-Arab state.' He added that it was impossible for the Palestinians to negotiate any such thing, and that they did not have the right to do so. As to the Jews, they had to be told that the Zionist movement had not solved their problems and they should go back to their own countries and find another solution. This was one of the PLO's old themes: Shuqairy had used it in a statement addressed to the Jews of Israel on 30 October 1967.[79]

An article written in 1969 throws an interesting light on the debate going on in Beirut.[80] There were two schools of thought on the question of the 'Jewish settlers'. The first proposed an 'Algerian solution'. If the Jews continued to oppose the idea of a democratic state, then the Resistance would encourage those Jews who wanted to remain in liberated Palestine and assist in the departure (with assistance money) of those who wanted to leave. It was clear that the latter group would be much the larger. In this context, 'all efforts must be directed towards military victory'. The other school proposed the 'one man, one vote' solution. This proposal rested on the fact that the development of the Palestinian armed struggle would make it possible for attitudes to change. Racial and national prejudices would be overcome and the bases laid of an alliance between Jews and Arabs.

The Pro-Syrian Ba'th and the Proposal

In these polemics, the pro-Syrian Ba'th curiously enough found itself on the side of Fatah. Although it proclaimed its devotion to Arab unity, and despite the fact that dreams of a Greater Syria were still alive in Damascus, the Ba'th developed novel attitudes when it came to power in February 1963.

The reason for this must be sought mainly in inter-Arab contradictions.[81] The breakdown of the tripartite negotiations on unity between Egypt, Syria and Iraq in 1963, the fall of the Ba'th in Iraq in November of the same year, the creation of a PLO dominated by Cairo and the relative isolation of Damascus in the Arab world — all these factors explain why Syria sought to make itself the champion of the Palestinian cause. This was reflected ideologically in a re-evaluation of the place of Palestine in Ba'thist doctrine. The existence of Israel was treated as the principal obstacle to Arab unity and the cause of the setbacks of 1961 and 1963. To achieve unity, the first thing to do was to liberate Palestine; thus linking up with Fatah's slogan 'Palestine is the road to unity.' In addition, stress was placed on the role that Palestinians must play in this fight. Thus a communiqué from the National Command published in Damascus in *al-Ba'th* on 5 March 1964 set out the features of the Palestinian entity then being debated.

> 1. It must be incorporated into a popular organization in which the Palestinians will be able to express their will in complete freedom; it will also have to be provided with an effective authority to make it fit to exercise the sovereign rights of the people of Palestine in its country.
> 2. It must have available to it an army made up of, and commanded by, Palestinians, directly linked to the authority directing the Palestine people's organization. This army will be the revolutionary body in a position to carry out its responsibilities in agreement with the other Arab armies. . .
> 3. The Arab states will have the duty to support the Palestinian entity both morally and materially and will have to abstain from putting pressure on it or preventing it from accomplishing its wishes.[82]

The main aim here was, we must repeat, to counter Egypt and the placing of the PLO under Egyptian tutelage; but this stand paved the way for collaboration with Fatah, which got underway in 1964. But it was not problem-free. Thus Abu Iyad, who cited Syria as being the only Arab country (other than Kuwait) where Fatah militants were not persecuted, asserted:

> The government and the Ba'th party in power looked on us as 'separatists' in that we did not share their pan-Arab visions. . . While they did not fight us, the Damascus authorities nevertheless engaged in various manoeuvres designed to contain and even control us.[83]

In fact, collaboration continued until 1967, with ups and downs, depending on inter-Arab relations and power struggles in Damascus. Fatah set up bases in Syria, and groups set off from Syria to carry out operations in Israel (but by way of Jordan and Lebanon). These ups and downs are clearly revealed in the graph of the various military operations published by O'Neill.[84]

This conflict-laden collaboration led the Ba'th to set up its own Palestinian organization, the Vanguards of the Popular Liberation War, at the beginning of 1967; its military arm was Sa'iqa, set up in May 1968. Fatah was then asked to withdraw its training camps to Jordan, but the collaboration still continued. Sa'iqa was the first organization to enter the executive committee of the PLO with Fatah in February 1969; it was to remain there without a break until the 1975-76 Lebanese civil war and its collaboration and identity of views with Fatah are striking. In the period up to 1971 this collaboration rested on the following political bases: rejection of Resolution 242, 'peace initiatives' and the Rogers Plan.

To sum up, it can be said that the interests of Syria (and hence of Sa'iqa) and Fatah broadly coincided during this period and that each side got something out of the situation. (Whether this alliance was a strategic one is another question; the 1975-76 Lebanon war and the later events of 1982 were to answer in the negative.) Abu Musa, one of the leaders of Sa'iqa, could assert on 12 July 1970[85] that there had been no disagreement between Fatah and Sa'iqa in the strategic goals of the two organizations and their practice during the preceding period.

The change of regime in Syria in late 1970, with the seizure of power by Hafez al-Assad, did not alter the situation. Despite a total reassertion of control over Sa'iqa, which had been in the hands of Assad's opponents (led by Salah Jadid), relations between Assad and Fatah improved: in an interview with the Beirut newspaper *al-Nahar*,[86] the Syrian president asserted unambiguously his support for Fatah goals and a democratic state.

He thus adopted the positions propounded by Sa'iqa during the previous two years. Although it was not a particularly 'ideological' organization, and had contributed little to the debate, the pro-Syrian organization gave its support to Fatah's line. Thus, in the *al-Anwar* debate mentioned above, the representative of Sa'iqa asserted:

> for us . . . the slogan of the establishment of a democratic state is not a question of tactics, but of strategy, although so far its content has not been spelled out. . . The Resistance is still at the beginning of the road, but when it gets nearer to victory, there will be no option but to put forward a comprehensive programme.

He of course reaffirmed the Arab character of Palestine, but he saw in it a means of solving the economic problems which would arise from the fact that Jews and Palestinians would remain in Palestine (even though he thought that a number of them, particularly Arab Jews, would want to return to their own countries); the difference with Fatah appears above all in the stress placed by Sa'iqa on the Arab character of a democratic state and on the fact that the problem was not solely a Palestinian one. That should not be surprising coming from an organization whose centre was in Damascus.

An Original Position: the PDFLP

The most original contribution to the debate came without doubt from the PDFLP, a leftist splinter from the PFLP. It was strongly expressed in a draft resolution submitted for the sixth PNC.[87] This text proposed in particular:

1. the rejection of all chauvinistic, reactionary, Zionist and imperialist solutions based on recognition of the state of Israel;
2. the rejection of chauvinistic solutions of Palestinian or Arab origin (massacring the Jews, driving them into the sea, and so on);
3. a popular democratic solution to the Palestine and Israeli problems. . .
   Such a solution would mean the setting up of a popular democratic Palestinian state for Arabs and Jews alike in which there would be no discrimination and no room for class or *national* [author's italics] subjugation and in which the right of both Arabs and Jews to perpetuate and develop their indigenous cultures would be respected;
4. the democratic state would be part of a federal Arab state;
5. national liberation, which would be the result of a long popular armed struggle and the total liberation of Palestine, would involve:
   the establishment of a democratic state in which Arabs and Jews shall enjoy equal *national* [author's italics] rights and responsibilities.

Three points need stressing: first, the clear-cut nature of the proposals concerning Jews and the denunciation of 'chauvinistic' Arab and Palestinian solutions — Fatah's proposals are indeed there, but formulated more forcefully and more precisely; secondly, the replacement of the concept of the 'coexistence of Muslims, Christians and Jews' by that of the 'coexistence of Arabs and Jews'; and finally, the reference to the cultural and national rights of Israeli Jews.

These last two points are interesting. They appear to mark a turning-point in Palestinian thought, since they seem to contain an implicit acceptance of the existence of two nationalities in Palestine. But this was not without contradictions. For example, the PDFLP sometimes spoke of two peoples;[88] it even referred to the Yugoslav and Czechoslovak models.[89] This might be thought to suggest recognition of a 'Jewish people' or an 'Israeli Jewish people'; but, as Harkabi very accurately points out, this would be a very special people, a people without the right to build its own state. Here the PDFLP, which claimed to be Marxist-Leninist, ran into an insurmountable theoretical contradiction. Lenin's writings[90] on nationalities could not be clearer. For a Leninist organization, recognizing the existence of a nation means recognizing its right to self-determination and hence to 'separation', to the creation of an independent state. Recognizing an Israeli Jewish nation meant recognizing the right to separation, to an independent state; in short it meant recognizing the state of Israel.

This was a step that the PDFLP could, of course, not take. The consensus in the PLO and among the Palestinian people at that time was clear:[91] Judiasm was a religion, it could in no way constitute a nationality. All that could be recognized were some cultural rights. Rodinson explains very clearly the difficulties Palestinians and Arabs have in envisaging the Jews as a nation[92] on the basis of the experience of coexistence between Jewish or Christian communities and Muslims in the Middle East.

The PDFLP did not go beyond such a framework. Through its secretary-general Hawatmeh,[93] it rejected even the idea of a binational state since such a state 'conflicts with the progressive proletarian approach for solving the Israeli and the Palestinian problems'. No clarification was given, either then or later, as to the nature of this conflict. This same position is confirmed in several PDFLP statements.[94]

It may then be wondered whether there was not some misunderstanding in Western Europe about the PDFLP's stand. When, for example, Chaliand writes: 'the PDFLP was the only movement to defend the thesis of a Palestinian state in which Jews would enjoy national rights',[95] is he not in fact putting a gloss on a thought that is much more fluid and contradictory?

Everything seems to point in that direction, in particular Hawatmeh's interview cited above, in which he stated:

> The PDFLP considers – and it is a ideological position – that Judaism is purely and simply a religion. The Front however believes in the legitimacy of 'Judiasm' as a culture for the Jewish communities and in particular for that community that is in the land of Palestine today.

While this does not detract from the merits of the PDFLP stand, it does put it in a more modest place,[96] especially as another aspect, which is often neglected, involved adherence to the slogans of Arab nationalism.

The leaders of the PDFLP, like those of the PFLP, had emerged from the ANM, and they had been influenced by Nasserism, and later by the myth of a socialist revolution in the Arab world. What was important for them in the democratic state was above all the solution of the Jewish question; the setting-up of an independent state seemed to them, in fact, a utopia. In a memorandum submitted to the sixth PNC, it was clearly stated: 'the popular democratic state of Palestine shall form an inseparable part of a federal Arab state in this area'.[97] In an interview appearing on 3 July 1970, on the relationship between the Palestinian revolution and the Arab revolution, Hawatmeh replied:

> The Palestinian revolution is an inseparable part of the Arab revolution and any attempt to 'Palestinianize' the Palestinian question is in the last analysis a rightist attempt and nationally suspect.[98]

41

This idea was defined even more clearly in May 1970 in a communication from the PDFLP to the first World Conference of Christians for Palestine:

> Foundations must be laid that guarantee the non-return of Zionism. This will be possible only if the Palestine of the future is an integral part of a socialist state embracing the whole area. . . as the removal of Zionism depends on the success of the Arab revolution, it is naive to imagine the Palestine of the future independently of the area. . . The fact that the unitary state will be socialist is enough to establish the objective foundations, so that Palestine should be truly democratic, with no trace of national oppression.[99]

Thus, through the myth of a socialist state, the PDFLP lapsed into Arab 'unitary' positions. The liberation of Palestine goes through Arab unity, but an Arab socialist unity.

Finally, we cannot end discussion of the position of the PDFLP without recalling that it was the first organization to launch the idea of a dialogue with an Israeli organization, Matzpen. This dialogue (which was not rejected by an organization like Fatah) was certainly limited by the tiny size of the organization in question; but it did mark a change that was to lead to the discussions with the Communist Party (Rakah), and later with a number of Zionist organizations after 1973. A form of recognition of the existence of an Israeli people was thus initiated.

Fatah in the Debate

The debate and the objections were not altogether futile: they led Fatah to clarify a number of its stands, and to review others. In addition to various statements, this section will rely mainly on two texts: one has been mentioned earlier, Dr Sha'ath's intervention in Kuwait; the other is entitled *La révolution palestinienne et les juifs* [The Palestinian revolution and the Jews], which is anonymous, but seems to have the same author as the first.[100] It is not claimed that these closely reasoned and finished texts represent the whole of Fatah's political thought in the 1968–71 period. Fatah is a movement with a variety of tendencies and sensitivities. Nevertheless they represent the thought of the leadership group around Arafat and they are confirmed by all the statements made by its leaders. Defining what the democratic state is and what it is not, Nabil Sha'ath asserts:

1. It concerns the whole of Palestine: there can be no question of a 'rump state' in the West Bank and Gaza.
2. It is not an Israel Mark Two; it will be a non-racist and non-sectarian state.
3. It can only result from the destruction of the Zionist state and armed struggle.

4. The new state will accept all the Jewish settlers who so desire.

5. It will not be a state like Lebanon or Cyprus.

6. We cannot go into details of the solution since we are only at the beginning of our struggle.

He then raises the two objections to his proposal:

1. Those who believe that it is a tactical slogan. The author recognizes that there are reservations about the 'settlers' and a certain tendency to turn them into a religious problem and to resort to anti-Semitic arguments in some Arab and Palestinian circles. Arafat himself had deplored this: 'We have been very hurt by the extremist declarations of the Arab world. . . since we are very attached to our Jewish friends.'[101] Sha'ath sees the solution in the revolutionary education of the younger generation that is increasingly less open to the arguments of the older generation, in the learning of Hebrew[102] and in contacts with progressive Jews. He also stresses the participation of Israeli Jews in the Palestinian armed struggle. Generally, Fatah was always to make a great propaganda play about Israeli Jews who joints its fight.[103]

2. Others, such as the PFLP, the PDFLP and the ALF, says Sha'ath, accept our approach to the Jewish problem, but do not want to talk of a state, and see the future in an Arab United State. This is not denied by Fatah, but, says Sha'ath, we see the Palestinian state as a step towards federation.

The anti-Arab character of Fatah propaganda in this period was quite marked; it often stressed that the first martyr of the revolution had been killed by 'an Arab bullet' when returning from a mission inside Israel.[104] It clearly set out its policy towards the Arab countries in saying that 'Fatah stood by the principle of non-intervention in the affairs of Arab states. At the same time, it wanted no interference in its own affairs and considered the independence of its revolution as a basic condition of its success.'[105] This led Yaari to say:

> Al-Fath, in contrast to Shuqairy, the 'Popular Front', and even Syria, never accepted the view that the downfall of the monarchic regime in Jordan is a condition for the struggle against Israel.[106]

Thus, while accepting the idea of Arab unity, Fatah confirmed its line: the liberation of Palestine and the formation of an independent Palestinian state must come first.

Sha'ath also denounces the ALF's violent attack on the idea of a democratic state, since 'it gives credence to the idea that the new vision of the Palestine of the future is subordinate to inter-Arab polemics thus destroying its credibility'. This attack, he says, was so violent that it prevented the amendment of Article 6 and thus enabled Israeli propaganda to attack the democratic state and the contradiction between the texts.

In the same framework of ideas, that of the relationship between the Arab character of Palestine and the democratic state, an important objection is often made concerning the Jewish 'majority', the non-Arab majority. Fatah's replies on this issue do not always agree, except on one point: Jews who so wish will be able to live in Palestine.

It is obviously impossible to understand the various types of arguments without taking into account the balance of power within the Palestinian Resistance and above all with other Arab countries. If an organization as small as the ALF (but representing Iraq) could secure postponement of the amendment of Article 6, it is because in its concrete tactics and its problems, it is difficult for the PLO and Fatah to forgo the aid of any Arab country. Sha'ath is correct in saying that these polemics undermine the credibility of the democratic state.

On the question of the 'majority', Arafat replied in August 1969:

> A democratic, progressive State in Palestine is not in contradiction to that State being Arab. . . Such a State can only acquire stability and viability by forming a part of the surrounding area, which is the Arab area. . . The majority of the inhabitants of any future State of Palestine will be Arab, if we consider that there are at present 2,500,000 Palestinian Arabs of the Moslem and Christian faiths and another 1,259,000 Arabs of the Jewish faith who live in what is now the State of Israel.[107]

On the same point, he later stated:

> Our demand is not connected to a certain number but to a basic notion according to which every Jew who will give up the. . . Zionist ideology and agree to live with us in the Palestinian state, within a framework which the Palestinian revolution will determine for its democratic state, will be welcomed.[108]

The book *La révolution palestinienne et les juifs* stresses other factors that will maintain the Arab majority: higher birth rate; increase in emigration brought about by the development of the revolutionary struggle; the possibility for Jews from Arab countries to return to their home countries.

While Sha'ath stresses the fact that the two communities represent the same number of individuals, he adds that the real problem lies elsewhere. However many Jews there are in the future Palestine, their rights must be guaranteed; their participation in the revolution will be another guarantee.

A preliminary survey confirms two points:

— the prominent place occupied by discussion on the democratic state in the Palestinian Resistance. At a time when the Resistance is engaged in a difficult struggle, both against Israel and against the Arab states, one cannot but be struck by the scale of the debate. This confirms the importance attached to this question by the PLO, which has sensed how decisive it will be for the future.

— the evolution of Palestinian political thought. This is confirmed by Abu Hatem and Dr Sartawi,[109] who both saw the battle of Karameh as the vital turning-point from the point of view of Palestinian 'collective psychology'.

We shall now examine how this evolution and debate were translated at the level of the various PNCs, that is at the highest level of the PLO.

The Discussion of the Democratic State in the PNCs

To appreciate the impact of the debate, it is important to underline what made up the consensus among the Palestinian organizations in the Resistance (except for the Communist Ansars):

1. Armed struggle as 'the only way leading to the liberation of Palestine'; hence the rejection of all negotiated solutions (on the basis of Resolution 242, and Rogers Plan, and so on). A democratic state is thus considered not as a plan, or a negotiable proposal, but as a strategic objective.

2. The liberation of the whole of Palestine as the necessary condition for the establishment of a democratic state. No compromise with the Zionist leaders is possible, no accommodation with the Zionist structures imaginable.

3. The rejection of the 'rump state', i.e. a state in part of Palestine, in particular the West Bank and Gaza.

But the debate was also dominated by the internal struggles among the Palestinian organizations; in this period 1967-70, Fatah's hegemony was far from being secure. The PFLP disputed this leadership, particularly during 1970.

> Throughout 1970 it was the PFLP which, by virtue of its growing strength on the ground, in Jordan, and through the adventure of the seizure of hostages in June in hotels in Amman and in September in airliners near Zarka, asserted itself, willy-nilly, over the PLO.[110]

This struggle had two immediate consequences for the debate: it forced Fatah, which without any doubt sought the broadest possible unity (for the reasons that we have examined), to make compromises and concessions; and it sometimes gave the discussion a significance that it did not possess. Thus Dr Sartawi stated that aspects of the internal conflict heavily influenced the discussion on the democratic state:

> We thought that we were dealing with a manoeuvre by Fatah and Arab reaction; we thought it was some sort of trap, but didn't know what sort. Hence our initial refusal and rejection of the Fatah proposals.[111]

As we have seen, the fifth PNC, in February 1969, was the first to talk of a democratic Palestine. The PFLP took no part in this PNC, however, being in the throes of an internal crisis.

The sixth PNC met in Cairo, in September 1969. The question of the democratic state was again strongly posed, but the PFLP sent only an observer and the ALF was absent. The memorandum presented by the PDFLP led to a wide-ranging debate at the end of which the slogan was adopted, but with some reservations. The resolution on policy laid down that the goal of the Resistance was to continue the struggle 'until victory and the construction of the Palestinian democratic state'.[112] But the recommendations of the commission on policy and information stated that while it was in favour of the 'retention of this slogan in its [the PNC's] policy resolutions and statements', it, at the same time, requested of the executive committee 'the setting up of a commission to study it and clarify it fully'.[113] The commission was asked to present the results of its work at the following meeting of the PNC. The result was thus positive for Fatah, but it also showed the limits of its action in the PLO and the strength of the reservations. These were also apparent in the problem of the amendment to Article 6 of the Charter. Dr Yusif Sayegh, the head of the PLO Planning Board, asserted in a letter published in *The Times* of 28 February 1970[114] that at the sixth PNC, Fatah, Sa'iqa and the PDFLP submitted an amendment to Article 6 of the Charter stating that all Jews freed from colonialist attitudes who agreed to live in peace with the Muslims and Christians would be able to live in Palestine. A sub-committee was set up to submit an amendment to the second session of the PNC. Why was the decision postponed?

In the first place, Article 33 of the Charter laid down that any amendment of the Charter required an extraordinary meeting of the PNC, convened for this purpose. The sixth PNC had not been so convened; but in that case, why not? Secondly, amendment of the Charter required a two-thirds majority. At this time, Fatah, Sa'iqa and the PDFLP had 53 votes out of 112,[115] they also had the support of a number of independents, but did they have a two-thirds majority? (Especially as Fatah seemed not to be unanimous on the question.)

The seventh session of the PNC, which had been postponed several times, was held in the Egyptian capital from 30 May to 4 June 1970. The political and military situation of the Resistance had undergone considerable change, and clashes with the Lebanese and especially the Jordanian government had grown in number. On the agenda were: national unity in face of the Hashemite regime, and the various proposals for a negotiated solution based on Resolution 242. The PFLP, as we have noted, was riding high. The February 1970 crisis with the Jordanian government had enabled it to come together with the other groups in the Unified Command, which brought together 11 Palestinian organizations. Combining internal and external pressures on the Resistance, aeroplane hijackings and a solid implantation in the refugee camps in Jordan, it had gradually succeeded in imposing its political line. This role was reflected in the agreement signed on 6 May 1970 between the various Palestinian organizations (11 organizations signed it, including the PFLP and Fatah; only the Ansars were not asked to ratify it), which made it possible to convene the seventh PNC. This agreement was one of the basic texts adopted by the PNC.

All reference to the democratic state had disappeared from the 6 May agreement. The only vague reference to it is in the following phrase:

> The objective of the Palestinian struggle is the liberation of the whole of Palestine to establish a community in which all citizens will coexist with equal rights and obligations within the context of the Arab nation's aspirations for unity and progress.[116]

Another resolution adopted by the PNC stated that the latter:

> refers the subject of the 'democratic state' to the executive committee for exhaustive study, the conclusions of which it shall submit to the [PNC] at its next session.[117]

There was no reference to amendment of Article 6 of the Charter. There had thus been a distinct retreat on the question; the evolution of the balance of forces in 1970 had not been favourable to Fatah.

But another offensive was underway during the seventh PNC, even though the PFLP was in the end only represented by one token delegate: it was waged on the grounds of the unity of the 'Jordanian-Palestinian theatre'. The Palestinian Resistance movements had been faced by the question of relations with Jordan since 1967. As we have seen, the 1968 Charter had removed all restrictions placed on PLO action in the West Bank; at the same time, the PLO did not lay claim to sovereignty over the West Bank. This contradiction was only really resolved after the PLO had accepted the idea of the creation of a state in the West Bank and Gaza.

There was another related problem: it was Britain that had separated Transjordan from Palestine after the First World War, and some Palestinian groups saw this as just one aspect of the division imposed by colonialism on the Arab nation. These organizations, particularly the PFLP and the PDFLP, were to use the Palestinian presence in Jordan and the special place they occupied in the armed strategy to demand 'the unity of the Jordanian-Palestinian theatre'; it was their way of asserting their 'Arab nationalist' character.[118]

The fifth and sixth PNCs had made little reference to Jordan, which was looked upon mainly as a support base. The 6 May agreement marked a turning-point in that it asserted 'the unity of the people in the Jordanian-Palestinian theatre' in point 2. This formulation was combined with a text with strong 'Arab nationalist' overtones. The final resolution further accentuated these aspects.[119] Another novelty at this PNC was the participation of a Jordanian 'popular' delegation in the proceedings.[120] It asked for an amendment to the Charter of the PLO and its Basic

Constitutional Law to allow Jordanians to participate fully in the PLO. Demands were even made for the Jordanian delegate to have seats in the PNC. Arafat opposed this. The final outcome was the setting-up of a Higher Committee of the National Movement in the East Bank and of the Palestinian Revolution. It should be stressed that this was a way of asserting the difference between the two movements: Fatah had yielded a great deal of ground at this PNC, but it could not yield on what it saw as essential – the autonomy of the Palestinian movement *vis-à-vis* all other forces in the Arab world, whether states or not.

The assertion of the unity of the people in the Jordanian–Palestinian theatre offered direct encouragement to those who thought that the liberation of Palestine involved the fall of King Hussein. The crisis of June 1970 and the PDFLP's slogan, 'All power to the Resistance', showed that the dividing line in the Palestinian movement had not disappeared. Fatah attempted to resolve the conflict with Hussein, the PFLP and PDFLP tried to aggravate it. Egypt and Jordan's acceptance of the Rogers Plan further deepened these divisions. The emergency PNC held in Amman in August 1970 condemned Nasser's attitude and threatened the Jordanian government; it reasserted the unity of the people in the Jordanian–Palestinian theatre and the 'refusal to divide the country into two small states, one Palestinian and the other Jordanian'.[121]

In the space of a few months, the Palestinian Resistance, cut off from Nasserist Egypt (and doubtless not having appreciated how much disarray its opposition to Nasser created among the Arab masses) and subject to ever stronger pressures from its extremist wing, lost much of its support. Faced with a Jordanian government and army whose only dream was to deal with it once and for all, it was unable to avoid the military confrontation of Black September in 1970 and its disastrous consequences.

Black September precipitated a crisis in all the Palestinian organizations; much ink was spilled in polemics over the causes of the defeat. The eighth PNC met from 28 February to 5 March 1971, in Cairo, against the background of continuing combats in Jordan which, in July, were to end in the elimination of the Resistance. The PFLP and the PDFLP stressed the need to struggle against the Jordanian regime, and unity between the Jordanian and Palestinian masses. In their view, the slogan of a democratic state was no longer on the agenda.[122] Sa'iqa was divided; it was one element in the hands of Salah Jadid's 'civilians' in their power struggle with Hafez al-Assad's 'military' in Damascus. There were also some stirrings in Fatah. It was in this context that the eighth PNC nevertheless reasserted the slogan of a democratic state:

> The armed struggle of the Palestinian people is not a racial or religious struggle directed against the Jews. That is why the future state that will be set up in Palestine liberated from Zionist imperialism will be a democratic Palestinian state. All who wish to will be able to live in peace there with the same rights and the same duties, in the framework

of the Arab nation's aspirations to national [*qawmiya*] liberation and total unity. . . particularly unity of the people on the two banks of the Jordan.[123]

In an interview on the outcome of the eighth PNC,[124] Arafat declared that for the first time the Assembly had taken up Fatah's slogan of a democratic state in Palestine. 'Although other assemblies have discussed this aim', he said, 'they had not endorsed it. This is an unprecedented event and a significant outcome.'

The contradiction between the assertion of the need for a democratic Palestinian state and the unity of the two banks of the Jordan runs through all the statements of the PNC. But it remains true that they marked a success for Fatah, the more so as it was clearly reaffirmed that the PLO had become the sole representative of the Palestinian people, and that it was up to the PLO to lead the revolution to victory. This affirmation, taken up by the emergency PNC in Amman in 1970, marked a great step towards the real recognition of Palestinian autonomy.

The final elimination of the Resistance in Jordan, the failure of attempts to overthrow Hussein and the proposal for a United Arab Kingdom in 1972 were to impose new responsibilities on the PLO. While the unity of the two banks looked like a utopia, the question of the PLO's sovereignty over the territories occupied since 1967 and the formation of a Palestinian state became very much a live issue. It took a long time before the PLO formulated this goal; after Black September, defence of the revolution (and no longer liberation) became the essential task. A change in the regional balance of power had to occur in order to make these new formulations possible. Then, in an about-turn often seen in political history, the opponents of a democratic state were to become its strongest supporters, to the extent that this slogan could be used to combat the slogan of a state in the West Bank and Gaza! In another irony of history, the question of 'the unity of the two banks' would re-surface after the elimination of the Palestinian Resistance in Beirut in 1982; then Fatah was to be somewhat favourable to the idea, whereas the PFLP and the PDFLP were to be decidedly reticent.

Before attempting to draw some conclusions from this debate on a democratic state in the period 1967-70, we shall examine briefly two aspects not so far mentioned: the problem of secularism and the problem of the social structure of the state.

The Secular Nature and Social Structure of the Democratic State

Contrary to a widespread notion, the idea of a democratic state is not associated with the idea of a secular state in Palestinian political thought.[125] In fact the idea of a secular state does not appear in any of the PLO's official texts of this period, nor in those of Fatah or any other organization, although it can be found in one or two declarations.[126] The term generally used is 'non-sectarian'. As Arafat explained: 'We did not issue the slogan calling for the establishment of a secular state. . . I am certain . . . that this is a distortion of the expression of democracy we proclaim.'[127] As an author reflecting the views of Fatah explained, Fatah did not define the Palestinian state as secular 'lest the Arabs might use this matter as a justification for abandoning the responsibility of supporting the Palestinian revolution'.[128] It is certainly true that the concept of a secular state (*ilmani*) is one very unlikely to win much of a hearing among the Arab masses, and only the Ba'th Party has adopted it.

Moreover this concept of a secular state did not appear in the later stages. Neither the various PNCs nor even the fourth Congress of Fatah in 1981 made any reference to it. It would appear that today, as a result of a curious shift of meaning, the term secular state is used by those who envisage the co-existence of religious communities, whereas an organization such as the PFLP avoids the term and envisages the coexistence of two national or quasi-national communities.

As for the social structure of the future state, it is not a major concern of the Palestinian organizations. Two trends can be discerned on this question: the first, with the PFLP and PDFLP, calls for a Marxist–Leninist socialist state;[129] the second, with Fatah, postpones this problem until victory. Arafat has stated this clearly: 'We do not debate the structure of the new state in detail because what we need now is the greatest possible national cohesion.'[130]

It is this latter thesis which is to be found in PLO statements, which only touch vaguely on the question. It takes a good dose of misunderstanding of the discussions in the PLO to be able to assert, as Jureidini does, that the idea of a democratic state was imposed on Fatah by the PFLP and PDFLP, thus confusing a democratic state and a state of people's democracy![131]

Conclusions

Discussions on the democratic state did not end with the holding of the eighth PNC. They continued, not on the slogan itself which was never again to be seriously questioned, but on the strategic issues raised in the course of four years of lively debate which had produced an evolution in Palestinian political thought. The later evolution cannot be understood without appreciating the qualitative leap involved in the adoption of the slogan of a democratic state.

First, by asserting the need for an independent Palestinian state, Fatah and the PLO confirmed their break with all the Arab nationalist theories that had dominated the Palestinian movement over the previous 20 years. They confirmed the necessity of the self-determination of the Palestinian people, and of its having its own organization, led by Palestinians and having autonomy *vis-à-vis* the Arab countries. Of course this autonomy was not total — the PLO was dependent on various sources of Arab support, and on inter-Arab contradictions — but it would attempt to use these to maintain its freedom of decision. The 'Arab nationalist' currents, in their various forms — particularly the 'revolutionary' one — were in a small minority, especially after Black September. Acceptance of the idea of a Palestinian state, parallel to that of Palestinian sovereignty, opened the way to new ideas. As a PLO official said:

> The slogan of a democratic state constituted an intermediate stage between the first period when chauvinistic slogans were put forward (driving the Jews into the sea) and the present period when we have accepted the idea of a state on any liberated part of the territory. Progressive ideas have thus begun to have real bases.[132]

The PLO would claim its rights in the West Bank and Gaza and then accept — in the event of the liberation of these territories — seeing a 'revolutionary government' and later an independent state set up there.

Secondly, there was the acceptance of the Jewish presence. This idea had two major consequences. First, it led to the recognition of the fact that Israeli Jews had a place in the future Palestine, whence the beginnings of a dialogue. Certainly, it was limited; but the scope quickly broadened: first to the Israeli Communist Party (Rakah) and then to a number of Zionist organizations and figures. This dialogue was not always straightforward but it was to lead to a new grasp of Israeli reality. The second consequence flowed from a contradiction inherent in the proposal itself. If the right of Israeli Jews to remain in Palestine was recognized — they would have the same rights and duties as the rest of the population — how at the same time could the structure of the state be decided without them?[133] What would happen if a majority of Israeli Jews refused to live with the Palestinians? Did not the acceptance of the Jewish presence imply the idea of the self-determination of Israeli Jews? This fear surfaced among various opponents of the proposal. Arafat himself recognized it when he said:

> The Palestinians first announced that they were willing to live in a democratic state in which Muslims, Jews and Christians would live on an equal footing. But this suggestion was rejected. Our second proposal envisages the setting-up of a Palestinian state on all the territories from which the Israelis withdraw.[134]

Thus the slogan of a democratic state contained the seed of future developments in Palestinian political thought. But this would require a lengthy transformation, linked not only to the internal debate within the PLO, but also and above all to the development of the regional and international situation, the attitude of the various factions of the Palestinian people and the emergence, after 1973, of the Palestinians in the occupied territories as a determining force.

The history of this evolution will be examined in Parts Two and Three. First, however, one last comment is necessary. The whole debate just discussed was marked by the total absence of thinking about the state as a legal entity, that is as defined by the following five elements: a territory; a population; a state apparatus; an international legal personality; and sovereignity.[135] Unlike the Algerian revolution or the Vietnamese revolution which had, through their political programmes, clarified these various elements, the Palestinian Resistance was incapable of doing so. And this was as true in 1984 as it was in 1970. It is easy to understand why when one examines each of the five elements mentioned. How could there be any talk, in legal terms, of the population of the future Palestinian state when the Palestinian Resistance could not even define who would be a 'Palestinian citizen' and who not? How could one speak of a state apparatus when it had not been decided whether there would be two nationalities – or one – making up Palestine? This difficulty was to be aggravated with the acceptance of the idea of a state in part of Palestine. What would be the status of such a state? By virtue of the principle of effectiveness in international law, did not the setting-up of such a state ensure mutual recognition between Palestine and Israel? These were all questions that were never touched upon, because the replies would have cut through the ambiguities that marked the PLO discussion of the state.

Notes for Part 1

1. See especially W. Quandt *et al.*, *The Politics of Palestinian Nationalism*, University of California Press, 1973.

2. For this section, see ibid., pp. 52-5 and 75-82, and Bard E. O'Neill, *Armed Struggle in Palestine*, Boulder, Colo., Westview Press, 1978.

3. Interview with Dr Sartawi, Paris, 22 December 1980.

4. *International Documents on Palestine 1970*, Beirut, Institute for Palestine Studies, p. 750. (Henceforth cited as *IDP* with the year of reference.)

5. *Al-wathaiq al-'arabiya al-filastiniya 1970* [Palestine Arab Documents], Beirut, Institute for Palestine Studies, p. 993. (Henceforth cited as *PAD* with the year of reference.)

6. Abu Iyad, *My Home, My Land: A Narrative of the Palestinian Struggle,* New York, Times Books, 1981, pp. 65 and 139.

7. R. Sayigh, *Palestinians: from Peasants to Revolutionaries*, London, Zed Press, 1979, pp. 175-6.

8. O'Neill, *Armed Struggle*, pp. 114-19, and J. Rabinovich and H. Shaker (eds.), *From June to October*, New Brunswick, N.J., Transaction Books, 1978.

9. O'Neill, *Armed Struggle*, p. 118.

10. Ibid., pp. 237-42.

11. *Middle East Record 1969-70*, Tel Aviv, Shiloah Center, 1976, p. 242. (Henceforth cited as *MER 1969-70*.)

12. See, for example, the press conference on the principles of the armed struggle in *PAD 1970*, pp. 228–34.

13. O'Neill, *Armed Struggle*, pp. 115–19 and table, p. 81.

14. *Al-kitab al-sanawi lil-qadiya al-filastiniya 1968* [*Annual Survey of the Palestine Question*], Beirut, Institute for Palestine Studies, p. 88. (Henceforth cited as *ASPQ* with the year of reference.)

15. Iyad, *My Home, My Land*, pp. 65 and 139, and *IDP 1968* p. 453.

16. Quoted in *Les palestiniens et la crise israélo-arabe*, Paris, Editions Sociales, 1974, pp. 167–8.

17. Interview with Abu Hatem (Muhammad Abu Mayzar), Fatah official responsible for international affairs, Beirut, May 1982.

18. For the stand of the National Liberation League, see M. al-Sharif, *Al-shiyu'iya wal-mas'ala al-qawmiya al-'arabiya fi filastin 1919–1948* [Communism and the Arab National Question in Palestine], Beirut, PLO Research Centre, 1981. See especially document no. 14: Address by the League to the British Prime Minister in October 1945.

19. See *IDP 1969*, p. 589.

20. Ibid, p. 666.

21. N.J. Mandel, *The Arabs and Zionism before World War 1*, University of California Press, 1980. See especially pp. 80 and 152 and ch. 9.

22. For this section, see Y. Porath, *The Emergence of the Palestinian Arab National Movement 1918–1929*, London, Frank Cass, 1974, especially pp. 70–122.

23. Ibid., pp. 199–216 and 274–94.

24. Abu Iyad, *My Home, My Land*, pp. 137–8.

25. See for example M. Colombe, *Orient arabe et non-engagement*, vol. I, Paris, P.U.F., 1973.

26. See for example Sayigh, *Peasants to Revolutionaries*.

27. See especially M. Colombe, 'Les problèmes de "l'entité" palestinienne dans les relations interarbes', *Orient*, Paris, 1st quarter, 1964, and O. Carré, *Proche-Orient entre la guerre et la paix*, Paris, E.P.I., 1974, pp. 91–5.

28. I. Sakhnini, 'Al-kiyan al-filastini 1964–1974' [The Palestinian Entity], *Shu'un filastiniya*, no. 41–2, January 1975.

29. See the list of those invited in R. Hamid (ed.), *Muqararat al-majlis al-watani al-filastini 1964–1974* [Resolutions of the PNCs 1964–1974], Beirut, PLO Research Centre, 1975. It includes particularly the names of Khalid al-Hassan, Khalil al-Wazir, Kamal Adwan and Yasser Arafat. But the last-named did not attend.

30. See F. Hourani, *Al-fikr al-siyasi al-filastini 1964–1974* [Palestinian Political Thought], Beirut, PLO Research Centre, 1980, 247 pp.

31. Ibid., pp. 30–1.

32. For the Arabic text of the Charter see the appendices to Hourani's book. For the debates at the first Congress, see chs. 1 and 2 of the same work.

33. Quandt *et al.*, *Politics of Palestinian Nationalism*, p. 56. See also the interview cited above with Abu Hatem, who sees the Algerian revolution as one of the main sources of inspiration for the Palestinians.

34. E. Yaari, 'Al Fath's Political thinking', *New Outlook*, November-December 1968.

35. Ibid.

36. Interview with Abu Adnan (Abd al-Karim Hamad), member of the political bureau of the PDFLP, Paris, December 1981.

37. Hourani, *Al-fikr al-siyasi*, pp. 120–1.

38. The idea of a Palestinian national authority is to be found in a November 1961 issue of *Filastinuna*, quoted by Sakhnini, 'Al-kiyan al-filastini'.

39. Yaari, 'Al Fath's Political Thinking', p. 23.

40. See Quandt *et al.*, *Politics of Palestinian Nationalism*, part II, ch. 3. See also App. 1 and 2 for biographies of Fatah leaders. A more detailed study remains to be done.

41. See the article in *Filastin al-thawra* of 10 November 1980 on the 1 March 1955 events in Gaza.

42. See particluarly Carré, *Proche-Orient*, pp. 91–2; Abu Iyad, *My Home, My Land*; and App. 2.

43. On the role of the 'leading group' and the importance of its cohesion for the influence of a party, see *Gramsci dans le texte*, Paris, Editions Sociales, 1975, pp. 458–9.

44. It should be noted, however, that this ideology was already in crisis following the collapse of the UAR (the United Arab Republic, the union between Egypt and Syria) in 1961 and the breakdown of talks between Egypt, Syria and Iraq in 1963. See particularly Rabinovich and Shaker (eds.), *From June to October*, p. 248.

45. A. Baha' al-Din, *Iqtirah dawla filastin wa ma dara hawlhu min muna-qashat* [The proposal for a Palestinian state and the debate that followed], Beirut, Dar al-Adab, 1968, 184 pp.

46. Ibid., p. 76.

47. Ibid., pp. 175–6.

48. Hourani, *Al-fikr al-siyasi*, pp. 151–2.

49. See the text of the resolution in Hamid, *Muqararat*.

50. Abu Iyad, *My Home, My Land*, p. 138.

51. Quandt *et al.*, *Politics of Palestinian Nationalism*, p. 17.

52. Dr Nabil Sha'ath, 'Palestine of Tomorrow', speech at the Second International Symposium on Palestine, Kuwait, 13–17 February 1971, in *Fateh*, 23 March 1971.

53. On the ANM see W. Kazziha, *Revolutionary Transformation in the Arab World*, London, Croom Helm, 1975.

54. Even then they must not be transposed mechanically. On this see Rodinson's analyses in *Peuple juif ou problème juif?*, Paris, Maspero, 1981.

55. Quoted by Sakhnini, 'Al-kiyan al-filastini'.

56. Quoted by *Fiches du Monde Arabe* (henceforth *FMA*), Palestiniens Fiche IP 14 (11 September 1979).

57. *IDP 1967*, pp. 727–9.

58. *IDP 1968*, p. 305.

59. Ibid., p. 300.

60. Abu Iyad, *My Home, My Land*, p. 138.

61. See for example Y. Harkabi, *Israël et Palestine*, Geneva, Editions de l'avenir, 1972.

62. *FMA* Fiche IP 14a (18 September 1979).

63. Abu Iyad, *My Home, My Land*, p. 139.

64. *Tribune Socialiste*, 30 January 1969.

65. Interview with Dr Sartawi, Paris, 9 March 1981. Similar comments by Dr Sha'ath.

66. Quoted by Harkabi, *Israël et Palestine*, pp. 139-40.

67. *IDP 1969*, pp. 767-71.

68. Declaration of 19 December 1969 cited by *ASPQ, 1969*, p. 123.

69. See the debate published by *al-Anwar* (Beirut), 8, 15 and 22 March 1970, on the democratic state. See also a more detailed statement of the ALF theses in *PAD 1970*, p. 325.

70. *PAD 1970*, p. 210.

71. Interview with Dr Sartawi, 22 December 1980.

72. Kazziha, *Revolutionary Transformation*.

73. Quotations taken from Sakhnini, 'Al-kiyan al-filastini'.

74. *IDP 1967*, pp. 636-42.

75. Ibid., pp. 723-6.

76. *PAD 1969*, p. 830.

77. *PAD 1970*, p. 336; on the same theme see the contribution by Ghassan Kanafani, a member of the politbureau of the PFLP, to the debate cited above in *al-Anwar*.

78. *PAD 1970*, p. 147.

79. *IDP 1967*, p. 690.

80. H. Sharabi, 'Palestine Guerillas: their Credibility and Effectiveness', *Middle East Forum*, vol. XLVI, nos. 2 & 3, Beirut, 1980.

81. For this section, see Quandt *et al.*, *Politics of Palestinian Nationalism*, especially the chapter 'The Palestinian Resistance and Inter-Arab Politics'.

82. Published in *Orient*, 1st quarter, 1964.

83. Abu Iyad, *My Home, My Land*, p. 45.

84. O'Neill, *Armed Struggle*, p. 172.

85. *PAD 1970*, pp. 528-9.

86. *IDP 1971*, p. 414.

87. *IDP 1969*, pp. 777-8.

88. Harkabi, *Israël et Palestine*, p. 142.

89. Interview with Hawatmeh in *Le Monde*, 31 May-1 June 1970.

90. See for example, 'Notes critiques sur la question nationale' and 'Du droit des nations à disposer d'elles-mêmes' in *Oeuvres complètes*, vol. 20 (December 1913-August 1914), Paris, Editions Sociales, 1959.

91. For a dissenting voice, see the article by the Israeli Communist leader Emile Touma, cited in *Les palestiniens et la crise israélo-arabe'*.

92. Rodinson, *Peuple juif*, pp. 246-53 and 328-61.

93. *IDP 1969*, pp. 805-7.

94. See the statement by the PDFLP representative to the newspaper *al-Anwar*, 8 March 1970.

95. G. Chaliand, *La résistance palestinienne*, Paris, Seuil, 1970, p. 102.

96. In my interview with the PDFLP leader Abu Adnan, he confirmed that there was a division in his organization on the question of an 'Israeli nationality'; this problem was discussed at their second Congress in May 1981. It was not settled.

97. *IDP 1969*, p. 777.

98. *PAD 1970*, p. 517.

99. Quoted by B. & N. Khader (eds.), *Textes de la révolution palestinienne 1968-1974*, Paris, Sindbad, 1975.

100. Fath, *La révolution palestinienne et les juifs*, Paris, Editions de Minuit, 1970. This book reprints three articles that appeared in March, April and May 1970.

101. *Le Monde*, 12 February 1969.

102. In 1969 Fatah published a book called '*Apprendre l'hebreu*'. Information given in *Journal of Palestine Studies* (Henceforth *JPS*), no. 1, Beirut.

103. See the series *Fateh*, published fortnightly in English, 1969–1970; for example, *Fateh* of 1 October 1969 on Kamal al-Nameri.

104. *Fateh*, 15 October 1969.

105. Ibid.

106. Yaari, 'Al Fath's Political Thinking'.

107. *IDP 1969*, p. 773.

108. Declaration of the 5 February 1970 reproduced in *MER 1969–70*, p. 336.

109. Interview with Abu Hatem, May 1982; interview with Dr Sartawi, 9 March 1981.

110. Carré, *Septembre Noir: refus arabe de la résistance palestinienne*, Brussels, Editions Complexes, 1980.

111. Interview with Dr Sartawi, 9 March 1981.

112. Hamid (ed.), *Muqararat*, p. 156.

113. Ibid., p. 151.

114. Cited by *Arab Report and Record* (Henceforth *ARR*), London, 1–15 November 1970. *Fateh* of 19 January 1970, cited by Quandt *et al.*, *Politics of Palestinian Nationalism*, asserts that Fatah called for an amendment of the Charter to remove the restrictions on Jews' obtaining Palestinian nationality.

115. R. Hamid (ed.), *Muqararat*, p. 31.

116. Ibid., p. 166.

117. Ibid., p. 162.

118. It would be interesting to have a full study of relations between 'Transjordan' and Palestine since the mandate. Until 1948 there was no particular participation by 'Transjordanians' in the Palestinian movement. On this see Porath, *Palestinian Arab National Movement 1918–1929*, pp.138–9. After 1948 the 'West Bankers' joined the Jordanian national movement and played a major part in the uprisings of 1956–57; but gradually, and particularly during the 1966 demonstrations, their demands took on a distinctly Palestinian flavour.

119. See Hamid (ed.), *Muqararat*, pp. 165–8.

120. For this section see *MER 1969–70*, pp. 308–10.

121. Hamid (ed.), *Muqararat*, p. 170.

122. Hourani, *Al-fikr al-siyasi*, p. 176.

123. Hamid (ed.), *Muqararat*, p. 178.

124. Cited by *Fateh*, 23 March 1971.

125. The notion is so generally accepted in France that Anouar Abdel-Malek, in his *La pensée politique arabe contemporaine*, Paris, Leuil, 1970, entitles the Fatah statement of 1 January 1970 'Pour une Palestine indépendante, démocratique et laïque' [For an independent, democratic and secular Palestine], although the word secular is nowhere used in the text quoted. If we are to believe Abu Hatem, however, it would seem that some Fatah leaders wanted to include the term in the statement but had to withdraw in the face of opposition to it.

126. *PAD 1970*, p. 247.

127. Interview cited by *MER 1969-70*, p. 335.

128. Farid al-Khatub, 5 February 1970, cited by *MER 1969-70*, p. 335.

129. Statement by the PFLP of 18 January 1970 cited by *MER 1969-70*, p. 335.

130. Interview of 6 January 1970 cited by *MER 1969-70*, p. 335.

131. P. Jureidini and W. Hazen, *The Palestinian Movement in Politics*, Lexington, Mass., D.C. Heath, 1976, p. 98.

132. Interview with Abu Ja'far (Abd al-Latif Abu Hijle), deputy head of the political department of the PLO, Paris, October 1981.

133. O. Carré, *L'idéologie palestinienne de résistance*, Paris, Armand Colin and Fondation Nationale des Sciences Politiques, 1972, p. 105.

134. *Le Monde*, 27 March 1980.

135. See P.-F. Gonidec and R. Charvin in *Relations Internationales*, 3rd edn, Paris, Editions Montchrestien, 1981.

Part II:
The Palestinians in the West Bank and Gaza and the Idea of a Palestinian State (1967-1973)

The idea of a 'Palestinian entity' or a 'Palestinian state' first saw the light of day after 1967 in the West Bank. In this Part we shall analyse the positions of the advocates of this proposal, the protagonists in the wide-ranging debate that ensued. It will also be shown how the discussion in the occupied territories, and the evolution of Palestinian national consciousness, ended up by impinging on the PLO, especially during 1973, both before and after the October war.

4. The First Phase of the Occupation

Face to Face with the Occupier

The occupation of the West Bank and Gaza in 1967 caused a new trauma for the people of Palestine, and a new flood of refugees. For the first time since 1948 (except during the occupation of Gaza in 1956) it left the Palestinians alone face-to-face with the Israelis. Just like the Gaza experience in 1956, the new occupation would play a major role in speeding up the development of Palestinian national consciousness. The first confrontation was between the Israelis and what Heller rightly calls 'the Jordanian establishment'.[1] This establishment had been installed by Amman after the annexation in 1950 but played a much more reduced role than during the period of the British mandate. This was not only because it had been affected by the *nakba*, but also because of the deliberate intention of the Hashemite government. This had begun by confirming Amman as the capital, and depriving Jerusalem of everything that might make it a power centre. The great Palestinian families, natives of Jerusalem, lost the dominant role they had gained between 1920 and 1948.[2] The result was that leadership became fragmented and each leader fell back on his local bases.

But the Hashemite regime had never completely trusted the Palestinians. While they were given posts as deputies, senators and even ministers, they never penetrated the real centres of power, in particular the army, especially the Arab Legion. In addition to these traditional elites, there were those of the opposition parties, the Arab nationalists of the ANM, the Ba'thists and the Communists, all banned since 1957.[3]

Faced with the occupation, the vast majority of the population and the establishment demanded the restoration of the *status quo ante*, the borders of 4 June 1967. Only a tiny minority, whose stand will be examined below, called for the creation of a 'Palestinian entity'. The majority attitude was not straightforward. In fact, a survey carried out in a refugee camp at Jalazun, north of Ramallah, in 1967-68 revealed the following picture:

> None of the respondents spoke of Jordan as 'our country' or of its government as 'our government'. On the contrary . . . refugees still spoke of the 'annexation of the West Bank by Jordan'.[4]

Most refugees showed little enthusiasm, under the political circumstances of the time, for the idea of establishing a Palestinian state in the West Bank but many of them nevertheless expressed their hopes for the eventual emergence of some kind of Palestinian statehood.[5]

While it is true that the West Bank refugees living in the camps were less integrated into the Jordanian state, the attitude of the rest of the population seems to have been similar. This had already been shown by the demonstrations of 1966-67. This lack of attachment to Jordan does not seem to be in contradiction with a low level of Palestinian national consciousness. Dr Ahmad Hamzeh, who returned to the West Bank in 1967 after studying and working abroad, and who is today a member of the PNC, stresses that 'the Palestinians outside were much more active in the Palestinian renaissance [before 1967]; Palestinian consciousness had been weakened in the territories by Jordanian policies'.[6]

Other factors, more conjunctural but powerful, impelled the population and the notables towards this attitude of a return to the *status quo ante*. First was the fear of seeing the West Bank in the situation of Galilee or the Triangle in 1948; these areas had not been claimed by any state (or by the Palestinians) and had thus fallen into the hands of the Israelis. By placing themselves under Jordanian control, the West Bankers would avoid the creation of a 'legal vacuum' which would have enabled a state recognized by the United Nations (i.e. Jordan) to claim sovereignty over the West Bank. International organizations, and the UN in particular, were the guarantors of such a situation since they would not recognize border changes resulting from the 1967 war. No one in the Arab world, not even the Resistance organizations, questioned this reality; the PLO was far too weak to demand anything different, such as laying claim to a sovereignty that would totally lack supporters.

The second reason was the need felt after 1967 to face up to what was not simply an occupation but also a determination to change the very character of the land of Palestine — 'Judaization'. Faced with this, stress was laid on the Arab character rather than the Palestinian character of the Resistance, and on the mobilization of public opinion in all Arab countries (even all Islamic ones when it came to Jerusalem). It seemed that only by uniting Arab efforts would it be possible to face up to the determination shown by the occupiers.

Thus this reassertion of the 'unity of the two banks' arose less from a deep attachment to Jordan than from reasons to do with the struggle. Nevertheless, 'from the period after the 1967 occupation, many people began to think about some other formula than the Jordanian formula' (Hamzeh). For the traditional elites, over and above the need to take account of public opinion, other factors were at work.

First, the Israelis — despite a number of contradictions which will be examined below — always considered Jordan to be their special interlocutor, thus giving Amman considerable weight. Secondly, maintaining contacts with Jordan, the 'open bridges' policy and Amman's payment of some civil servants in the West Bank gave King Hussein various opportunities to apply pressure, to which the notables were very sensitive.

This was very soon evident from reactions to the occupation. On 21 July 1967 the members of the Jerusalem municipal council informed the Jerusalem authorities of their refusal to join the 'amalgamated' municipal council of both parts of Jerusalem. They stated their rejection of the *faits accomplis* and illegal annexation measures.[7]

In an undated statement reprinted in a newspaper on 16 August 1967, over 100 West Bank leaders made known their rejection of the annexation of the city of Jerusalem which was 'an Arab city and an integral part of the Hashimite Kingdom of Jordan', condemned 'all attempts to establish a Palestinian entity under whatever name and in whatever form' and declared that 'the elimination of the effects of aggression demands comprehensive Arab responsibility'.[8]

In an article laying out the programme of the Jordanian Communist Party in July 1967, a member of the leadership asserted that resistance to the occupier:

> explains the lack of success of all attempts embarked on by the aggressors to secure adoption of their solution of the Palestinian problem, a solution that is a disgrace for the Arabs of Palestine and contrary to their interests since it envisages the creation of a puppet Palestinian community wholly dependent on the goodwill of the Israeli leaders.[9]

But the state of mind of the Palestinian masses and elites was best expressed in the National Charter of the Arabs of the West Bank for the Current Phase, adopted on 4 October 1967. It was signed by 129 prominent figures linked to the Jordanian regime (including Hikmat al-Misri, former president of the Chamber of Deputies, and several mayors), to the Palestinian nationalists (Kamal Nasser, a future member of the executive committee of the PLO), and to the Communists (Fayiq Warrad), and by religious leaders, both Christian and Muslim.

The very terminology 'Arabs of the West Bank' is interesting, even if the text mentions the right of Palestinian Arabs to a homeland. After recalling the need for collective Arab action, the signatories reaffirmed that 'Jerusalem is part of the West Bank, which is united with the East Bank by the Jordanian entity. We insist on this unity being maintained.' After criticizing the attitude of the Jordanian governmental apparatus and its responsibility in the defeat, they asserted their confidence that the necessary reforms would be carried out. Finally, they rejected:

> the pernicious proposal for the establishment of a Palestinian state intended to form a buffer between the Arabs and Israel, but to be closely linked with the alien Zionist presence. This proposal is an attempt to remove the Palestine problem from its Arab context and divest it of its national significance, and to isolate the Palestinian Arab

people from the Arab nation. The establishment of such a state could only result in the final liquidation of the Palestine problem, the dissolution of the Palestinian people and the dealing of the death-blow to the Arab liberation movement.[10]

This statement is interesting in several respects. First, because of the broad consensus that it reveals; all the major currents are represented. Some phrases reflect laborious agreements worked out among various factions: for example, in the formulation of the criticisms of Jordan. There seems conversely to have been no disagreement among the various tendencies about the condemnation of the idea of a Palestinian state or about acceptance of the return of the West Bank to Jordan.

The signatories' description of themselves as representatives of the 'Arabs of the West Bank' takes up the dominant ideas in the Arab world that were examined in Part One. 'Palestinian consciousness', autonomous in relation to the Arab world, was still little developed.

This consensus could not hide contradictions that were to grow throughout this period: in particular between the 'activists', often former members of the opposition to the King, and those who sought a *modus vivendi* with the occupiers and who were often 'loyal' to Hussein. But these contradictions only emerged later: in the meanwhile, all opponents — even moderate ones — suffered repression and deportation.

This latter method was much used by the Israelis to decimate the political elites in the West Bank. According to a survey by Lesch,[11] which includes the names of all deportees, the number of them was as follows:

    1967:   5 (plus one tribe)
    1968:   69
    1969:   223 (plus one tribe)
    1970:   406

The author stresses that until 1970 these deportations affected all tendencies indiscriminately (whereas in Gaza, where the situation was totally different, they affected mainly the fedayeen).

Outside this majority tendency, however, another trend began to emerge immediately after the occupation, composed of supporters of a Palestinian entity. This tendency grew partly out of opposition to the Hashemite family, but also because of certain equivocations or ambiguities in Israeli policy. The following section provides a broad outline.

Tel Aviv's Policy

On 7 June 1967, even before the war was over, General Moshe Dayan gave instructions not to establish an Israeli administration in the occupied territories (except East Jerusalem which was annexed), but to use the existing apparatus. The victors were prepared for this new situation, not only because they had never for a moment doubted the outcome of the war, but also because of their experience in Gaza and Sinai in 1956–57 and in controlling Israeli Arabs.[12]

Within this framework, the mayors and municipal councils were called upon to play an increased role: the mandate of those in the West Bank, which ended in September 1967, was extended by the occupying authorities. On 26 June 1967 Dayan declared that, until a decision had been taken on the future of the West Bank, no central Arab authority would be set up 'above' the municipal level.[13] Jordanian governors, senators and deputies who had not fled saw their role considerably reduced.

The occupiers called this a policy of 'non-interference'. It left the local administration in place and thus made available an 'intermediary which massaged national feelings but could easily be bypassed'.[14] A Ministry of Defence notice put it in concrete terms:

> It could be said, in principle, that the aim of the military government is that an Arab resident of the zone could be born in the hospital, receive a birth certificate, grow up and be educated, marry and bring up his children and grandchildren to old age, all without the help of an Israeli clerk or government official and without even having seen one.[15]

This idyllic vision had little to do with everyday reality, but it sums up the occupiers' philosophy very well. Moreover it raised a number of criticisms from 'left-wing' figures, close to Mapam, who thought that the West Bank should be 'democratized' and Israeli laws enforced there.[16] It was, in short, a new form of left-wing colonial ideology.

But these proposals, imposed by the powerful Minister of Defence, went hand-in-hand with a number of unofficial contacts with West Bank figures on the problem of a Palestinian entity. Thus Abd al-Jawad Salah, mayor of the town of El Bireh until his expulsion in 1973, says that the first three years saw several Israeli proposals for self-administration or autonomy.[17] The then mayor of Nablus, Hamdi Kan'an, also asserts that he had several contacts with Israeli officials on the problem of a Palestinian state.[18] It appears that these contacts involved initiatives by individuals without the agreement of the Israeli government. A debate on the proposal in the Knesset and various government statements show that such a proposal was far removed from the goals of Tel Aviv.[19]

Some of these goals were far from easy to discern, especially at the time. As the plans multiplied — the Dayan plan, the Sapir plan, and above all the Allon plan — so questions were raised and concern arose. The Allon plan[20] made the following proposals: a 15-kilometre-wide security belt would be established along the Jordan to be controlled by Israel; some parts of the West Bank would be annexed, notably Jerusalem and areas near Latrun and Hebron; and finally, the most densely populated areas would be either returned to Jordan or (if agreement proved impossible) given an autonomous status.

All these ambiguities had important consequences. First, as we shall see later, they created an association in the minds of many Palestinians — and in particular of the PLO — between the proposal for a state in the West Bank and the Allon plan and Israeli 'plots'. Secondly, they encouraged, internally, the emergence of a few supporters of the idea. Linked as they were with the occupiers, they expected a concrete response to their proposals. They never got one because, in reality, the ruling Labour Party was seeking an agreement with Jordan; it did not want to give too much encouragement to 'secessionists' who would not find favour with the leaders in Amman. And this remained true even though Labour used supporters of a West Bank state as a means both of dividing the Palestinians and of putting pressure on King Hussein.[21]

Israeli reservations about the idea of a mini-state were summed up by Cygielman in an article in *Le Monde Diplomatique*:

> 1. It would be difficult to persuade a tiny Palestinian state squeezed in between Jordan and Israel to make territorial concessions (Latrun, Kalkiliya) which would reduce even further the size of an already very reduced territory.
> 2. Since Amman was not its capital, it would demand back the Arab part of Jerusalem with the likely support of sympathetic international opinion.
> 3. As a nationalist movement developed there, its territorial demands would be made, not against a 'brother country', Jordan, which was moreover little developed, but against Israel.[22]

There was a degree of hesitation in the government, especially during the first months of the occupation. After Black September some leaders, notably Yigal Allon, then deputy Prime Minister, attempted to relaunch a plan for local autonomy. But it was dropped after being rejected at a meeting of the Labour Party.[23]

A Palestinian Leadership for a Palestinian State?

From the very beginning, the proposal for a Palestinian entity was linked to the problem of Palestinian leadership in the West Bank and Gaza. As we have seen, this was weak and divided. The Israeli authorities themselves seem not to have responded to the various requests from a number of figures to give them a greater role.

As early as 11 June, 1967, when the full scale of the Arab defeat was clear, a number of Palestinian figures contacted Israeli officers and suggested the convening of a meeting of 50 local leaders in Ramallah; these would constitute themselves into an assembly which would then request the Israeli government to recognize them as representatives of the Palestinian people, and negotiate with the Jewish state the establishment of a separate Palestinian entity on the lines of the 1947 Partition Plan.[24] It seems that, a few days later, three West Bank notables made offers to co-operate with Israel in exchange for the setting-up of an Arab state in the West Bank. Their offer was rejected by the Prime Minister's office.[25] This was confirmed in an interview with Aziz Shihada, a Ramallah lawyer: 'We presented the idea of a Palestinian state for the first time immediately after the [1967] war.'[26]

In addition to Aziz Shihada, the main advocates of these proposals were Dr Hamdi Taji al-Farouqi, a former leading member of the Jordanian Ba'th, and Shaikh al-Ja'bari, the mayor of Hebron.[27] Al-Ja'bari, the more influential, was an old pro-Jordanian figure; his move in favour of a Palestinian leadership was no doubt linked to his desire to become leader of the entire West Bank. Being a traditional leader rather than an intellectual, he left few writings about his ideas. Nevertheless he set out his proposals for a state in a statement:

> 1) Repatriation or compensation for Palestinian refugees, at their choice; 2) the establishment of an independent Palestinian state in the West Bank, the Gaza Strip and those areas of Palestine annexed by Israel in 1948 and allocated to the Palestinian state in the UN Partition Plan; 3) close ties between the Palestinian state and the East Bank.[28]

His ideas were generally much less fixed, however, and referred more to a type of autonomy than to a Palestinian state.

What distinguished Shaikh al-Ja'bari's stand were his ultimately fruitless attempts to establish a Palestinian representation:

> The time has come for the Palestinians to decide their own future. Only a decision taken by the Palestinians' own leaders could serve as a firm basis for solving the Palestine problem.[29]

Various attempts were made to call a meeting of Palestinian leaders. Thus in March 1970 a 'Committee for Public Affairs', headed by al-Ja'bari, was authorized to discuss local affairs with Israel and the Arab states. Al-Ja'bari tried to secure permission for a wider meeting, which would have meant recognizing a 'Palestinian entity', but the Israelis refused.[30]

The other two figures, Dr Hamdi al-Farouqi and Aziz Shihada, were linked to the opposition to King Hussein before 1967.[31] The former halted his activities after the attack on his house by fedayeen in December 1967. The latter was typical of the generation of intellectuals opposed to the Hashemite regime who – in the name of this opposition – put forward the idea of a Palestinian entity.

Shihada's analysis of the situation was published in a series of articles in the journal *The New Middle East*. We shall take as an example the article published in December 1968, 'The Voice of the Forgotten Palestinian'.[32]

1. He lumped the Arab and Israeli governments together and blamed them for their intransigence which was blocking the situation: the Arab governments demanded unconditional Israeli withdrawal from the occupied territories, the Israeli government demanded direct negotiations between itself and the Arab states.

2. The Palestinian Arabs must take the initiative in the handling of their own problems; even though, 'we would have preferred it if this initiative did not have to be independent of the rest of the Arab world'.

3. The Arab setbacks were to be explained by lack of solidarity and rivalries but also by the:

> subjection of the Palestinian Arab leaders. . . to pressures from abroad. . , largely economic ones . . . It is this which prevents the considerable proportion of the population from thinking and acting along more independent lines.

4. No peace is possible without the Palestinians and without recognition of the right of Palestinians to a state on the basis of UN resolutions.

> Why then not take this problem by its horns and decide in the first place to restore to our country (not to Israel) the name of Palestine?

The precise stand taken as to a Palestinian state was as follows:

— Once Israel recognized the Arab state [in Palestine], other problems could be solved and an overall settlement with the Arab states could be achieved.
— The establishment of such a state ought to precede a peace settlement with the Arab states.
— Such a state would 'be based on a modification of the UN Partition Plan [of 1947]'; its capital would be East Jerusalem.
— After a short period of peace with Israel, it could join Israel in some of federation; and perhaps later, with Jordan.
— The state must be fully sovereign.[33]

Finally, Shihada condemned the democratic state proposed by Fatah — in which Jews would be in a majority — since:

> the position of the Palestinian Arabs will not differ in the proposed Palestine state from what it actually was, and still is, in Israel. Their rights and privileges will be the same but they will continue to be a minority.[34]

What was the real influence of this group? Shihada claimed: 'We had with us a large silent majority. I think that if there had been a referendum we would have had 70 to 80% of the votes.'[35] This is an optimistic estimate, to say the least. Israeli leaders hold a different opinion. On 25 November 1968 Prime Minister Levy Eshkol declared:

> We talked at length with Palestinian personalities whom we know to be

influential . . . For the time being, most of them are looking to Jordan, as long as there is still hope for a settlement with Jordan.[36]

Moshe Dayan supported this stand and said that the Palestinians did not want a separate peace. E. Sasson, who was Eshkol's adviser for the affairs of the occupied territories, asserted brutally that 'not a single recognized West Bank leader subscribed to the concept of a Palestinian Arab state in the Israeli-held territories'.[37]

Shihada sees these explanations as rationalizations. In his interview, he asserted that:

> there was a golden opportunity when we first presented the idea of the Palestinian state . . . the opportunity was missed by the Israelis. The Arab states had lost the war, they had no authority among the ordinary people; it was a good opportunity.

General Herzog, the first military governor of the West Bank, was of the same opinion:

> Following the occupation of June 1967 I held a number of talks with local Arab leaders. It was then possible to meet the Arabs of various political persuasions who spoke very freely. It is regrettable that we didn't take advantage of the opportunities presented to us then.[38]

It is likely that in the first few weeks, with the trauma of defeat, and the hatred felt by a section of the population for the Hashemite monarchy, a certain wait-and-see attitude prevailed; and that the very idea of a Palestinian entity did not arouse opposition. But that did not last long, as a teacher in Nablus said to Eric Rouleau:

> It did not take long for our relative optimism to evaporate. From the very first weeks of the occupation the Israeli leaders made numerous annexationist statements. To listen to them one would think we were living in their liberated homeland. At best, some of them were disposed to envisage granting autonomy to the West Bank, called Palestine, and intended to become a rump state, a sort of Israeli Bantustan.[39]

In April 1969 *The Observer* newspaper also stressed the isolation of supporters of separation of the West Bank.[40] This relative isolation of supporters of a Palestinian entity seems to have been real. It is important to grasp the reasons for this and also to try to answer the question: were they right too soon?

In the first place, there was the easily comprehensible opposition of the Hashemite family. Secondly, there was the attitude of supporters of a Palestinian entity *vis-à-vis* the Arab world. While the prestige of the Arab countries waned after 1967, few Palestinians thought it possible to secure an end to the occupation by relying solely on the strength of the inhabitants of the occupied territories. But the supporters of an entity seemed to be sympathetic to autonomous initiatives. Linked to this was the relationship with the Israelis. Shihada declared that 'some people misunderstood our motives and thought that we were going to become quislings'. The fact was that some of their proposals were ambiguous. What, for example, did Shihada mean when he said that the establishment of a Palestinian state ought to precede peace with the Arab states? What did the repeated appeals to Israel mean? They contained overtones of a 'separate peace' which would be difficult to accept and moreover not very realistic. The essential issue was Israel's evacuation of the occupied territories; but on this problem most of the 'plans' were very unclear. It should also be noted that none of the advocates of an entity or a state played an active role in the concrete resistance to the occupation. During several recent visits to the West Bank I was able to observe that they are still today widely looked upon as 'collaborators'.

Neither did these people get any real support from Tel Aviv, a situation which compounded the effect of certain Israeli hesitations and ambiguities. This seriously affected their credibility, the more so as, in 1967-69, no one believed that the occupation would last very long. If that were the case, why should anyone compromise himself by associating with people who risked dire retribution if the West Bank were to be returned to the bosom of the Hashemite Kingdom?

One last point to take into account is the heterogeneous nature of the group, ranging all the way from people claiming to be leftists to well-known conservatives. Some were thinking in terms of a state, others of an autonomous unit, others again of federal links with Israel.[41] This confusion did nothing to help widen their support.

The Communists and the Palestinian State

We cannot close this brief survey of positions in the occupied territories without looking at the position of the Communists: first that of the Jordanian Communist Party, which played a growing role in the national struggle in the West Bank; and then that of the Israeli Communist Party, which represented a significant fraction of Israeli Arabs and whose stands influenced the Palestinian national movement.

For the Jordanian Communist Party, the period 1967-71 saw the unfolding of a very bitter internal struggle over the Palestinian issue and the role of armed organizations.[42] One tendency, led by Salfiti (then Party secretary), denied the Palestinian character of the struggle in the West Bank; this line found its fullest expression in an article published in October-November 1968 by the *Nouvelle Revue Internationale* which provoked widespread opposition and polemics with some Arab Communist Parties. In March 1969 the Jordanian Communist Party rectified its stand,[43] spoke of the struggle of the Palestinian people and referred to the 1947 Partition Plan. In June 1969 at the International Congress of Communist and Workers' Parties in Moscow, Fuad Nassar, the party's First Secretary stated:

> The struggle of the Arab people of Palestine is. . . a legitimate and sacred struggle since its goal is to drive the invader out and recover the territories usurped by Israel in 1948 in violation of UN decisions, to bring the refugees back to their homes and to fulfil their right to self-determination on the territory of their homeland.[44]

By this reference to the Partition Plan, the Jordanian communist Party was taking up a novel position — struggle against the occupation and for the right of Palestinians to self-determination and, at the same time, acceptance of the existence of Israel. The Jordanian Communist Party did not, however, specify what forms this right to self-determination would take.

If reference is now made to the stand of the Israeli Communist Party, this is for two reasons: first because it gradually came to assert itself as a party representing the Palestinian national minority in Israel, and secondly because its stand had, for this reason, an impact in the West Bank and Gaza.[45]

The fact was that the 1967 war had had divisive consequences for the Palestinian people. As Emile Touma, a member of the politbureau of the Israeli Communist Party, said, it 'broke down all the barriers that had separated the Arab national minority in Israel and the Palestinians in the West Bank and Gaza'.[46] This reunion had consequences that were both human (reuniting families) and social (comparison of different experiences); but, according to Touma, it was above all on the political level that the consequences were the most significant:

> The Palestinian minority in Israel has been able to draw up its own political programme for the solution of the Palestinian problem, in direct contact with other Palestinians, and with a very concrete understanding of this problem. . . What is most important is that it has been able to influence the process that began after the Six Day War and brought the PLO to its position in 1974.

Without examining it in depth, it is important to understand that this influence made itself felt through several channels: concrete solidarity with the Palestinians in the occupied territories struggling against oppression (the role of Communist lawyers such as Felicia Langer, the role of the Arab-language press, and so on), the place of the culture and works of Israeli Arabs in the overall Palestinian culture (the role of figures such as Emile Touma, Tawfiq Zayyad, Emile Habibi, and of a cultural journal such as *al-Jadid*).

The political line of the Israeli Communist Party was defined in the resolution of the sixteenth Congress which was held from 30 January to 1 February 1969:

The 16th Congress emphasizes that our party had fought throughout all the years for a political peaceful solution of the Israeli-Arab conflict and of the Palestinian question on the basis of mutual recognition of the just national rights of the two peoples of Palestine, the people of Israel and the Arab people of Palestine. We said that the people of Israel had realized its national rights, while the rights of the Palestinian Arab had been deprived. Therefore we correctly considered that the path to peace lies in Israel's recognition of the national rights of the Palestinian Arab People, and first of all the right of the Arab refugees to choose either to return to their homeland or to receive compensations, according to the UNO decisions. We said that the national question, including the territorial question, has to be solved on the basis of the right to self-determination of the peoples and in accordance with the general interest of peace, progress and anti-imperialist struggle.[47]

The resolution then went on to stress the importance of UN Resolution 242 in all its aspects: withdrawal by Israel from all the occupied territories; recognition of Israel by the Arab states. In a section headed 'About the Natural Right to Resist Occupation', the Israeli Communist Party stressed the failure of the occupation policy and the importance of political resistance. It condemned 'the irresponsible acts on part of extremists in the Arab resistance movement' (it mentioned the attack on the central bus station in Tel Aviv, the explosion of a mine near a market in Jerusalem and the attack on an Israeli aeroplane in Athens). It also condemned the political programme of the Resistance leaders who want 'not only the liberation of the occupied territories and the attainment of the just rights of the Palestinian Arab people, but also the liquidation of the State of Israel'.[48]

The resolution also denounced a

plan of establishing an autonomous 'Palestinian state' in the occupied territories. . . The plan. . . under the prevailing circumstances [i.e. the occupation] is nothing but the establishment of an Israeli colony and the perpetuation of the Israeli occupation.[49]

In a speech at the Congress Habibi denounced the Mikunis-Sneh group which advocated the establishment of a Palestinian Arab state in part of the occupied West Bank.[50]

When asked about this problem of a state, Touma confirmed that the Israeli Communist Party could not accept the proposals of a number of groups (for example, Uri Avneri's) which stressed that the right of Palestinians to self-determination and made no mention of the evacuation of the occupied territories. According to him, this was a trap.[51]

The Debate in Gaza

The reason that so far the Gaza Strip has hardly been mentioned is that its history still remains to be written. In 1967 there were nearly 400,000 Palestinians there, including 200,000 refugees, 100,000 of whom were living in camps, and Gaza played a major role in the development of the consciousness of the leadership group in Fatah. The Resistance began to organize immediately after the occupation in 1967; at least until 1971 the armed struggle there was on a scale never seen in the West Bank. The camps provided both a reservoir of Palestinian militants and also a field of action where the Israeli soldiers found it difficult to penetrate. The three main organizations were Fatah, the ANM and the United National Front (which brought together the Communists, the Ba'thists, the Palestine National Liberation Front and a number of independents). While it is impossible to detail the positions of all three organizations, a recent book makes it possible to define the positions of the third,[52] and, at least so far as concerns the points in the present study, it is likely that these reflected the state of mind of the Resistance organizations.

On 20 September 1967 the Front published its 'Charter'. It mentioned that the 'Zionist aggressors' were continuing their manoeuvres and in particular:

> the attacks against the United Arab Republic, to spread alternative proposals to a return to Arab administration including annexation to Jordan, internationalization or setting-up of a puppet Palestinian entity under the protection of the bayonets of the occupying Power.

The text ends by setting out among the goals of the struggle:

> The return to Arab administration as the starting-point for the liberation of Palestine ... and the rejection of all alternatives to a return to Arab administration, such as annexation to Jordan, internationalization or the setting-up of a puppet Palestinian entity.[53]

A few weeks later, the Front's newspaper violently attacked Aziz Shihada and his proposals for a Palestinian entity. It denounced those in Gaza who, with the help of the Israelis and the American embassy, were holding meetings to convene a 'Palestinian Congress'. The article ended by denouncing

> slogans ... on 'independence' and 'self-determination', for the reason that real independence and the right to free self-determination cannot be achieved under the occupation.[54]

It can be seen that this contains the same concerns as in the West Bank: putting an end to the occupation and returning to the pre-1967 situation as conditions for the implementation of Palestinian rights.

Defence of the UAR was all the stronger because some people were trying to blame it, whereas the Front saw Nasser as one of the Palestinian people's most valuable allies. Thus Mahmud Najib, president of the Gaza city chamber of commerce, after congratulating the Israeli authorities on their attitude, declared, in March 1968, that the majority of inhabitants wanted the implementation of the Partition Plan without a return to Jordanian or Egyptian rule.[55] The *Jerusalem Post*, quoting 'authoritative Israeli sources', noted that 80% of the population were opposed to a return to Egypt and preferred attachment to the West Bank to form a Palestinian state or entity.[56] This Israeli support for a break with Egypt could only increase Palestinian suspicions.

In Gaza, too, attempts to propagate the idea of a Palestinian entity were linked to a desire to create a local leadership. This leadership was even weaker than in the West Bank, however, and was under heavy pressure from the armed struggle. Attempts which surfaced to set up a local representative body had little success.[57]

5. The Second Phase of the Occupation

The Changes in the West Bank and Gaza

The period 1967–70 saw the beginning of major economic changes in the occupied territories whose social and political consequences soon began to make themselves felt.[58] The 'open bridges' policy inaugurated by Dayan, which had both political and economic objectives, continued.

> Freedom of movement between the occupied West Bank and Transjordan was intended . . . to prevent 'the development of a dangerous feeling of frustration among the Arabs'. It made it possible to market both crops harvested in the West Bank, which competed with Israeli agriculture, and some industrial goods produced by the Jewish state.[59]

But what was really happening was the economic integration of the two regions. Tens of thousands of men from Gaza and the West Bank became integrated into theIsraeli economy, going every day to work in Israel. For the West Bank alone, their number rose from 5,000 in 1968 to 14,000 in 1970, 25,000 in 1971 and 37,000 in 1973 and from 6% of the labour force in 1968 to 12.2% in 1970, 21.4% in 1971 and 29.1% in 1973. For wage-earners this rose from 12.2% to over 50%.[60]

Although a degree of prosperity ensued, Tamari is right to stress its negative consequences. This prosperity had an artificial character and it arose essentially from wages earned by contributing to Israel's output and not that of the West Bank. Work in Israel was to the detriment of work in the West Bank, where industry and agriculture could not employ workers at the same rates of pay. The confiscation of Arab lands and the establishment of settlements accentuated this feature.[61]

These economic changes had important consequences on the social structure. In the first place, the number of people working in agriculture and the craft sector diminished while the number working in construction and industry increased.[62] A significant proportion of the latter group became incorporated into a modern-type structure, the Israeli economy. Traditional society began to break up, and the type of relations based on patron–client relationships began to decline.[63] All this was accentuated by the growing proportion of young people and a high school-attendance rate.[64]

Against this background, the position of the traditional elites underwent a relatively rapid, albeit contradictory, transformation. Changes in the social structure, the refusal of the Israelis to allow them to play a political role and their inability to create organizations at a time when the social struggle made it increasingly difficult to continue the patron–client system, were all factors that undermined their authority.

Of course, they retained some power through the municipalities, from the financial assistance they received from Jordan (plus its political support), and from the fact that after 1970 the Israelis initiated a policy of making a sharp distinction between pro-Jordanian and pro-PLO elites and came down very harshly on the latter.

The well-educated younger generation slowly began to take up the reins. Engineers, doctors, journalists, intellectuals or teachers, often more heavily affected economically (they suffered inflation without seeing any substantial increase in pay, since they were working in the West Bank and Gaza), identified more and more with the PLO as the breach with Amman deepened.

Nevertheless it was not until five years after Black September that the transformation was complete, as was to be shown in the municipal elections of 1976.

Black September and Abu Shalbaya's Proposals

King Hussein's massacre of the Palestinians in Amman in September 1970 accelerated the changes: the differences between supporters of the PLO and pro-Jordanians deepened. But the first reaction was indignation. Social organizations, trade unions, leading figures and chambers of commerce all protested; even figures close to the King such as the former governor of Jerusalem, Anwar al-Khatib, demanded his abdication.[65] This was followed by shock, which is well captured in the following commentary made during the massacres and quoted by Lesch:

> The people here, they feel now that whatever they do it's no use. We tried petitions, demonstrations, strikes – nothing worked. We tried grenades and sabotage – no use. We are punished and nothing changes. Now we just go about our business and hope something will happen and the Israelis will go away.[66]

This widely shared feeling created the belief that all opposition had disappeared and that the occupation had succeeded. Thus in 1972 an Israeli author wrote of the West Bank having entered a period of normalization.[67] This indeed was the analysis made by most observers, especially those who were Israeli. The 1973 war brought a rude awakening, but we shall return to that later.

The despondency and shock did not prevent the continued spread of new ideas, however, in particular that of a state in the West Bank and Gaza. In an interview published on 10 November 1970 in *al-Ahram*, Arafat explained[68] that a delegation of prominent figures from the West Bank had come to inform him that they were going to declare the separation of the West Bank from Jordan. Arafat convinced them not to do so, saying that it was an Israeli–American plan.

> Nevertheless, a trend began to emerge that supported the idea of a separate state on the West Bank and the Gaza Strip. Its adherents demanded that the occupation end and that a referendum be held under UN auspices so that the Palestinians could exercise their right to self-determination and create an independent state. The plan for a separate state was spelled out by the journalist Muhammad Abu Shilbaya in *No Peace without a Free Palestinian State*, in the fall of 1971. He proposed a five-year UN administration during which Palestinian refugees would return. IDs and passports would be issued, political parties organized, free elections held, and a national assembly convened that would elect a provisional government for the independent republic of Palestine. The book caused a furor on the West Bank, although Abu Shilbaya himself was — and remained — marginal politically. Given the widespread animosity toward Jordan, the idea of a separate Palestinian state attracted considerable interest. However, most political figures believed that West Bank residents alone lacked the power to end Israeli rule and achieve independence, and so they feared that the outcome would differ little from the 'autonomy' supported by Shaykh Ja'bari. Therefore Abu Shilbaya was criticized as politically naive and defeatist. His articulation of this concept of statehood was still premature and heretical, but the study at least began to air the idea of establishing a state located in that part of Palestine which retained a substantial Arab majority.[69]

There can be no doubt that a trend existed which favoured the idea of a Palestinian state; but it is difficult to differentiate between a number of 'collaborators', who were in reality sympathetic to autonomy under the occupation, and those who truly wanted an independent state. This difficulty no doubt arises from the fact that supporters of the first option also used the slogan of a Palestinian state. As we have seen above, the concrete political practice of these people did not oppose the occupation; their contacts with the Israelis were considered suspect. It is interesting to note that ten years later, during a trip made in October 1981, I was able to observe that people like Abu Shalbaya (who was working on the Arabic-language Israeli journal *al-Anqa'*) who had supported the Camp David agreements were still seen by all PLO supporters as 'collaborators'.

This difficulty in distinguishing between the two trends partly explains the negative positions taken up by the PLO (see Part Three). However, one author, who is totally committed to the PLO, today asserts that during the period 1970–73 there did indeed exist two trends of thought in the West Bank. One was secessionist, isolationist, overcome by despair; the other truly national and pro-independence. He concludes by saying that the negative stand taken by the Resistance did not help the development of the second trend.[70]

The secessionist trends expressed themselves in several ways after Black September. Some involved the continuation of demands expressed before; others were new. One idea above all came back into favour, the idea of a temporary UN trusteeship. This took up a proposal put forward by Musa al-Alami in 1968.[71] The proposal envisaged an Israeli withdrawal to the borders of 4 June 1967; demilitarization and a neutral mandate for five years; and a plebiscite giving the choice between an independent state and a federation with Jordan. This proposal was immediately condemned by the fourth PNC. On 16 October 1970 the Jerusalem newspaper *al-Quds* asked for a free referendum under UN auspices; al-Ja'bari proposed a five-year trusteeship followed by the holding of a referendum,[72] as did Abu Shalbaya.[73] It should be noted that this idea was taken up much later in various proposals put forward by the PLO or Arab states.[74]

Efforts were again made to develop a new leadership. A number of young intellectuals launched a manifesto in the name of 'The Congress of the Coalition Party of Nationalist Youth'. The four principles adopted were: rejection of the occupation; unity of the Palestinian and Jordanian peoples, while clearly distinguishing between the Jordanian people and the regime; a just peace that would ensure the right of the Palestinians to self-determination; and co-ordination between the Palestinians under occupation and those outside the occupied territories.[75] But these attempts remained stillborn: not being placed within the framework of the PLO, there seems to have been no real place for them in the context of the political forces operating in the territories.

We cannot conclude this survey without once again mentioning the proposlas made by the journalist Abu Shalbaya. He seems not to have had much influence, although, according to him, his book on the Palestinian state sold 15,000 copies in three days.[76] He was however the person who did most to popularize these proposals.[77] Abu Shalbaya claimed to belong to the school of thought that accepted the 1947 Partition Plan and voiced positions violently hostile to Jordan (he had been imprisoned by the King for five years). He even went so far as to write: 'If our people is put before a choice . . . [between] the occupation or the regime of King Hussein . . . a large proportion would opt for the occupation.'[78] He also opposed the proposal for a United Arab Kingdom.

The plan he proposed involved:

— UN trusteeship over the West Bank, Gaza and East Jerusalem;
— the return of refugees to these areas;
— free elections and restoration of a liberal parliamentary regime.

Refugees from areas now in Israel would be offered a choice between return (which most would refuse) or compensation. He posited the coexistence of two states, one Jewish, with its capital in West Jerusalem, the other Arab, with its capital in East Jerusalem. It should be noted that the author nowhere clearly deals with the problem of the presence of Israeli troops or the settlers.

The Proposal for a United Arab Kingdom and the Hashemite Position

The massacres of 1970-71 and the weakening of the armed organizations confirmed for some people that the only realistic solution was a return to Jordan (even though other solutions were beginning to emerge). 'We shall settle accounts with the King after the Israeli evacuation and after the re-unification of the two banks of the Jordan',[79] some leaders were saying.

But the King was fully alive to the assertion of Palestinian nationhood and the dangers that this represented to his own authority. The Hashemite ruler had always asserted that the West Bank was an integral part of his king-dome and had done so right from 19 June 1967.[80] As early as 7 August 1967 the Jordanian government decided to pay all the civil servants in the West Bank their salaries on condition that they did not co-operate with Israel,[81] and on 15 August his cabinet set up a Ministerial Committee for West Bank Affairs.[82]

Then, faced with Palestinian self-assertion, he began to echo some of the criticisms that the 'Arab nationalists' were making against Fatah on the subject of the democratic state. One of the tactics used by the Israelis 'from time to time', the King said, was to say that the problem was one between the Israelis and the Palestinians, in which the Arabs should not interfere, thus looking to 'the building of a phoney state or a phoney entity with which [Israel] would collaborate fully', which would enable it to settle the problem once and for all.[83]

Moreover, it was right from October and November 1967 that the Amman press began to launch a campaign against supporters of the idea of a Palestinian state.[84] During 1968 a number of civil servants were dismissed for 'collaboration'.[85] 'The strongest attacks on us came from Jordan', said Shihada.[86] It is for these reasons that the polemic over the so-called statements by King Hussein to *The Observer* in December 1968, favourable to the creation of a Palestinian state, can be considered an enormous misunder-standing.[87]

In 1971 changes in the balance of power and the development of Palestinian national consciousness led the King to 'reconsider the relationship' that existed between the two banks to ensure they remained 'a single family.[88] He even added that 'the choice is left to the Palestinians, to our kinsfolk over there [in the occupied territories], to decide their own future'. Only to say later that it was not worth the trouble consulting them because they 'would resist . . . all attempts to divide them'.

After the events of 1970 the Hashemite regime developed a two-pronged campaign. First it rejected the Palestinian state. There are many examples of this stand: the statement by Jordanian parliamentarians sent to the heads of state and presidents of parliaments in the Arab states on 24 February 1971,[89] or the letter of 2 April 1971 from notables in the refugee camps in Jordan to the Arab heads of state, in which they proclaimed their devotion to Jordanian–Palestinian unity.[90]

This encouragement given to expressions of devotion to the unity of the kingdom went hand-in-hand with attacks on anyone in the Palestinian Resistance who supported the proposal for a Palestinian state. These attacks were stepped up from mid-1971 when Hussein was preparing to put an end to all armed Palestinian presence in Jordan. On 2 June 1971 the King launched a tirade against those who wanted a Palestinian state or a government-in-exile and thus divided the Arab nation.[91] His prime minister, Wasfi Tall, stated on 5 June 1971 that:

> some fractions [of the Palestinian Resistance] want a Palestinian government even over 20 feddans. But this will not succeed, although we know that they are getting encouragement in this design from several quarters.[92]

The aim of this onslaught was to counter the idea of a state, but it was also designed to discredit the Palestinian Resistance in East Jordan by accusing it of dividing the people, and of dividing the Arabs. (And this was at a time when the Palestinian Resistance, as we shall see, categorically rejected both the idea of a Palestinian state and the idea of a government-in-exile.) This attack was a skilful one, since it forced the Palestinian Resistance to reaffirm its attachment to the unity of the two banks and thus to defend positions similar to King Hussein's: the PDFLP was well aware of the contradiction.

The second aspect of the Hashemite campaign was to assert the King's position among the Palestinians, particularly those in the occupied territories. The King also attempted to set them against the Palestinian Resistance organizations. Thus he responded to a question about a Palestinian government-in-exile as follows:

> It is up to the Palestinians, particularly those living under the occupation, to choose who will represent them and they will not allow an organization far removed from Palestinian realities to represent them.[93]

But that was not enough: the Palestinians had to be offered territory and a vision for the future; and this was the purpose of the proposal for a United Arab Kingdom. It is my feeling that there has been much misunderstanding of this proposal. This was partly the fault of the Palestinian Resistance which attacked it from the standpoint that it was an 'Israeli-American-Jordanian plot' for a compromise solution; but the fact remains that, on 16 March 1972, the day after the proposal had been announced, Golda Meir condemned it and declared that Hussein 'is disposing of territories that he does not possess'.[94]

In fact the King's main object lay elsewhere. What was at stake was the problem of the future of the West Bank (and ultimately Gaza) and hegemony over the Palestinians. He wanted to offer them the only realistic solution after the liquidation of the Resistance: 'Hussein is better, since it is the only way to get rid of the occupation.'

A few days after the King's declaration, the Jordanian Minister of Foreign Affairs stated that the proposal was not aimed at a political settlement. Concerning the Palestinians, he added:

> Our main concern, in reality, is the Palestinians living in Jordan and Palestine, since they form the overwhelming majority of the Palestinian people. And this vast majority of Palestinians is living in the occupied West Bank and the Gaza Strip and another large number, totalling some 800,000, live on the East Bank. It is they who must have self-determination and decide their future, who will represent them, who will be their leaders... As for the rest, the door is open, and Jordan is Palestine and Palestine is Jordan, and Jordan hails every Palestinian who seeks to do his duty to his cause and his country.[95]

King Hussein returned to the point several times in his attempts at clarification. Thus, in an interview in early December 1972, he explained that his proposal was 'a setback for ideas that some people have got into their heads that the solution to the Palestinian question will be found through a state on the West Bank'.[96] Two months later, he added that the proposal had killed the idea of 'an alternative homeland for the Palestinians on the East Bank'[97] and he made it clear that his proposal could not be implemented under the occupation.

What was at issue then was indeed the answer to the question, 'Who represents the Palestinians, the PLO or King Hussein?'[98] This central goal did not prevent the King from trying to sell his proposal to the Americans. As Henry Kissinger, then US Secretary of State, notes in his Memoirs:

> Hussein, alone of all the Arab leaders at that time, was prepared to make specific peace proposals. He gave me [at their meeting in February 1973] a document setting out the points he had described, to Nixon and myself, a few weeks earlier. Jordan would negotiate directly with Israel over the West Bank. There would be a few border adjustments on condition that the Gaza Strip was handed over in exchange.[99]

But these proposals had already been rejected by Israel, and there is no reason whatsoever to think that they were a basis for negotiations acceptable to Tel Aviv (or indeed to the Americans).

The explanations and the proposal, as they were set out by the Jordanian monarch, confirm the overriding determination to win over the inhabitants of the occupied territories.[100] The King first explained the creation of the Kingdom of East Jordan in 1921, its place in the Great Arab Revolution and the fact that it was the very existence of this kingdom that had made it possible to keep the East Bank out of the Balfour Declaration.

In 1948, he went on, it was the Jordanian army that had saved the West Bank from the Israelis; its incorporation into the kingdom was the outcome of a request from the Palestinians. This was the first real step on the road to Arab unity. (It is interesting to note how Hashemite pretentions to hegemony and the unity of the Fertile Crescent are identified with the desire for Arab unity.) The unity of the two banks had taken deep root since they were one people, not two.

After 1967, and the new catastrophe, the Jordanian state's goals were: 1. resistance to aggression against the West Bank; 2. the liberation of the West Bank. Then followed a long section about 'plots against the Palestinian people and the whole Arab nation', meaning proposals for a separate status for the West Bank. The King referred both to the Palestinian Resistance and to the West Bank notables who were advocating a Palestinian entity; he denounced the proposed municipal elections as part of this plot.

Against this background, Hussein put forward a proposal that was:

> based on our absolute determination to regain the legitimate rights of the Palestinians and it is directed to place them in a position to enable them to regain and safeguard these rights ... This [plan] is now our answer to all those who choose to doubt [our] pledge [to give your people the right to self-determination] ; ... planning for the new phase has come as a result of continuous meetings which were held with the representatives and leaders of both Banks. There was a unanimous consensus.

He then presented his proposal, which is reproduced here *in extenso*:

1.   The Hashemite Kingdom of Jordan shall become a United Arab Kingdom, and shall be thus named.
2.   The United Arab Kingdom shall consist of two regions (*qutr*):
A.   The Region of Palestine, and shall consist of the West Bank and any further Palestinian territories to be liberated and whose inhabitants opt to join.
B.   The Region of Jordan, and shall consist of the East Bank.
3.   Amman shall be the central capital of the Kingdom and at the same time shall be the capital of the Region of Jordan.
4.   Jerusalem shall become the capital of the Region of Palestine.
5.   The King shall be the Head of the State and shall assume the Central Executive Power, assisted by a Central Council of Ministers. The Central Legislative Power shall be vested in the King and in the National Assembly, whose members shall be elected by direct and secret ballot, having an equal number of members from each of the

two regions.

6. The Central Judicial Authority shall be vested in a 'Supreme Central Court'.

7. The Kingdom shall have a single 'Armed Forces' and its 'supreme Commander' shall be the King.

8. The responsibilities of the Central Executive power shall be confined to matters relating to the Kingdom as a sovereign international entity ensuring the safety of the union, its stability and development.

9. The Executive Power in each region shall be vested in a Governor-General from the Region, and in a Regional Council of Ministers also formed from citizens of the Region.

10. The Legislative Power in each Region shall be vested in a 'People's Council' which shall be elected by direct secret ballot. This Council shall elect the Governor-General.

11. The Judicial Power in each Region shall be vested in the courts of the Region and nobody shall have any authority over it.

12. The Executive Power in each Region shall be responsible for all matters pertinent to it with the exception of such matters as the constitution defines to be the responsibility of the Central Executive Power.

The proposal was a clever one and showed the King's desire to respond to Palestinian aspirations: first, in the formation of a Palestine region, with Jerusalem as its capital; and secondly, in the fact that he claimed all Palestinian territories that were liberated, not only Gaza, but also — at least in theory — Galilee or the Triangle.

Reactions to this proposal in the West Bank were summed up in an article by the Israeli journalist Amnon Kapeliouk. The federation proposals:

> raised hardly any enthusiasm in the West Bank. Some saw them as 'castles in Spain', others as a new retreat by Jordan from its undertakings to the Palestinians, still others as a new phase in the struggle waged by the King against Yasser Arafat to win the support of the Palestinians. Some even saw in them the danger of collusion with Israel. In any event, the plan was doomed to failure among the people in the West Bank, most of whom heartily detested the King.[101]

This position was also expressed in a letter from residents of the West Bank to the Palestine People's Congress that opened in Cairo at the end of March 1972.[102] This letter condemned the refusal of the Israeli authorities to allow them to attend the Congress and, on the subject of the United Arab Kingdom proposal, declared:

> [1.] Dayan's representative asked us to accept this proposal, saying that Israel's opposition would not last long [; 2.] King Hussein has no right to speak for us ... The proposal is rejected and we reject any link between our people and the Hashemite family [; 3.] We believe that we

are one people and we reject all attempts to divide our people between a people living under the occupation and a people not living under the occupation.

In my opinion, these reactions explain why the King's plan had such little success. In fact his determination to secure control over the Palestinian people already seemed illusory: not only did people still remember Black September but Palestinian national consciousness had grown considerably. This national consciousness was emphasized above all: it can be seen in the letter above and in the rejection of any link between the people of Palestine and the Hashemite family.

An Illusion of Normalization

At the end of 1968 the mayor of Nablus, Hamdi Kan'an, made a statement in favour of the holding of municipal elections.[103] This call was part and parcel of the attempts by various leaders in the West Bank to secure a status as recognized leaders. This first attempt, which was violently attacked by the Jordanians,[104] hung fire.

In December 1971 the Israeli authorities announced their decision to hold municipal elections in the following spring. This provoked a storm of protest in the Arab world and the Palestinian Resistance. The day after the announcement, the Jordanian government condemned the new elections.[105] All the forces opposed to the emergence of a Palestinian leadership in the occupied territories came together. Concern was heightened in Jordan and the PLO by the fact that they were well aware of the existence of pro-independence and separatist trends.

The PLO and the Jordan government thought increasingly that the Israelis and Americans were aiding and abetting these trends. Again I can do no more than repeat that this was simply not the case. The refusal, after the elections, to give the mayors the least political role amply confirms the point. All the attempts made by al-Ja'bari, for example, went unanswered.[106] The Israelis hoped to show that the situation had been 'normalized' and that the inhabitants of the occupied territories were running their own affairs. Perhaps they also saw the elections as a means of exerting pressure, a sort of threat against Hussein if he continued to reject a settlement.

The PLO called for a boycott of the municipal elections. For Dr Hamzeh:

> The national movement was weakly organized in the territories because of the refusal of the majority of the Palestinian organizations to carry on political work. It is for this reason that the movement was not strong enough to win the elections. So it found excuses to boycott the elections, such as the idea that elections could not be held under the occupation ... In 1976, by which time the movement was strong enough, it was the opposite that was proved.[107]

The Israelis did everything to ensure the success of the elections. The pressures organized in Nablus to force candidates to stand are proof enough of that.[108] The evolution of King Hussein's attitude also helped the success. From total rejection, he moved to encouragement of candidates backing him. The first round, on 28 March 1972, which covered the towns in 'Samaria', saw a turn-out of 84% among the 17,000 eligible voters (there was a property franchise), helped by the fact that identity cards were stamped. The failure of the boycott led the PLO to reconsider its stand. For the second round, on 2 May, the PLO and the Communists called for the re-election of incumbent mayors.[109]

The Israelis and the French press[110] presented these elections as a victory for the Tel Aviv government. It may be wondered whether it was not above all the result of mistakes made by the PLO: the situation had not really been 'normalized'. As a student in Nablus said at the end of 1972:

> Don't be taken in by the surface calm . . . We all believe that what they want in the long run is to drive us out and take our land . . . But we won't leave . . . Even if the whole outside world forgets us, and the Arab governments continue using our cause for their own political ends. If we leave, the Palestinians will be nowhere and will become non-persons. And that won't happen.

The year 1973 was to mark the end of Israeli hopes of 'normalization'.

The Year 1973

This year marked the end of dreams of normalization fondly held by the Israelis. At the same time, it was the year when Palestinian national consciousness was openly displayed, even before the October war. The Palestinian 'awakening' in the occupied territories struck many observers all the more strongly because they had been fooled by the relative calm of 1971 and 1972.

There are various reasons for the Israeli failure. The first and most important one relates to the very character of the occupation. Portrayed by its defenders as 'liberal' — and in a few limited ways it was — the Israeli occupation was basically different from many other similar 'experiences'. For the Israeli leaders, the West Bank was Eretz Israel, the land of Israel; the Arabs were 'intruders' to whom, at most, a status of autonomy could be granted, as second-class citizens. The spread of settlements, the confiscation of lands, the annexation of Jerusalem and also the experience of the Arab minority in Israel were a daily reminder — even to those who wanted to forget it — of the real character of the Israeli conquest. The social base of the 'collaborators' was thus gravely limited. This was even more true than among the Israeli Arabs, who had for 20 years been cut off from all contact with the Arab world, which had given them little scope for resistance.

The second reason is more prosaic. Foreign occupation, whatever the intentions of its promoters, has its own logic. It is a lesson that history has taught repeatedly and occupiers, just as frequently, forget. In the West Bank, while the effectiveness of the repressive measures taken against armed resistance was formidable, it was accompanied by collective punishments, thousands of arbitrary arrests, torture and maltreatment which only fuelled hatred of the occupier. In this daily struggle — against colonization and repression — the inhabitants of the West Bank and the Gaza Strip found themselves, for the first time since 1948 (except for the Gaza experience in 1956), alone, face-to-face with the Israelis. This helped to strengthen their national consciousness, which was confirmed by the ineffectiveness of the Arab countries and by the attitude of Jordan in 1970–71.

The third reason for this renewal of the Palestinian struggle is related to the economic and social upheavals that we have examined above. By undermining the hold of the traditional elites, and strengthening that of a new generation — one that was better educated and more nationalistic — the changes brought about by the occupation promoted a radicalization of the Resistance in the occupied territories. To use a well-known expression, the occupation 'had dug its own grave'.

The last reason has to do with the PLO itself. It had survived the defeat of 1970 and redirected its struggle. It was placing increasing importance on the occupied territories. It remained a force and a symbol which Palestinians recognized as their own wherever they were, especially in the West Bank and Gaza.

The first sign of this change came after one of the most spectacular operations by the Israeli army. In the night of 9–10 April 1973 commandos belonging to the Tsahal (Israeli army) landed near Beirut. They operated for several hours with impunity and killed three PLO leaders in their homes: Abu Yussef (Muhammad al-Najjar) and Kamal Nasser, members of the executive committee, and Kamal Adwan, a member of the Fatah central committee.

This attack had numerous consequences, both internationally and in Lebanon. But the most alarming ones for the Tel Aviv leaders appeared in the West Bank. There were many demonstrations, especially at Bir Zeit, Kamal Nasser's home town; Palestinian municipalities protested, and newspapers published dozens of death notices which testified to the support of the population. The Jerusalem newspapers *al-Quds* and *al-Sha'b* attacked the Israeli leaders and compared the raid on Beirut to the one on Deir Yassin in 1948.[111]

'The unprecedented scale of the mourning and protest demonstrations', said the *Le Monde* correspondent, '. . . have worried the authorities.'[112] That was putting it mildly. The Israeli Minister of Finance, Pinhas Sapir, declared that 'all the talk about the gradual *rapprochement* between Israel and the Arabs in the occupied territories over these last six years has begun to evaporate in the light of harsh reality'.[113] General Dayan condemned the identification of the Arabs in the territories with the leaders of the fedayeen.[114]

The Israeli government newspaper *Davar* wrote:

> Israelis who have really begun to get to know the people in the West
> Bank are more and more aware that the term 'peaceful coexistence'
> is a stupidity . . . The Israelis will soon have occupied the West Bank
> for six years. The reactions of the people of the West Bank prove that
> peaceful coexistence has not advanced one inch.[115]

Two other facts should nevertheless be stressed that clearly show how the
April 1973 demonstrations marked a turning-point. They are both mentioned
by Isa al-Shu'aybi. The first is the appearance of the Palestinian flag — for the
first time, it seems — in the demonstrations. It symbolized the assertion of
'Palestinian consciousness', whereas until then the Jordanian flag had acted
as the rallying-point. The second fact is the convergence that was revealed
between the Palestinians in the occupied territories and Palestinians outside,
not only in the fact that the demonstrations occurred at the same time
(200,000 people attended the funeral of the murdered PLO leaders in Beirut)
but in the *de facto* recognition of the PLO by all Palestinians. They were not
yet at the point of the slogans of the 1974 demonstrations: 'No to the occupation, no to a return to Jordan, yes to the PLO', but they were moving in
that direction.

Two political declarations of great significance underline the evolution of
Palestinian thought in the occupied territories. The first was an appeal from
over 100 prominent citizens of the West Bank and Gaza to the President of
the Security Council and the Secretary-General of the UN.[116] It should be
noted at the outset that it was a text signed jointly by representatives from
Gaza and the West Bank; this confirmed the 'unification' that was gradually
coming about between these two fractions of the Palestinian people in
addition, the list of signatories was very broadly based and included most
of the mayors, except for al-Ja'bari, and Elias Freij and Rashad Shawa,
the mayors of Bethlehem and Gaza respectively.

The text was short; it condemned the Israeli occupation in all its forms
and demanded an end to it. It also demanded that the inhabitants of the West
Bank and Gaza should have 'the right to self-determination and to sovereignty
over their territory'. There was no reference to either Jordan or Egypt. The
wording was necessarily vague: but the affirmation of the right to self-
determination, even if the framework in which it could be exercised was not
defined,[117] is further proof of the rise of national consciousness.

It must also be stressed that these stands had an impact on the debates
running through the PLO. Indeed, this is perhaps the most striking fact —
the eruption of the Palestinians in the occupied territories onto the political
scene in Beirut. We may note that three of the signatories of this appeal were
to join the executive committee of the PLO in June 1974.

This declaration also confirmed the links that had been created between
the inhabitants of the West Bank and those of Gaza. Economic integration

and freedom of movement had, as we have seen, reunited the Palestinians. The fact that representatives of the two areas jointly signed statements (in marked contrast to what had happened in 1967–68) was symptomatic. The rallying of the mayor of Gaza, Rashad Shawa, to King Hussein[118] was a symbol of this evolution and also, no doubt, of the diminution of Egyptian influence in Gaza. Moreover, at the beginning of 1972, the Israelis had separated the administration of northern Sinai from that of Gaza and joined this territory to the West Bank.

The second statement was the one accompanying the setting-up of the Palestine National Front (PNF) in the occupied territories in August 1973.[119] The establishment of this Front was the outcome of a decision by the tenth PNC and the activity of Communist activists in the West Bank. The Front's efforts produced significant concrete results: massive abstentions by Arabs in Jerusalem at the Histadrut elections in September 1973, abstentions by Arabs at the municipal elections in Jerusalem in December of that year, and so on.

The Front's programme was issued on 15 August 1973.[120] Among the main points concerning the problem of a state and Palestinian national goals should be stressed the recognition of the 'right to self-determination on their land and to the return to their homes', and the rejection of all proposals seeking to liquidate the Palestinian problem such as 'the Palestinian entity, local administration, autonomy, the Allon plan, King Hussein's plan', and so on. While the political groups participating in the Front (Fatah, the PDFLP, the Ba'th, the PFLP, the Communist Party) reflected the whole spectrum of the PLO, there was no reference to the democratic state which all, except the Communists, had ended by endorsing. According to Lesch,[121] the absence of any such reference was at the insistence of the Communists; but, on the other hand, they were unable to secure an explicit mention of a return to the 1967 borders.

Conclusion

Thus, on the eve of the October war, the Palestinian national movement in the occupied territories found itself in a new situation. It had in effect largely broken the ties that bound it to the Hashemite kingdom; it had reasserted its own demands — in particular the right of the Palestinian people to self-determination — and above all its links with the whole Palestinian people and the PLO. This was affirmed in the call for the creation of the PNF, which was defined as 'an inseparable part of the Palestinian national movement represented in the PLO'.[122]

Without yet having gone so far as to recognize the right of Palestinians to a state in the territories occupied in 1967, the national movement in the West Bank and Gaza had moved through the necessary stages that would enable it, after October 1973, to play an active part in the internal debates of the PLO. Its very influence in the occupied territories acted as confirmation for the PLO leadership of the dangers involved in setting up a state which it did not lead.

The actors were ready for the next act. And all the more so since the PLO in Beirut had undergone a parallel evolution in its thinking which we shall now attempt to examine.

Notes to Part 2

1. For the whole of this section, see M. Heller, 'Political and Social Change in the West Bank since 1967', in J.S. Migdal (ed.), *Palestinian Society and Politics*, Princeton, Princeton University Press, 1980, pp. 185–211.

2. See Y. Porath, *The Emergence of the Palestinian Arab National Movement 1918–1929*, London, Frank Cass, 1974, p. 187.

3. E. Rekhess and A. Susser, 'Political Factors and Trends in the Israel-Administered Territories', in J. Rabinovich and H. Shaker (eds.), *From June to October*, New Brunswick, NJ, Transaction Books, 1978, pp. 269–91.

4. S. Shamir, 'West Bank Refugees between Camp and Society', in Migdal (ed.), *Palestinian Society*, p. 152.

5. Ibid., p. 154.

6. Interview with Dr Hamzeh, Paris, 25 April 1981.

7. *The Resistance of the Western Bank of Jordan to Israeli Occupation 1967*, Beirut, Institute for Palestine Studies, 1967, pp. 9–10. This issue reprints 37 documents on the rejection of Israeli occupation by Palestinians.

8. Ibid., pp. 57–60.

9. A. Salem, 'Le Parti poursuit son action en Jordanie', *Nouvelle Revue Internationale*, January 1968, pp. 174–7.

10. The full text and the names of the signatories are reprinted in *International Documents on Palestine 1967*, Beirut, Institute for Palestine Studies, pp. 682–6. (Henceforth cited as *IDP* with the year of reference.)

11. A. Lesch, 'Israeli Deportation of Palestinians from the West Bank and Gaza 1967–70', *Journal of Palestine Studies* (henceforth *JPS*), Beirut, no. 30, Winter 1979.

12. L.-J. Duclos, 'Description de l'occupation militaire israélienne', *Politique Etrangère*, no. 4, 1972, pp. 499–534. The book by N.M. Kerber, *Les droits de l'homme dans les territoires administrés par Israël*, Editions A. Pedone, 1978, p. 239, may be mentioned as an interesting curiosity. The author gives an idyllic – and false – picture of the occupation, from which we will quote but one extract: 'While awaiting a political settlement, the Israeli authorities are endeavouring to administer the territories, responsibility for which has devolved [*sic*] on them in the best interests of the people who live there' (p. 2).

13. *Middle East Record 1967*, p. 278. (Henceforth cited as *MER* with the year of reference.)

14. Duclos, 'Description de l'occupation.

15. Ibid.

16. Heller, 'Political and Social Change'.

17. 'Isa al-Shu'aybi, *Al-kiyaniya al-filastiniya 1947–77* [The autonomous

Palestinian consciousness], Beirut, PLO Research Centre, 1979, p. 145.

18. Ibid., pp. 145–6.
19. Ibid., p. 146. See also the statements by Eshkol, Dayan and Allon, *MER 1968*, p. 259, and by Eban and Dayan, *MER 1969–1970*, p. 116.
20. Bard E. O'Neill, *Armed Struggle in Palestine*, Boulder, Colo., Westview Press, 1978, pp. 47–8.
21. See the statements by A. Eban in July 1968, *MER 1968*, p. 245.
22. *Le Monde Diplomatique*, November 1970.
23. *MER 1969–1970*, p. 387.
24. *MER 1967*, p. 282.
25. Heller, 'Political and Social Change', p. 200.
26. Interview with Aziz Shihada, Ramallah, 14 October 1981.
27. Rekhess and Susser, 'Political Factors', p. 271.
28. *MER 1968*, p. 449.
29. Ibid.
30. *MER 1969–1970*, p. 377.
31. There are several references to their activities in A. Plascov, *The Palestinian Refugees in Jordan 1948-1957*, London, Frank Cass, 1981, p. 268.
32. See also 'Why Fatah does not Speak for Democratic Palestine', *The New Middle East*, March 1969; 'Remember Sparta!', ibid., October 1969; 'Must History Repeat Itself?', ibid., January 1971, etc.
33. *MER 1969–1970*, p. 390.
34. *The New Middle East*, March 1969, pp. 11–12.
35. Interview with A. Shihada, 14 October 1981.
36. *MER 1968*, p. 245.
37. *MER 1969–1970*, p. 391.
38. Discussions organized by *Ha'aretz*, 20 February 1970, reprinted in S. Avineri (ed.), *Israel and the Palestinians*, New York, St Martin's Press, 1971, pp. 109–32.
39. See the series of articles by E. Rouleau, 'Israël: le ghetto des vainqueurs', *Le Monde*, 2-7 July 1969.
40. *MER 1969–1970*, p. 391.
41. *MER 1967*, pp. 282–3.
42. See in particular Ya'koub Zayadin, *Al-bidayat* [The beginnings], Beirut, Dar Ibn Khaldoun, 1980 (these are the memoirs of one of the leading members of the Jordanian Communist Party), and A. Flores, 'The Arab C.P.s and the Palestine Question', *Khamsin*, no. 7, pp. 21–40.
43. *Al-wathaiq al-'arabiya al-filastiniya 1969* [Palestine Arab Documents], Beirut, Institute for Palestine Studies, pp. 117-18. (Henceforth cited as *PAD* with the year of reference.)
44. *Conférence internationale des Partis communistes et ouvriers Moscou 1969*, Prague, Editions Paix et Socialisme, 1969, pp. 81–4.
45. The reference here is, of course, to Rakah. The Israeli Communist Party split in 1965. The other fraction, led by Mikunis and Sneh, soon lost all influence, especially among the Arab minority.
46. Interview with E. Touma, Haifa, 16 October 1981.
47. *Information Bulletin; Communist Party of Israel*, Tel Aviv, no. 3-4, 1969, p. 119.
48. Ibid., pp. 125–7.
49. Ibid., p. 127.

50. Ibid., pp. 80–6.
51. Interview with Emile Touma, 16 October 1981. On the stand of the Israeli Communist Party, see the very interesting article by E. Touma, 'L'état palestinien' mentioned above, which is reprinted in *Les palestiniens et la crise israélo-arabe*, Paris, Editions Sociales, 1974.
52. Abd al-Qadir Yasin, *Tajribat al-jabha al-wataniya fi qita' Ghaza* [The experience of the National Front in the Gaza Strip], Beirut, Dar Ibn Khaldoun, 1980.
53. Ibid., pp. 91–5.
54. Ibid., pp. 112–14.
55. *MER 1968*, p. 458.
56. Ibid., p. 459.
57. *MER 1969–1970*, p. 399.
58. See particularly Heller, 'Political and Social Change', and the outstanding study by S. Tamari, 'The Palestinians in the West Bank and Gaza, the Sociology of Dependency', in K. Nakhleh and E. Zureik (eds.), *The Sociology of the Palestinians*, London, Croom Helm, 1980, pp. 84–111.
59. Rouleau, 'Israël'.
60. Heller, 'Political and Social Change'.
61. On the settlement programme during the first five years, see A. Kapeliouk, 'L'implantation des colonies israéliennes dans les territoires occupés crée des faits accomplis irréversibles', *Le Monde Diplomatique*, June 1972.
62. *Palestinian Statistical Abstract 1980*, Damascus, Palestine National Fund, 1980.
63. See Heller, 'Political and Social Change'. For a detailed description of attitudes and how they were changing, see S. Khalifa's novel, *Chronique du figuier barbare*, Paris, Gallimard, 1978.
64. *Palestinian Statistical Abstract*, 1980.
65. See *PAD 1970*, pp. 854–5; *IDP 1967*, p. 926; A.M. Lesch, *Political Perceptions of the Palestinians in the West Bank and the Gaza Strip*, Washington DC, The Middle East Institute, 1980, p. 39; and *MER 1969–1970*, pp. 383–7.
66. Lesch, *Political Perceptions*, p. 39.
67. A. Cohen, 'West Bank Sentiments 1967–73', M. Curtis *et al.* (eds.), *The Palestinian People, History, Politics*, New Brunswick, NJ, Transaction Books, 1975, pp. 88–96. Despite the title, this piece was written, as the author notes, in 1972.
68. *IDP 1970*, p. 991. Arafat was to refer to this incident several times.
69. Lesch, *Political Perceptions*, pp. 38–41.
70. Al-Shu'aybi, *Al-kiyaniya*, p. 158.
71. *MER 1968*, pp. 449–50.
72. *MER 1969–1970*, p. 389.
73. M. Abu Shalbaya, *La salam bighayr dawla filastiniya hurra* [No peace without a free Palestinian state], Jerusalem, n.d. (1971?), p. 73.
74. See Khalid al-Hassan's statements in *Le Monde*, 22 April 1980; and Afif Safieh's statements in *Monday Morning*, Beirut, 24 August 1981.
75. *MER 1969–1970*, pp. 388–9.
76. Interview with Abu Shalbaya, Jerusalem, 17 October 1981.
77. See his articles in *The New Middle East.*

78. Abu Shalbaya, *La salam*, pp. 75–6.
79. Quoted by A. Kapeliouk, *Le Monde*, 13 November 1970.
80. *IDP 1967*, p. 606.
81. *MER 1967*, p. 288.
82. Ibid., p. 410.
83. *PAD 1968*, p. 713.
84. *MER 1967*, p. 283.
85. Ibid., p. 607. See also the attacks in the Jordanian press on Hamdi Kan'an, mayor of Nablus, in late 1968, for the same reasons, *MER 1969–1970*, p. 375.
86. Interview with A. Shihada, 14 October 1981.
87. See the amount of space given by *Le Monde* to the problem at that time (17 December 1968).
88. *PAD 1969*, pp. 76–8.
89. *PAD 1971*, pp. 155–6.
90. Ibid., pp. 252–4.
91. Ibid., pp. 416–17.
92. Ibid., pp. 439–41.
93. Ibid., 23 August 1971, pp. 700–73.
94. Cited by X. Baron, *Les Palestiniens, un peuple*, Paris, le Sycomore, 1977, p. 280.
95. *PAD 1972*, pp. 139–40.
96. Ibid., pp. 495–6.
97. *PAD 1973*, pp. 46–50.
98. It seems that the assassination of Wasfi Tall on 28 November 1971 contributed to the reassertion of Jordanian sovereignty over the West Bank. The Prime Minister (according to V. Pann, *The Jordanian Entity*, p. 239) saw the loss of the West Bank as a good thing since he considered the Palestinians to be foreigners. But the debate seems to have continued. 'Already there were those in the palace and outside — including the King's influential mother — who were suggesting that the kingdom's affairs would be in a much better state if it was relieved of the burden of the ever dissident population of areas such as Nablus and elsewhere', Neville Brown, 'L'idée d'abandoner la rive occidentale du Jourdain gagne du terrain dans le royaume hachemite', *Le Monde Diplomatique*, September 1972.
99. H. Kissinger, *Les Années Orageuses*, Paris, Fayard, 1982, Vol. I, pp. 261–2.
100. See the full text of King Hussein's speech on the United Arab Kingdom in *IDP 1972*, pp. 289–93.
101. A. Kapeliouk, 'En Cisjordanie: Les Israéliens ont misé sur les élections pour normaliser la situation', *Le Monde Diplomatique*, April 1972.
102. *PAD 1972*, pp. 206–7.
103. Rekhess and Susser, 'Political Factors', p. 274.
104. *MER 1969–1970*, p. 375.
105. *PAD 1971*, pp. 891–2.
106. Rekhess and Susser, 'Political Factors', p. 282.
107. Interview with Dr Hamzeh, 25 April 1981.
108. *Le Monde*, 28 March 1972.
109. Lesch, *Political Perceptions*, p. 46.
110. *Le Monde*, 30 March 1972.

111. Ibid., 15–16 April 1973.
112. Ibid.
113. Quoted by al-Shu'aybi, *Al-kiyaniya*, p. 183.
114. Ibid., p. 184.
115. Quoted by *Le Monde*, 17 April 1973.
116. Quoted by al-Shu'aybi, *Al-kiyaniya*, pp. 268–70. The English text is in *JPS*, no. 9, pp. 187–89.
117. Lesch, *Political Perceptions*, p. 53.
118. *PAD 1972*, pp. 332–3.
119. On all forms of national struggle against the Israelis, see al-Shu'aybi, *Al-kiyaniya*, pp. 191–3.
120. *PAD 1973*, pp. 252–3.
121. Lesch, *Political Perceptions*, pp. 53–4.
122. *PAD 1973*, p. 252.

Part III:
The Resistance and the Proposal for a State in the West Bank and Gaza (1967-1973)

The rejection by the Resistance of all proposals for a Palestinian state in the West Bank and Gaza was unambiguous, from the morrow of the 1967 war. It was linked to rejection of any political solution, particularly Resolution 242. Three periods can nevertheless be distinguished. The first went from June 1967 to September 1970. Here the rejection was stated, but it was secondary, and the main focus remained the development of the struggle against plans for a political solution, such as the Rogers Plan. The second period went from Black September in 1970 to the end of 1972. The issue of the rejection of a state became central, and this was so for several reasons. First, because the Resistance saw in it a concrete proposal, sponsored by the United States and Israel and their 'agents' in the occupied territories. Next, because the PLO had to respond to the attacks by Jordan, which criticized it for being behind the proposal for a state, for having a policy of dividing the Arab world and for creating a breach between the two banks of the Jordan. Finally, because the weakened PLO felt itself incapable of controlling such a state: if it was set up, this would be done without the PLO. The third period began in 1973 *even before the October war* and ended in 1974 with the twelfth PNC. Part Three will attempt to show that, at the beginning of 1973, a major shift occurred in the Palestinian Resistance. In particular, the PDFLP began to try to set out a policy of 'phases' which led in August 1973 to the demand for self-determination for the Palestinians in the occupied territories. These developments created the conditions for the required changes in Palestinian political thought. It took the October war and the new regional balance of power for this decisive shift of opinion to be fully completed; but this did not occur without a series of discussions and clashes, as we shall see in this next Part.

6. The First Period (1967-1970)

This first period was marked, as previously mentioned, by the rejection of a state in the West Bank and Gaza, but it was not the dominant issue. This position was above all linked to the few moves in this direction made in the occupied territories. Thus a Fatah leader declared at the end of 1967 that:

> The occupation forces are trying to establish . . . a Palestinian state which would have no power of self-determination, and over which they would have full control. The enemy has been seeking support for this idea from among our people, but in vain. In fact, this idea was only adopted because a few traitors had consented to it.[1]

While the July 1968 National Charter did not mention the question directly, it stressed the unity of Palestine within the borders of the British mandate (Article 2). The resolutions adopted at the same time, on the other hand, explicitly condemned 'the suspect proposals for the creation of a spurious Palestinian entity'.[2]

The arguments used were the following. First, this entity would owe its existence to Israel and it would legitimate the presence of the 'Zionist entity'. Secondly, the creation of the entity would in practice enable Israel to clear the Arab lands of their inhabitants and then annex them. Thirdly, the existence of an entity would allow the creation of a Palestinian administration subservient to Israel and the Israelis would use it against the Palestinian Resistance.[3] The few other statements and declarations confirmed these stands and the policy resolution of the fifth PNC, in 1969, condemned those 'who make themselves the spokesmen for the liquidation of our cause and the establishment of a spurious Palestinian entity which would be an agent of Zionism and imperialism'.[4]

At the beginning of 1969 a new theme made its appearance, that of the responsibility of the US in the plan for a mini-state. In an interview published in March 1969, the vice-chairman of the PLO, Dr Ibrahim Bakr, declared:

> The first to raise the problem of the creation of a Palestinian entity was the Zionist wing collaborating most closely with American imperialism, represented by the Rafi, led by Ben Gurion, Dayan and

Peres who later united — except for Ben Gurion — with the Mapai and Hadout Avoda to form the Israeli Labour Party. After unification, the leaders of this party have continued to be involved in the question of a Palestinian entity right down to the present day. And, for example, one might point to the contact between Moshe Sassun and a group of West Bank traditional leaders.[5]

After describing these contacts and explaining that they had begun just after the occupation, Bakr denounced the existence of a detailed plan to:

separate the East Bank from the West Bank and the Gaza Strip from Egyptian administration; make a corridor between the Gaza Strip and the West Bank; and set up a Palestinian state in the West Bank and Gaza which would come to terms with Israel and thus liquidate the Palestinian question, and arrange that this state should establish a permanent relationship with Israel economically, politically and militarily, and have two outlets to the sea to reach Haifa and Ashdod.[6]

Bakr went on to stress that a second trend existed in the Labour Party (Eshkol–Eban) which was for a solution with Jordan, but 'was not opposed to the establishment of a Palestinian entity if no agreement could be reached'.[7]

After noting that the American embassy and consulate in Jerusalem supported the proposal for an entity, Bakr stressed that the recent changes in the PLO had led to the stepping-up of preparations for the proposal so as to sow confusion and weaken the armed struggle.

The threat facing Palestinian activity lies in the possibilities of implementing Security Council Resolution 242 and in the fact that either an entity is established in part of Palestine or there is a return to the situation before 5 June 1967.[8]

It seems to be true that at this time a number of American diplomats were exploring the 'Palestinian way'; but these contacts were still unofficial and appear not to have reflected a general policy. They may however have worried the PLO leaders. Thus Shaikh al-Ja'bari had talks with President Nixon's special envoy, William Scranton, in Jerusalem.[9]

The debate on a democratic state also led all the Resistance organizations to clarify their positions. In fact, Fatah saw itself violently accused of seeking a compromise that jeopardized the 'historic rights' of the Palestinians over the whole of the land of Palestine. Thus, a statement against the Palestinian state, published in March 1970 by the Arab Higher Committee for Palestine, said that the proposal for a state was first put forward by the Israeli secret services a few days after the occupation and that this state was envisaged in East Jordan, that is in non-Palestinian territory.[10]

To this, Fatah and Arafat repeated *ad nauseam* that the slogan of a democratic state:

came after the main slogan, which is liberation of the land and annihilation of the Zionist entity . . . If we wanted another way than that of liberation, we would have accepted the offers made on numerous occasions to establish a Palestinian entity alongside the Zionist state and entity. But we have rejected it.[11]

In this debate, a factor stressed by Harkabi,[12] and one which was doubtless important for Fatah's position, was that of the attitude of circles close to the Jordanian government. The demand for the establishment of a state in the West Bank would inevitably involve a conflict with the monarchy which would undermine the struggle against Israel. During the period 1967–70, when the Palestinian Resistance was still weak, it was certainly not seeking to aggravate the contradictions that already set it against King Hussein.

The year 1970 was marked by the repeated rejection of a state in the West Bank, even though this rejection seems not to have played a very important part in the statements of the various organizations. It may simply be stressed that point 7 of the agreement of 6 May 1970 denounced the proposals for a peaceful settlement and 'the reactionary and colonialist conspiracies to establish a Palestinian state in parts of Palestinian territory', and that the resolutions of the special PNC of August 1970 confirmed the refusal to divide the Palestinians and Jordanians into two states.[13]

7. Black September and its Consequences

It was the events of September 1970 in Jordan and the change in the balance of power to the detriment of the Resistance that were to give a major new impetus to the debate on a state. In this debate, one factor was to play a major role and deserves some consideration — the position of the United States.

The 'American Plans'

There is no denying that the year 1970 saw an 'advance' in American political thinking on the Middle East:[14] the Palestinians ceased to be looked upon simply as refugees. Senator Fulbright was the first American official to express public recognition for some form of Palestinian self-determination, on 23 August 1970:

> the Palestinians are entitled to some form of self-determination on the non-Israeli territory of Palestine. Whether they will wish to form an independent Palestinian state or rejoin the Kingdom of Jordan, or federate with it in some way, is beyond the reach of a foreigner's judgement.[15]

After September 1970 more and more voices spoke out along the same lines. Richard Wolte, a former US ambassador, supported the idea of a state in the West Bank and Gaza. Joseph Sisco, assistant Secretary of State for Near East Affairs, said in a briefing on 12 October 1970: 'more and more the Palestinians are thinking in terms of a given entity, wherever that may be'. Securing peace would require 'giving expression to the Palestinian movement and very likely in the form of some entity'.[16] He added:

> The Palestinians will have to be active participants in a peace settlement and this settlement will have to take account of their aspirations ... We know ... that more and more Palestinians are thinking in terms of a given entity'.[17]

Mention has been made of this evolution — which was backed up by frenzied activity by the US embassy in Israel and the consulate in Jerusalem among Palestinians in the occupied territories — because it makes it easier to understand the PLO's reaction. At this time, for all the Palestinian organizations, Israel and the United States were one and the same. The US was seen as the country most responsible for the unhappy situation of the Palestinian people. Anti-Americanism was a basic feature of Palestinian ideology. It is therefore in no way surprising that the various American proposals should appear as 'plots designed to liquidate the Palestinian Resistance' — especially as the US still saw the PLO as a terrorist organization.

The PLO and the New Situation

The Palestinians in the occupied territories were the first to put forward the idea of a Palestinian state in the West Bank after Black September. Arafat himself reported:

> After the fighting stopped, a delegation of nationalist personalities and elements in the West Bank came and met with me in Amman, and told me that they had decided to announce the separation of the West Bank from the Kingdom of Jordan.
>
> I asked them who was going to superintend the execution of this decision; had they contacted an Arab country?
>
> They said, No.
>
> I told them that . . . I could not accept this decision. I realized, I told them, that they wanted vengeance for what had happened, but circumstances did not permit of this. On the contrary, I said, the Palestinian revolution would punish any attempt to implement this decision . . .
>
> The imperialist attack that is at present being carried out against the commandos, the vanguard of the Palestinian people, is a malevolent and planned attack.
>
> The American–Israeli scheme is at present trying to establish a Palestinian state linked with Israel.
>
> This is the insidious theme they are harping on: You have had enough fighting, enough battles. The only solution of the Palestine problem is to establish a Palestinian state in the West Bank or the West Bank and Gaza Strip.
>
> This is the most dangerous proposal that could be made. In the name of the Palestinian revolution I hereby declare that we shall oppose the establishment of this state to the last member of the Palestinian people, for if ever such a state is established it will spell the end of the whole Palestinian cause.[18]

This first rejection was accompanied by a second: that of the policy of 'phased' stages. In a long interview with the Tunisian press, the Palestinian leader explained his position:

> Our situation cannot be compared to Tunisia's in its struggle against France. The Tunisian revolution was able to accept some compromises; but what we are asked in exchange for a state is to give up part of our land. And that we cannot do.[19]

This rejection went for all fractions of the Palestinian Resistance. And the threat looked sufficiently serious at the end of 1970 for each of them to publish a whole series of communiqués proclaiming their rejection of the proposal for a Palestinian state.[20]

The eighth PNC, in February–March 1971, confirmed this line and rejected 'the establishment of a Palestinian statelet in a part of the territory of Palestine'. Abu Iyad gives a good summary of the shared reasons of the Palestinian organizations. First, to accept the state would mean accepting the defeat of the 20 previous years and hence the existence of the state of Israel. Secondly, this state would be a bridge between Israel and the Arab world, and would be a means of economic conquest by the Israelis of the Arab world. Finally, Israel would not give up either Jerusalem or Gaza or other parts of the occupied territories.[21]

In addition to these reasons, there was yet another one — that the state would aggravate 'the local [*iqlimi*] conflicts between Palestine and Jordan'.[22] This last argument merits a closer look. It will be recalled that the Palestinian Resistance was the target of a vast military and ideological campaign in Jordan. It was accused by King Hussein of wanting to divide the Jordanian and Palestinian peoples. Arafat even went so far as to say that the proposal for a Palestinian state had no real basis but was a means of setting the Jordanians living on the East Bank against the Palestinians.[23] Blocked on every side, the Palestinian Resistance was on the defensive. This was true at the ideological level, where it did no more than try to refute the Jordanian arguments without making any concrete proposals of its own. Worse, its stand seemed in the eyes of the Palestinian masses to be similar to the one put forward by the Jordanian monarch: the return of the West Bank to Jordanian sovereignty. And this was happening just when the Palestinians in the occupied territories wer beginning to reject the Jordanian government.

The PDFLP deserves the credit for understanding these inconsistencies, even though it was not really able to propose a satisfactory solution to them.

The PDFLP's Memorandum to the Ninth PNC

This long memorandum[24] was addressed to the ninth session of the PNC, held in Cairo during the summer of 1971. The question of a Palestinian state in the West Bank was dealt with at length. In the first place, it is interesting to note that this discussion occurs in section 3, entitled 'The present situation in Jordan and our tasks', whereas it is section 5 that is devoted to the problems of a peaceful settlement of the Middle East crisis. What was the PDFLP's argument?

Two trends, it argued, had developed after the July 1971 events, and each had popular support: the first was regional (*iqlimi*) and East Jordanian, the second Palestinian and separatist. After explaining the social bases of the two trends, the memorandum showed that the development of the Palestinian Resistance in Jordan had driven reaction to adopt two apparently contradictory slogans: finish with the Palestinians once and for all; and condemn all separatist activity by Palestinians.

According to the memorandum, the reactionary forces were anxious to liquidate the Palestinian Resistance, but also wanted to remain masters of the Palestinian question: Jordan and no one else represented the Palestinians. This was all the more important because Jordan received funds from the imperialist countries for this very purpose. But this policy did not truly accord with the interests of the masses on the East Bank; it was illusory and the only true solution lay in carrying out the tasks of the National Democratic Revolution. Moreover, this chauvinistic policy only made possible a solution to the East Jordanian crisis by virtue of the fact that it ensured foreign assitance to the Hashemite regime in its wish to dominate the Palestinian question. At the same time, the policy of repression made the King's assertion that he represented the Palestinians less credible. For, the memorandum continued, royal policy attacked all Palestinians; it pursued a policy of segregation against them; it was filling the Palestinian masses with a determination to secede. This feeling reflected the present desire of the Palestinian masses to pay any price to put an end to the policy of terror.

The conclusions that the PDFLP drew from this analysis were cautionary ones: if the Palestinian Resistance appeared unable to bring about the downfall of the Jordanian regime or to ensure the triumph of the rights of Palestinians in Jordan in some reasonable time, 'separation' (*infisal*) would come to seem the only solution. And then, added the statement, the Palestinian bourgeoisie would put forward its slogan of a Palestinian state.[25]

But this solution, said the PDFLP, was itself illusory since it would not constitute even a temporary solution to the permanent repression that the Palestinian people were suffering. This was for three reasons:

1. The new state would lack the means to bring together the majority of Palestinians and would fall into the clutches of imperialism and be forced to accept its plans and give up the historic right of the Palestinian people over the whole of its land.

2. The new state would be unable to face up to Zionist expansionism or the provocations of the Jordanian regime.

3. As none of the Palestinians living on the East Bank would be able to enter the new state, the problem of repression would not be solved.

In the light of this, the Palestinian Resistance must reaffirm its opposition to this slogan and all its concrete manifestations (government-in-exile, and so on). It must reaffirm the unity of the two banks. 'All that is necessary, but not sufficient',[26] added the memorandum. This was because this reaffirmation of 'the unity of the two banks' would not be enough (at the time, it was one of the main slogans of the Hashemite regime itself). In fact, 'our struggle for the return to the unity of the two banks is profoundly linked to the struggle for the fall of the traitorous regime and the establishment of a national democratic regime'. The statement continued:

> In the event that the nightmare of the occupation is ended on the West Bank, our people will not allow its reconquest by the terrorist government of national treason; it will form [on the West Bank] a liberated zone which will serve as a base of revolutionary support to the struggle for the downfall of the traitor regime, and the building of a national democratic regime in the whole of Jordan, and will be a necessary step in the pursuit of the armed struggle to liberate the whole of the national territory and put an end to the Israeli entity.[27]

The contradictions in the text are striking: we shall return to them later, but first we will look in detail at another significant idea put forward in this resolution. In section 5, the statement returned to the idea of a Palestinian state. The desire to see such a state established must not be met, it stated, with a simple rejection or by long-term slogans (unity of the two banks, liberation 'from the river to the sea'). Principles must of course be asserted, but so too must the conditions that would make it possible to attain these objectives. But the slogan of 'non-interference in the internal affairs of Arab states' (Fatah's slogan), at a time when the masses were suffering repression, tended to disarm them. The rights of the Palestinian people as a whole would only be achieved after total liberation; this was true, but it did not mean, as reaction [i.e. the Hashemite regime] said, that partial rights must be abandoned, in particular the rights of Palestinians in Jordan. The principle of 'all or nothing' must be rejected.[28] And the PDFLP put forward the idea: there is no possibility of attaining the final goal without securing implementation of our rights in Jordan, without the downfall of the traitor regime.

The statement went on to develop — and reject — King Hussein's arguments on his attachment to the unity of the two banks and on the fact that the Palestinians would be able to exercise self-determination after liberation. Yes to the unity of the two banks, replied the PDFLP, but not at any price.

It is worth outlining the main ideas in this statement referring to a Palestinian state because they seem to provide a good summary of the contradictions in Palestinian political thought at this time. In the first place, in this statement, just as in most other statements by leaders of the Palestinian Resistance at the time, there was no mention of the fact that what was being advocated was 'a state in the West Bank and Gaza'. They spoke of a Palestinian state only to condemn it. Reference to a democratic state tended to disappear. We shall see later in what circumstances the slogan of a democratic state resurfaced during 1973. But this was in the future. The Palestinian Resistance, accused by the Hashemite regime of developing secessionist thinking and conscious of the rise of support for a Palestinian state, remained on the defensive. It demanded the preservation of the unity of the two banks, and thus found itself espousing the same line as King Hussein.

Having grasped this contradiction, the PDFLP asserted clearly that it did not want a return to Jordan under Hashemite rule; hence the overthrow of the Jordanian monarchy must be the essential goal. And if the West Bank were to be evacuated before that was achieved, it would become a liberated base for continuing that struggle. This reasoning contained the 'Arab nationalist' tendencies that had always been present in the PDFLP, and which were examined in the discussion of the democratic state in Part One.

This otherwise alluring analysis had one major defect, however: it failed to take into account the real relations of force. Only a few days later the Palestinian Resistance was to be totally eliminated in Jordan and the prospect of overthrowing the regime would appear totally utopian. The contradiction nevertheless had to be resolved; this would happen not by overthrowing the King, but by the Palestinian Resistance accepting a state in the West Bank and Gaza. But it took two years for this idea to be formulated and accepted.

This contradiction was, moreover, the criticism that Fatah made, indirectly, of the PDFLP's theses. In an article in September 1971 analysing relations between the Resistance and the Jordanian government, a Fatah leader recognized:

> we do not have the means, at this stage . . . to develop a struggle against the Jordanian government with the aim of putting an end to it . . . The problem between us and the regime in Jordan will not be resolved, at this stage, through military action and armed struggle . . . But the struggle, essentially, will be political, to win Arab political support.[29]

The aim was to isolate the Jordanian regime and force it to change its attitude,[30] certainly not to overthrow it. Fatah never had any illusions about taking power in Amman.

The Ninth PNC (July 1971)

Following the PDFLP, all the Resistance organizations condemned the idea of a Palestinian state, both in the run-up to the ninth PNC and during its proceedings. The ALF condemned proposals for surrender:

> which seek, step by step, to lead a fraction or fractions of the Palestinian people to participation in capitulationist solutions, such as the proposal for a Palestinian state, and [we] fight the evolution of any organization towards deceitful regionalist [*kiyaniya*] positions, such as

the proposal for a government-in-exile.[31]

The PFLP adopted a similar position with an allusion to people, in the ranks of the Resistance, who were thinking of capitulationist solutions.[32]

The recommendations of the political and information committee of the ninth PNC confirmed the rejection of the proposal for a state in part of the national homeland.[33] Curiously, the closing communiqué, while affirming that the unity of the two banks must be achieved democratically and that the PLO rejected all solutions opposed to the historic rights of the Palestinian people, said nothing about the proposal for a state.[34]

Notwithstanding the various references to those in the Palestinian Resistance who did not have a clear-cut position on the proposal for a state (doubtless aimed at the PDFLP which claimed it did), and the closing communiqué's silence on the question of a state, it does not appear — at least from currently available information — that there was any organized trend within the PLO at this time championing this proposal.

8. The Dark Years (1971-1972)

The Situation in the Palestinian Resistance

The Palestinian Resistance, eliminated from Jordan, was living through its darkest years. The PLO no longer represented a serious threat to Israel, and it had failed to broaden its base and its political appeal; it might disappear altogether from the Middle East stage. And yet it was during this period that the PLO began to lay the bases for a new type of activity. Greater importance was given to the diplomatic scene and international relations. Political work, especially in the occupied territories, began to be undertaken seriously. The Resistance, which had taken refuge in Lebanon, built up its relations with progressive forces and the Lebanese National Movement — relations which it had been incapable of forging in Jordan. At the same time, however, the Resistance embarked on large-scale terrorism. The Black September organization was its most striking symbol.[35] Abu Iyad, who disputes its terrorist character, gives a good definition of its role:

> It acted as the auxiliary of the Resistance, at a time when the latter was no longer in a position to assume fully its military and political tasks . . . [its members] expressed the deep feelings of frustration and anger felt by the whole Palestinian people towards the killings in Jordan and the complicities that had made them possible.[36]

It was also in this period that the Resistance developed most strongly what might be called 'an encirclement complex'. It saw 'plots' everywhere,[37] which is not to deny that some were very real. It gave up putting forward concrete proposals — even the democratic state seemed to have been if not abandoned, at least shelved — and restricted itself to a defensive position.

It is against this background that must be placed the reiterated rejection of the Palestinian state, a rejection that was all the more absolute in 1971-72 because the PLO had no illusions as to who would rule such a state — the 'collaborators'. And yet, unlike the preceding stage — and connected with the proposal for a United Arab Kingdom — the problem of a Palestinian state was to occupy an ever more important place in the debate within the Palestinian organizations, even though the rejection, at least verbally, persisted.

In the second half of 1971 condemnation of all proposals for a Palestinian entity continued. Several new arguments were put forward. First, and very forcefully, was that of the risks of division: not only between Palestinians inside the occupied territories and those outside, or between Palestinians and Jordanians, but also between those accepting the proposal and those rejecting it.[38] The concern about the development of secessionist tendencies in the West Bank was palpable, but so too was the fear of political divisions within the Palestinian people, which would provide fertile ground for manoeuvres and 'plots'.

Secondly, there was the danger represented by the division of the Arab world into a series of mini-states.[39] A mini-state in the West Bank and Gaza would be weak, and thus, caught between Jordan and Israel, it would fall into the lap of imperialism, particularly American imperialism,[40] and would be dependent on external aid.

Finally, the creation of a mini-state would result in institutionalizing the Palestinian Resistance and making it lose its revolutionary character. Arafat himself took up this point in arguing against the idea of a government-in-exile:

> I affirm that we are not acting to set up just any form of government. We have always said that we were a national liberation movement with the goal of liberation and return and we are not anxious for a new showcase which would be a burden on our national liberation struggle. And a Palestinian government to us means greater 'officialization' and complications.[41]

Before looking at reactions to the proposal for a United Arab Kingdom put forward by Hussein, we must stop briefly to look at the idea of Jordaninan-Palestinian unity.

The Problem of Jordanian–Palestinian Unity

We have seen how far the demand for Jordanian-Palestinian unity, under the impact of the PFLP and the PDFLP, grew within the PLO from 1969 onwards. This idea had its effects on the problem of a state in the West Bank. It was difficult to assert that there was only a single people in the West Bank and East Jordan and at the same time justify the setting up of two states. The eighth PNC declared:

> Jordan is linked to Palestine by a national relationship and a national unity forged by history and culture from the earliest times. The creation of one political entity in East Jordan and another in Palestine would have no basis either in legality or as to the elements universally accepted as fundamental to a political entity.[42]

The statement added that the masses in East Jordan and in Palestine formed a single people. As we have already observed, this statement contained contradictions, since it asserted at the same time that the PLO was the sole representative of the Palestinian Arab people and thus tended to distinguish it from the Jordanian people which, for its part, must build a national front in Jordan. These contradictions, which reflected the confrontation between Fatah on the one side and the PFLP and the PDFLP on the other, constituted a major blockage in the evolution of Palestinian political thought.

Despite the setbacks in Jordan and the expulsion of the Palestinian Resistance in July 1971, the evolution reflected by the PLO's official statements and texts was slow.

The ninth PNC adopted texts containing the same type of contradictions. They nevertheless contained a stronger affirmation of the Palestinian personality. The political declaration asserted that: 'recognition of the national [*qawmiya*] rights of the Palestinian people and its right to liberate its homeland does not mean renunciation of its present national rights'.[43] The closing communiqué added that the assertion of the unity of the two banks could not be established on the basis of the actions of the Jordanian government which was encouraging regionalist (*iqlimiya*) tendencies, but only on democratic bases.[44] This demand for a new type of unity of the two banks can certainly be seen as a step towards Palestinian autonomy. Significantly, the ninth PNC adopted a special resolution on the occupied territories which gave 'priority' to the demands inside the occupied territories and decided to enlarge and develop the Office for the Affairs of the Occupied Territories.[45]

It was not until the tenth PNC, held in Cairo in April 1972, in response to King Hussein's proposal for a United Arab Kingdom, that the myth of 'the unity of the Jordanian-Palestinian theatre' was finally buried. The tenth PNC, which opened in Cairo on 10 April 1972, was preceded by a People's Congress made up to 500 representative members of the various armed popular organizations and independent figures. Numerous Arab organizations participated in its proceedings. The Congress was opened by President Sadat, who used the occasion to announce the breaking-off of diplomatic relations with Jordan in reprisal against the proposal for the United Arab Kingdom.

The final communiqué of the People's Congress, which was endorsed by the PNC, devoted a long section to Jordanian-Palestinian relations. For the first time reference was made to a Jordanian people and a Palestinian people, and to the necessity for an alliance between the Jordanian movement and the PLO to strengthen the struggle of the two peoples.[46] The text went on to call for the unity of the two banks on new bases: 'complete regional [*iqlimiya*] equality of rights and duties'.[47] Thus not only was the role of the PLO as the sole representative of the Palestinian people confirmed and the existence of two peoples affirmed, but also the unity of the two banks was now conceived as a unity of two distinct entities, united only by shared interests.

The full import of this text is apparent if we refer to the recommendations of the political committee of the PNC. The text, which was not voted on but 'transmitted' with the comments of members of the PNC to the executive committee, was typical of the state of mind of many participants. It asked for nothing less than:

> the expulsion of the Hashemite regime from the Arab League in accordance with the spirit of the resolutions of the Council [of the Arab League] on the joining of the West Bank to the East Bank in the framework of the Hashemite Kingdom of Jordan.[48]

This was a direct reference to the resolutions of the Arab League adopted in 1950 when annexation of the West Bank by the Hashemite dynasty looked inevitable.

> Jordan was charged with annexing Arab Palestine against the League's declared policy, and holding secret talks with Israel ... The League realized it was too weak to impose anything on him [i.e. the King] which would prevent these final steps [i.e. towards annexation]. The Iraqi Prime Minister, Nuri Sa'id, therefore engineered a kind of compromise, reached without Jordan, which was contingent upon a declaration that Jordan would not undertake separate peace negotiations with Israel, and that its actions would not prejudice the final settlement of the Palestine issue. The League's declaration regarded the West Bank as a pledge in the hands of Abdullah 'until the liberation of Palestine'. It did not compel Jordan to ratify or reverse any of its administrative measures.[49]

This reference to the annexation of the West Bank and its provisional character was typical of the way the Jordanian hold over the Palestinians was removed. But it did not yet go right to its logical conclusion, secession.

The PLO and the Municipal Elections and the Proposal for a United Arab Kingdom

The announcement that municipal elections in the West Bank would be held in 1972 strengthened organizations in the PLO's interest in the occupied territories. On 23 December 1971 Sa'iqa denounced the Israeli plot and the attempts to develop a new Palestinian political leadership.[50] For this indeed is what it was really all about. Who represented the Palestinians in the occupied territories? Was there to be an alternative to the PLO? This was the danger denounced by the PDFLP when it asserted that the Israeli aim was to encourage the emergence of a representative Palestinian leadership opposed to the Palestinian Resistance which would coexist with Israel.[51] In the name of the executive committee of the PLO, Kamal Nasser denounced the attempts to transform the contradictions between the people and the occupying power into contradictions between various sections of the people, in particular between 'the Palestinian masses inside the occupied territories and the Palestinian masses outside'[52] Khalid al-Hassan spelled out these arguments when he commented on the proposal for a United Arab Kingdom:

> The West Bank as a whole, or what will remain of it, will not embrace all Palestinians, which means that there will be a Palestinian region and a Palestinian government without the power, economically and geographically, to absorb the Palestinians who at present number some three million. This means the end of the Palestinian identity of Palestinians outside the Palestinian region; they will become, in time, citizens of the countries giving them shelter.[53]

He added that, since the majority of citizens in the East Bank were Palestinians, a new separation would be created between them and those in the West Bank by the creation of two regions.

This threat was taken seriously by the leaders of the PLO for two reasons. First, they had completely neglected political work in the occupied territories in favour of military action; but this action had now considerably declined, even in the Gaza Strip. The second factor was the attitude of King Hussein, who had moved from rejection of the elections to undeclared acceptance. Therein lay a risk of Israel and Jordan coming together, with unforeseeable results.

The upshot was, first, the call for a boycott. (This boycott was based on dubious arguments, since in 1976, without there having been any change in the circumstances, the PLO would agree to elections.) The arguments in favour of a boycott were that the elections would not be free, that one could not vote under the occupation, that the number of electors was 17,000 out of 630,000 inhabitants, and so on. Secondly, and especially after February 1972, the attacks on King Hussein were stepped up. He was denounced by the PLO for having created a climate favourable to the elections.[54] For the PDFLP, the governments in Amman and Tel Aviv had the same aim — to get rid of the Palestinians — but each was acting in its own interest. The Jordanian government wanted its candidates to win:

> in a framework where the West Bank secures autonomy under the occupation, and then participates in a union with the East Bank under the authority of the traitorous Jordanian throne; in this way a common state [*dawla mushtaraka*] would come into being under the temporary control of Israel and the traitorous government in Amman.[55]

Put more clearly, this would mean that Israel and Jordan would share authority over the West Bank, which would enjoy an 'autonomy' that would make it possible to meet some Palestinian demands.

One can already observe the outlines of the arguments that the PLO was to marshal against the proposal for a United Arab Kingdom. This proposal immediately provoked an outburst of protest in the Palestinian Resistance.

The PDFLP was the first to reject the proposal.[56] It used two main arguments:

1. Despite the King's statements, the proposal was one endorsed by Israel, the United States and most Arab countries (including Saudi Arabia) and it would be implemented immediately.

2. This proposal included — as the King himself had stated at a meeting of prominent Palestinian figures that he had summoned on 12 March — abandoning Jerusalem (except for the Jordanian flag which would fly over the Muslim holy places and the Vatican's flag which would fly over the Christian holy places); the realignment of the border in the area of the triangle (Jenin, Tulkarem, Qalqiya); the non-penetration of Arab armed forces into the West Bank; and the continuance of Israeli settlements in the Jordan valley.

The PFLP also saw in the proposal 'an Israeli–Jordanian agreement'.[57] Fatah condemned the Jordanian proposals in a communiqué on 17 March.[58] It should be observed that neither the Americans, who expressed their reservations at the time of Hussein's visit to Washington in March 1972,[59] nor the Israelis, who categorically rejected the plan because of 'its political territorial programme [i.e. the withdrawal of Israeli forces from all the occupied territories], not [because of] the federal principle in the internal structure of the Kingdom of Jordan',[60] confirmed the fears of the PFLP and the PDFLP.

The most interesting reaction, however, was the long report submitted to the PLO executive committee on 16 March 1972 by Khalid al-Hassan, the head of the political department.[61] In a long introduction, he refuted the role that, according to King Hussein, the Hashemite monarchy had played since 1920. In particular he said that the Arab League:

> at a special meeting held on this subject, had issued a resolution on the non-recognition of this annexation [of the West Bank], considering the West Bank, the Gaza Strip and al-Himma as having been given in trust to the three Arab states (Syria, Egypt, Transjordan) and this resolution is valid today.[62]

This idea came up again at the tenth PNC. Al-Hassan went on to stress the discrimination against the Palestinians, 'second-class citizens in the so-called Hashemite Kingdom of Jordan'. He then refuted the arguments of the King, who put himself forward as the guardian of the Palestinian cause. He added that:

> the essential aim of the formation of the Emirate of Transjordan, the annexation of the West Bank, and its transformation into a kingdom — as is confirmed by facts and documents, and the Israeli contacts with Emir Abdullah from 1930 onwards and with King Hussein before and

after the June 1967 war — was: a) eliminating the fighting Palestinian personality; and b) putting an end to the existence of the Palestinian people.[63]

This introduction was indicative of the evolution towards a stronger assertion of the Palestinian personality and the questioning of anything that limited it.

There followed a long discussion of the timing of the presentation of the proposal for a United Arab Kingdom, from which it emerged that what was involved was a vast Israeli–Jordanian–American plot. Israel had rejected only the way the proposal was presented, not its content. In return, King Hussein would secure the reactivation of the proposal for a Fertile Crescent under his leadership [*sic*]. After briefly examining the consequences of implementing the proposal at the Arab level, al-Hassan examined the consequences at the Palestinian level.[64] The success of the King's proposal 'or even the fact that he does not withdraw his proposal' would, according to him, have the following results. It would make the Palestinians participate, through their regional government, in negotiations with the 'Zionist enemy' and in the recognition of Israel; it would bring about the end of the liberation struggle, given that Israel would be recognized by the Arab countries and the Palestinians.

> The formation of a Palestinian regional government is, in reality, the formation of a traitorous traditional official Palestinian power, in opposition to the revolutionary power of the Palestinian people represented by the PLO.[65]

This would lead to the existence of several bodies representing the Palestinians, the possibility of King Hussein continuing to proclaim himself as the representative of the Palestinians, and the existence of a contradiction between the Palestine region of the United Arab Kingdom and the 'Palestine' which was a member of the Arab League through the PLO. Finally, the United Arab Kingdom would be a bridge between the Arab states and Israel.

This text demonstrates the importance placed on the rejection of any political settlement involving recognition of the state of Israel and also on the role of the PLO which, alone, must be able to determine the future of the Palestinians (and which, *alone*, could represent them). This point was asserted most forcefully in the executive committee press release published at the end of this meeting.[66] It was repeated several times in this release that the PLO was 'the legitimate leadership responsible for the future of the Palestinian people and that the Palestinian people denies anyone the right to decide its future and that of its national question in its stead', that the PLO was 'the sole representative of the Palestinian people', and so on.

The stress put on this last point shows the PLO leadership's awareness of one — if not the only — essential issue at stake in the proposal for a United

Arab Kingdom: who would represent the Palestinians? It was also this issue that led the PLO gradually to abandon the myth of 'the unity of the Jordanian-Palestinian theatre', as the prospect of King Hussein's being over-thrown began to look more unlikely. This question was indeed examined in the final part of al-Hassan's report and already the outlines of the positions that were later adopted at the tenth PNC are visible.

The Palestine People's Congress condemned the proposal for a United Arab Kingdom and linked it directly to the municipal elections. It violently denounced the proposal for a 'Palestinian region', which would only be a weak entity 'nominally under the authority of the King and a few indi-viduals collaborating with him, but in reality — administratively, economic-ally, socially and culturally — in the hands of the Zionist occupiers'.[67] The Congress called rather for the establishment of a 'Palestinian national state';[68] the term 'democratic state' did not appear. Stress was put throughout on the representative nature of the PLO. The municipal elections were explicitly denounced as an attempt by the 'Zionist occupiers' to give the mayors a political representativeness that 'goes beyond the framework of the West Bank'.[69]

The PLO and the Proposals Put Forward in the West Bank

Having several times condemned any proposal for a state in part of Palestine, the PLO was bound to be concerned about the ideas developing in the West Bank. Arafat had touched on this problem soon after the events of September 1970. In an interview he gave me, Abu Shalbaya claimed that he had never been attacked by the PLO; it seems that this is not accurate. Thus the editorial in *Fath Informations*, no. 4,[70] was wholly devoted to this problem. It was entitled, 'The real reasons behind the call for the creation of a Pales-tinian state in the West Bank', and denounced the proposals made by Abu Shalbaya in 'No peace without a free Palestinian state'. It is interesting to observe two assertions in the article which are at first sight contradictory. The first was that:

> the occupying forces and the Israeli and American intelligence services . . . have made contacts and embarked on activities to propagate the idea of a buffer state.

The second was that:

> despite statements by the Golda Meir government saying that there was no room for two states between the sea and the desert, one being Israel and the other called Jordan or Palestine . . , supporters of a Palestinian entity refuse to accept that in reality Israeli policy, under cover of a local representation in the West Bank, is seeking *de facto* annexation.

This amounted to saying that the idea of a Palestinian state was a propaganda slogan for the Israelis, 'a legal basis for maintaining the occupation'. How then could the writer of the editorial go on to say that the proposal was 'a dangerous colonialist proposal'? If the proposal was pure propaganda and the Israelis had no wish to implement it, why then did the PLO denounce its contents? The PLO was later to explain itself on this point by saying that the relations of force before the October war made it impossible to envisage such a state being truly independent, which seems likely.

It should also be observed that this editorial mentions, as an example of resistance, the National Charter of the Arabs of the West Bank for the Current Phase adopted in 1967 (see p. 65), and it gave an extract: 'The West Bank is provisionally an integral part of Jordan and in this way an integral part of the Arab world.' It goes without saying that the word 'provisionally' is not to be found in the original text.[71] Its use in 1972 was symptomatic of the state of mind of Palestinian leaders at this time, even before the propposal for a United Arab Kingdom.

Various statements by Palestinian organizations, in particular the PFLP and the PDFLP, and various issues of *Fath Informations*[72] confirmed the attacks on supporters of a Palestinian entity. The situation seemed sufficiently worrying for the executive committee of the PLO to meet on the question, in early September 1972. The communiqué adopted[73] denounced al-Ja'bari, Shawa and al-Khatib by name, as men whose activities had increased over the previous period and who had 'fraudulently arrogated to themselves the right to speak in the name of some sections of the Palestinian people'. The French version of the communiqué added an appeal by the executive committee for a variety of actions to fight these manoeuvres through the:

> setting up of a National Unity Front in the West Bank and Gaza to fight the occupation and the machinations of the collaborators, denounce their plans and strengthen the will to national resistance among our people in these areas.[74]

This call foreshadowed the decision that was to be taken at the eleventh PNC in January 1973.

9. The Turning Point of 1973

There is no text in which we can follow the internal debate in Fatah and the actual evolution of the PLO before October 1973. But the fact remains that, immediately after the events in Jordan in 1970, a wide-ranging debate began and some cadres declared their acceptance of the objective of a state in the West Bank and Gaza.[75] Perhaps an echo of this debate can be heard in a declaration by the leader of Sa'iqa on the eve of the October war. When questioned about the disagreements between his organization and Fatah, he replied that, on the question of a Palestinian state, 'the leadership of Fatah has not taken a clear stand'.[76] At any event, the main leaders of Fatah were certainly asking themselves questions, and some had already come out in favour of a political solution. This was to be seen in the debate precipitated by the new proposals put forward by President Bourguiba of Tunisia.

President Bourguiba's Proposals

During the spring and summer of 1973 President Bourguiba made a series of proposals for a return to the 1947 UN Partition Plan. A war of words then erupted in the Palestinian Resistance and among the Arab regimes — although it was much less virulent than the one that had been provoked by the Tunisian president in 1965.

Tunisia's position on the Palestinian problem has always been a somewhat special one.[77] In January 1964, at the first Arab Summit, Bourguiba took a position in favour of the Palestinians' struggle and maintained that the continuing conflict was not an Israeli–Arab one, but rather an Israeli–Palestinian one. 'Is the Palestinian people ready to play its leading role in this fight as the main interested party, the direct victim of aggression, deprived of its own country?'[78] This was one of Fatah's favourite themes at the time. But Bourguiba added that the struggle would be a long one and that it 'will inevitably involve phases ... outside a policy of phases, there is no effective way'.[79]

Bourguiba spelled out this still vague policy of phases during a visit to Jordan in 1965. After several times mentioning the need for a phased struggle, based on the Tunisian example,[80] he declared, at a press conference in Jerusalem:

Arab statesmen must not deceive their people. They must be frank and not let their feelings carry them away . . . Let us put weapons aside and let politicians look up and ahead . . . Arabs and Israelis will be able to live in harmony when they have rejected hatred and got rid of their complexes and their extremists . . . The 1947 partition would not have been such a bad solution to the problem . . . in the present circumstances, it is a lesser evil.[81]

On 21 April of the same year, Bourguiba appealed to Israel to declare its readiness to return to the Partition Plan. Israel refused, which did not prevent a serious crisis breaking out in the Arab world: on one side, Nasser and the PLO, and on the other, Tunisia. Bourguiba had broken too many taboos; denunciations and condemnations rained down on him.[82] But Nasser failed to get Bourguiba condemned by an Arab Summit.

The stands taken in 1965 did not prevent Tunisia from placing itself resolutely alongside the Arab countries in 1967, however, nor from supporting the PLO led by Arafat. It was in strong defence of these stands that Bourguiba returned to the attack eight years later, in 1973.

On 22 May 1973 Bourguiba gave an interview to the Milan newspaper *Corriere della Sera.*[83] In it he asserted that President Sadat was ready to negotiate with the Israelis and that he himself was ready to meet any Israeli convinced 'of the need to establish peace'. He returned to this theme in a series of interviews. He advocated a return to the Partition Plan;[84] but the clearest and most comprehensive expression of his thinking is contained in his interview with the Lebanese newspaper *al-Nahar*, at the beginning of July 1973.[85] After recalling that he had already submitted these proposals in 1965, he called on the Palestinians to accept the 1947 Partition Plan. When asked about Jordan, he asserted that the Emirate of Transjordan was a British creation whose purpose was to satisfy Abdallah. 'Jordan is only the name of a river. Whereas Palestine is a reality with a history going back to the Pharaohs', he asserted, leaving it to be understood that the East Bank of the Jordan could be included in the new Palestine. After stressing that there had been no positive response to his proposal from Israel, he went on: 'My idea has failed and produced no results, but I believe that time is on our side.'

The Jordanian reaction was very sharp[86] and resulted in diplomatic relations being broken off on 17 July 1973. On the other hand, the reaction of other Arab countries was more moderate, or even sympathetic. As early as 15 June Egypt, through its Minister of Foreign Affairs, suggested a return to the Partition Plan.[87] The most interesting reaction came from the PLO, which did not reject the Tunisian President's proposals.[88] It thus confirmed its movement towards acceptance of a political solution.

While the proposals made by President Bourguiba did not succeed, they were both the reflection of an evolution in the Arab world and a contribution to that evolution.

The Last Debate

The need for the Palestinian Resistance to set out the intermediate stages in the struggle had begun to make itself felt in 1972. It was the PDFLP, as we have seen, that was the first to put forward this idea. At the time, its policy could be summarized as follows: today the intermediate stage for the liberation of Palestine is change in Jordan.[89] But all through 1972 and at the beginning of 1973 two features in the political situation became clearer: the prospect of overthrowing King Hussein began to recede; and the struggle of the Palestinians in the occupied territories took on new dimensions.

Abu Adnan, a member of the historic leadership of the PDFLP, explained how this organization saw the problem:

> From 1972 onwards we thought that there was a need for a political programme different from Shuqairy's National Charter; a programme was needed that would take account of our historic rights, the problem of the Jews and the real relations of force. A long debate took place at the level of our political bureau and central committee. Four or five months before the October war we adopted what we called the programme for a national authority, which envisaged: the withdrawal of the Israelis from the territories occupied since 1967; and the setting-up of a national authority in the West Bank and Gaza.
>
> For the first time [he added] a programme was put before the Palestinians which did not speak of the territories occupied in 1948 and stressed those occupied in 1967[99]

A gap emerged, however, between these slogans and the way in which the PDFLP publicly presented its stand.[91] This public stand can be summarized as follows: drive out the occupier; implement the right to self-determination of the people in the occupied territories (those occupied in 1967); and, starting from the right to self-determination, work for the renewal and improvement of the unity of the two banks under the control of a national democratic regime.[92]

When asked about the gap between these two positions, Abu Adnan said:

> We paid attention to the way in which our proposals were presented; there still existed in the Resistance a sort of unitary national [*qawmiya*] romanticism, but within the Democratic Front, we were agreed on a national authority. The affirmation of the right to self-determination, and of the fact that it is the people who will decide on relations with the East Bank, was a response to the attacks against us.[93]

These attacks, it should be observed, were all the harsher because simultaneously several proposals were being floated (Bourguiba, the Egyptian Minister of Foreign Affairs Zayyat) which looked to many Palestinians, once again, like imperialist proposals.

It was at this point that the slogan of a democratic state came back into favour. Those very people who had fought against it now used it against the various proposals for a state in the West Bank and Gaza. Faced with those who said: thanks to our sacrifices we have won international recognition, so why not use it for a state in the West Bank?, George Habash replied on behalf of the PFLP: we are not fighting in order for the end result to be recognition of the state of Israel and the continuation of national and class oppression. He added, 'The aim of the Palestinian revolution is a free democratic state on all the land of Palestine . . . The strategic objective is the democratic state.'[94]

We shall now attempt to deal with the debate and the polemic provoked by the PDFLP's proposals. *Al-Hurriya* immediately stressed that the debate under way was due to the new situation brought about by the development of the national movement in the occupied territories.[95] The journal attacked those who thought that 'the setting-up of a Palestinian state was the real goal of American–Israeli policy', whereas in reality this goal was 'the liquidation of the Palestinian revolution and the disappearance of any form of expression of the Palestinian national personality'.[96]

When it came to clarifying its attitude to the proposals of Zayyat and Bourguiba, *al-Hurriya* pointed out that the former was a limited diplomatic initiative whose declared goals (a Palestinian state in the borders of the Partition Plan) bore no relation to the means suggested for bringing them about. Bourguiba's proposal was similar, except that it envisaged the disappearance of Jordan and an 'alternative' homeland for the Palestinians.

> These proposals are not rejected because they will lead to the setting-up of a Palestinian state in part of the land of Palestine (they will not reach that stage anyway). They are rejected because they only lead to dividing the ranks of the revolution and weakening the people.[97]

The problem then for the PDFLP was the balance of forces. This was unfavourable to the Palestinian Resistance and favourable to imperialism and reaction; but the revolutionary forces were in the process of recovering, as was shown by the May 1973 confrontations with the Lebanese army. The PDFLP rejected the proposals made by a number of Arab regimes, not because these proposals were looking for political solutions, but because the solutions were placed in the existing balance of forces, without attempting to alter them.[98] The PDFLP's proposal was one for the present phase, but only on the basis of a change in the balance of forces, and this change was only possible by advancing an intermediate slogan: drive out the occupier, and secure the right to self-determination of the people in the occupied territories.

Three conditions were necessary for total liberation: the victory of the national democratic revolution in several Arab countries; a change in the balance of forces at the international level; and the development by the Palestinian Resistance of generalized people's war. Between the present relations of force and the one necessary for total victory, there could be a relative change, making it possible to expel the occupiers from the territories occupied since 1967.[99]

This was the heart of the problem. Total liberation seemed far off and unlikely to be achieved all at once. Even Habash was obliged to recognize that:

> Of course, the strategic slogan of the Palestinian Resistance is: a democratic state in the whole soil of Palestine as the result of the struggle of the revolutionary forces and Arab and Jewish exploited classes. It is difficult to envisage this goal being attained in a single stage. But there is a difference between the liberation of a region of occupied Palestine where the fight continues to complete the liberation of the entire soil of Palestine, and a Palestinian state in part of occupied Palestine proposed by imperialism.[100]

In fact, this last statement remained very unclear. It may be thought that the PFLP leader was here referring to the theory of 'liberated zones' as in the Chinese or Vietnamese revolutions. But other texts show that the PFLP's thinking was not so specific. Thus the weekly *al-Hadaf* asserted:

> Any partial geographical solution, not only does not alter the nature of Israel and the Arab situation, but also tends to freeze the struggle, weaken revolutionary action and close the way to the possibilities of a progressive strategy . . . From that perspective, the phased programme, in our opinion . . . must not raise the problem of driving the occupier out to the detriment of revolutionary activity.[101]

Two major differences can be observed between the PDFLP's proposals and those of its various adversaries. The first was the distinction made by the Front between the territories occupied in 1967 and those occupied in 1948. The second related to the Front's assertion of the right to self-determination of the Palestinians in the occupied territories.

We shall look at each of these problems in turn. The possibility of securing the liberation of the territories occupied in 1967 was related to the 'radical difference in kind between the Israeli presence in the territories occupied in 1967 and this presence in the land usurped in 1948'.[102] The former was an occupying presence, the latter a colonial presence. It was clear, the PDFLP continued, that it was easier to wage the struggle in the areas where the Palestinians were living. In addition, it was necessary to take account of the difference in the attitude of the Israeli masses (or part of them) to the 1948 and 1967 territories.

It must be observed that these ideas mark a major break with a whole literature that had flourished in the Palestinian Resistance after 1967 (the more so as, up to the present day, no official PLO text speaks explicitly of a state in the West Bank and Gaza, but only in 'all liberated or evacuated territory'.) In the name of the struggle against Resolution 242, a distinction was no longer made between the West Bank and, for example, Galilee. This attitude, reflected in the slogan 'Haifa before Jerusalem', had played a large part in isolating the Palestinian Resistance. The new position taken by the PDFLP, which thus moved closer to the positions adopted by the Arab Communists, therefore marked a major turning-point. This is true even though, in the mind of the Front, it was not a matter of implementing Resolution 242, but of forcing the Israeli forces to withdraw *unconditionally*. The PDFLP added that acceptance of Resolution 242 could be contemplated as a tactical withdrawal, but that the nature of the Arab regimes would turn this concession into a capitulation.[103]

The second idea was that of self-determination. It must be stressed once again that neither in the statements of the PDFLP of the time, nor in interviews with Hawatmeh, was the goal of a 'national authority' clearly spelled out. The Front said that after driving out the occupier, it was necessary to enforce the 'right to self-determination of the Palestinian people in the occupied territories and its national sovereignty over the occupied territories'.[104] But it left hanging the question of a state and the question of unity with the East Bank, which would be settled by the people in the framework of the new relations of force thus created. To those who accused it of seeking to divide the Palestinian people, the PDFLP responded with the example of Vietnam and the Democratic Republic proclaimed in the north in 1954, which later became the rear base for the struggle in the south. It must be stressed that such a position was the result of the real development of the Palestinian struggle and the influence of the PLO in the occupied territories.

Particular attention has been paid to the positions of the PDFLP because they constituted a considerable advance on the PLO's positions, as well as on the Front's own positions examined above. The immediate objective was no longer the fall of the Hashemite regime, but the liberation of the territories occupied in 1967. The Front even condemned explicitly the idea that the latter objective should be subordinated to the former.[105] The downfall of the Hashemite regime was a long-term struggle, but the regime could be forced into partial withdrawals: the ending of discrimination, the recognition of the national rights of the Palestinian people, participation in the struggle against Israel, and so on.[106]

There was a long-drawn-out polemic between, on the one side, the PDFLP and, on the other, the PFLP, the PFLP-GC (General Command) and also the editors of *Filastin al-Thwara* and *Wafa*. These two papers, in theory under the PLO, were in fact under the direct influence of Fatah. Their participation in the attacks on the PDFLP shows that the situation in Arafat's organization was far from clear. While the leading figures had developed their thinking, the same does not seem to have been the case for the intermediate-level activists.

In conclusion, while the period 1967–73 was marked by a declared rejection of all 'political solutions', a slow evolution was undoubtedly under way in the PLO. While it affected only small groups, it also had an impact on the main leaders of the PLO. It took the shock of the October 1973 war, however, for this evolution to manifest itself in precise political positions. On

10 October 1973, in the middle of the war, Arafat sent the American Secretary of State Henry Kissinger a message asserting the PLO's willingness to take part in peace negotiations.[107]

Notes to Part 3

1. *International Documents on Palestine 1967*, Beirut, Institute for Palestine Studies, pp. 727–9. (Henceforth cited as *IDP* with the year of reference.)

2. *Al-wathaiq al-'arabiya al-filastiniya 1968* [Palestine Arab Documents], Beirut, Institute for Palestine Studies, pp. 523–33. (Henceforth cited as *PAD* with the year of reference.)

3. Ibid.

4. *PAD 1969*, pp. 41–2.

5. Ibid., pp. 95–8.

6. Ibid.

7. Ibid.

8. Ibid.

9. *Middle East Record 1968*, p. 450. (Henceforth cited as *MER* with the year of reference.)

10. *PAD 1970*, pp. 147–8.

11. Ibid., pp. 28–30; 20 January 1970.

12. Y.K. Harkabi, 'The Palestinians and the Arab–Israeli Conflict', in S. Avineri (ed.), *Israel and the Palestinians*, New York, St Martin's Press, 1971, pp. 12–13.

13. *PAD 1970*, pp. 692–5.

14. For this section see W.B. Quandt, *Decade of Decisions: American Policy towards the Arab–Israeli Conflict, 1967–1976*, Berkeley and Los Angeles, University of California Press, 1977, and M.K. Shadid, *The United States and the Palestinians*, London, Croom Helm, 1981.

15. Quoted by Shadid, *United States and Palestinians*, p. 89.

16. Quoted by Quandt, *Decade of Decisions*, pp. 130-1.

17. Quoted in *Le Monde*, 17 October 1970.

18. *PAD 1970*, pp. 945–8.

19. Ibid., pp. 992–8.

20. For the ALF see *PAD 1970*, p. 1010; for the PDFLP see *PAD 1970*, p. 1014; for the PFLP see *PAD 1971*, pp. 45–6.

21. *PAD 1971*, pp. 34–5.

22. Interview with Abu Latif, *PAD 1971*, pp. 176–9.

23. *PAD 1971*, pp. 377–80.

24. Ibid., pp. 495–516.

25. Ibid., p. 505.

26. Ibid., p. 506.

27. Ibid.; the same idea was taken up by the PDFLP in a draft resolution submitted to the ninth PNC, see ibid., pp. 524–6.

28. Ibid., p. 507.

29. Ibid., pp. 759–61.

30. Ibid., pp. 761–5.

31. Ibid., pp. 527–9.
32. Ibid., pp. 547–56.
33. Ibid., pp. 590–3.
34. Ibid., pp. 599–600.
35. For an incomplete study, but one that contains a number of documents, see G. Mury, *Septembre Noir*, Paris, Sindbad, 1972.
36. Abu Iyad, *My Home, My Land: A Narrative of the Palestinian Struggle*, New York, Times Books, 1981, p. 98.
37. See, for example, the PDFLP's statement of 28 August 1972, *PAD 1971*, pp. 707–10, which accused Dayan of saying that he favoured the establishment of a 'permanent government' in the West Bank, and of thus favouring the 'secessionists', whereas in fact Dayan's statement advocated that Israel consider itself as the established government of the occupied Arab territories (*IDP 1971*, pp. 234–5).
38. *PAD 1971*, pp. 759–61.
39. Ibid., p. 766–8.
40. Statement by the PDFLP, ibid., pp. 707–10.
41. Interview in April 1970, *PAD 1970*, pp. 208–9.
42. R. Hamid (ed.), *Muqararat al-majlis al-watani al-filastini 1964–1974* [Resolutions of the PNCs 1964–1974], Beirut, PLO Research Centre, 1975, p. 178.
43. Ibid., p. 183.
44. Ibid., p. 192.
45. Ibid., pp. 188–9.
46. Ibid., p. 233. In fact, the first public expression of the existence of two peoples came in the report by K. al-Hassan to the executive committee on the proposal for a United Arab Kingdom and the press release that followed. See especially *PAD 1972*, p. 837, and *PAD 1972*, pp. 132–5. We should note that the PFLP was not a member of the executive committee at this time.
47. *PAD 1972*.
48. Ibid., p. 212.
49. A. Plascov, *The Palestinian Refugees in Jordan 1948–1957*, London, Frank Cass, 1981, p. 15.
50. *PAD 1971*, pp. 917–18.
51. *PAD 1972*, pp. 53–4.
52. Ibid., p. 54–5.
53. Ibid., p. 136.
54. Ibid., pp. 54–5.
55. Ibid., pp. 53–4.
56. Ibid., p. 120.
57. Ibid., p. 121.
58. Ibid., pp. 136–7.
59. *Le Monde*, 30 March 1972.
60. *IDP 1972*, pp. 172–3.
61. *PAD 1972*, pp. 126–33.
62. Ibid., p. 126.
63. Ibid., p. 127.
64. Ibid., pp. 131–3.
65. Ibid.

66. Ibid., pp. 133–5.
67. Hamid, *Muqarat*, p. 209.
68. Ibid.
69. Ibid., p. 213.
70. *Fath Informations*, Paris, 23 February 1972.
71. *IDP 1967*, pp. 682–6.
72. See for example issue no. 13–14 of 1 August 1972.
73. *PAD 1972*, p. 379.
74. *Fath Informations*, no. 17, 15 October 1972.
75. Interview with Abu Hatem (Muhammad Abu Mayzar), Beirut, May 1982.
76. *PAD 1973*, pp. 285–8.
77. J.-P. Chagnollaud, *Maghreb et Palestine*, Paris, Sindbad, 1977.
78. Ibid., p. 107.
79. Ibid., p. 108.
80. *PAD 1965*, pp. 78–82.
81. Chagnollaud, *Maghreb et Palestine*, p. 110.
82. For 'immediate' reactions, see *PAD 1965*, in particular for those of the PLO, pp. 112–14, the ANM, pp. 119–21, Fatah, pp. 141–3, and the Ba'th, pp. 180–3.
83. *PAD 1973*, pp. 162–3.
84. Interview with *Le Monde*, 30 June 1973.
85. *PAD 1973*, pp. 208–10.
86. Ibid., pp. 210–11, 220, and 224–5.
87. Ibid., pp. 193–4. 'Zayyat Proposal'.
88. Chagnollaud, *Maghreb et Palestine*, pp. 224–5, and press release from the executive committee of the PLO, *PAD 1973*, pp. 299–300.
89. See for example the PDFLP's press conference, 4 April 1972, *PAD 1972*, pp. 193–6.
90. Interview with Abu Adnan (Abd al-Karim Hamad), member of the politbureau of the PDFLP, Paris, December 1981.
91. See a series of articles in *al-Hurriya*, published just before the October war, in the book *Adwa'min fikr al-jabha al-dimukratiya al-sha'biya li tahrir filastin hawla al-muhimat al-rahina lil-thawra al-filastiniya* [Aspects of the thought of the PDFLP on the present tasks of the Palestinian Resistance], n.p., n.d., 155pp.
92. Ibid., p. 149.
93. Interview with Abu Adnan, December 1981.
94. *PAD 1972*, pp. 213–14, see also *PAD 1973*, pp. 250–1.
95. *Adwa'min*, pp. 4–5.
96. Ibid., p. 14.
97. Ibid., p. 28.
98. Ibid, p. 33.
99. Ibid., pp. 45–7.
100. *PAD 1973*, p. 251.
101. Quoted in *Adwa'min*, p. 64.
102. Ibid., p. 60.
103. Ibid., pp. 72–4.
104. Ibid., p. 106.
105. Ibid., p. 117.
106. Ibid., p. 42.
107. Kissinger, *Les années orageuses*, Paris, Fayard, 1982, vol. I, pp. 581–2.

Part IV:
The Great Turning Point: the Decision-Making Process in the PLO (1973-1974)

The October war of 1973 marked a decisive point in the evolution of Palestinian political thought. By opening up concrete prospects of an overall settlement, it placed the Palestinian Resistance in a dilemma. It could either reject such a settlement and risk confrontation not only with Israel but with the Arab regimes closest to it (Damascus and Cairo); this is what it had done in August 1970 over the Rogers Plan, with the results we have already seen. Alternatively, it could try to enter into the peace process, while attempting to secure the maximum number of guarantees and make the minimum number of concessions. It was this second path that, generally, it was to attempt to follow, with the successes and setbacks that we shall see.

Within this strategy, the question of a state occupied a central place. Standing by a democratic state as the sole slogan meant demanding the destruction of the state of Israel and thus deferring the rebirth of a Palestinian state to the distant future. Accepting a transitional solution (but which one?) meant tryint to put forward a solution acceptable to the allies of the Palestinian Resistance; it was thus the only realistic solution in the short term.

In this Part we shall try to follow the debate that shook the Palestinian Resistance from the October war to the adoption of the slogan of a 'national authority' by the twelfth PNC in June 1974.

We shall also endeavour to understand the decision-making process in the PLO and, through this process, a number of the organization's characteristic features, which are all the more important because they enable us to explain — or clarify — how and why the PLO takes any particular decision today.

10. The Positions and Forces within the PLO

In order to understand the debate within the PLO, three essential factors must be taken into account. The first was purely internal — the relationship between the various Palestinian organizations. In this debate, the Palestinians inside the occupied territories came to play an ever greater role. The second factor was Arab: the positions of Cairo and Damascus, and to a lesser extent those of the other Arab capitals, which affected the PLO — mainly externally, but sometimes internally through organizations under the thumb of Arab regimes. The third factor was international: the PLO, recognized by a growing number of states, had to take account of the position of these states, and in particular those providing it with a large amount of support.

There were two essential and linked questions to which the PLO had to respond during this period. First, could one accept an intermediate objective which would not be that of the liberation of the whole of Palestine and the establishment of a democratic state? Secondly, should the PLO go to the peace conference to be held in Geneva, and if so on what terms?

The Palestinians inside the Occupied Territories

One section of the Palestinian people, that living in the occupied territories and represented by the PNF, was immediately in a position to give a reply to the questions asked. Having lived under the occupation for six years, the population had no wish to see it prolonged for the sake of a more or less mythical democratic state. The liberation of the West Bank and Gaza and the setting-up of a state in these territories were concrete objectives that met their aspirations. For these reasons, but also because of the failure of the armed struggle in the occupied territories, the most extremist organizations had little influence. The enemy was seen as the pro-Jordanians who were preparing for the return of the occupied territories to Jordan; they could only be fought by offering a realistic alternative to their proposals. Finally, the Communists, the backbone of the PNF, had long since accepted the idea of the partition of Palestine. In a discussion with Eric Rouleau, two important Communist leaders, Barghuti and Zayadin, told the French journalist:

> If Israel accepts the principle of the total evacuation of the territories occupied since 1967, under the guarantee of the great powers, the Arab states should be ready eventually to enter negotiations directly with Tel Aviv.

They added, not without irony:

> We have often been denounced as traitors because for 26 years we have consistently advocated the existence of the Jewish state alongside a Palestinian state. Today we are demanding that the right to self-determination based on the resolutions adopted by the UN since 1947 be accorded to the Palestinian people. The implementation of this right should also be the subject of negotiations.[1]

The population's support for the idea of a Palestinian state was made forcefully clear, in an opinion poll carried out by an Israeli institute among the inhabitants of the West Bank.[2] First, 61% of the people questioned spontaneously defined themselves as Palestinians, 28% as 'from the West Bank of the Jordan' and only 6% as 'from Jordan'. Next, 44% hoped to belong to a future independent Palestinian state, whereas only 19% wanted a return to Jordan. This broad assertion of Palestinian identity among the inhabitants of the West Bank gave the PNF an unprecedented audience and authority. There are some other facts which testify to this audience. For example, on 3 December 1971 the extremely conservative Jerusalem Higher Muslim Council published a statement supporting the resolutions of the Algiers Arab Summit which recognized the PLO; it was a sharp defeat for the supporters of Hussein.[3] On 31 December 1973 the Arabs in East Jerusalem obeyed the PNF call to boycott the elections; only 10% voted as against 18% in 1969. Finally, the Israelis, through their repression of the PNF, were implicitly recognizing its audience: on 10 December 1973 eight of its leaders were expelled to Jordan. This step was followed by a wave of demonstrations and strikes.[4]

In addition, the PNF's positions were strengthened by numerous discussions with the leaders of the PDFLP and especially of Fatah. While the latter, for reasons that will be examined below, could not yet take clear-cut positions, they asked the PNF to be the most radical spokesman for what Hourani calls the 'realistic revolutionary trend'.[5]

Out of these discussions emerged an important letter from the PNF to the executive committee of the PLO.[6] Dated 1 December 1973, this was the most comprehensive summary of the PNF's positions.[7] The letter began by touching on the decisive problem being debated on the Palestinian, Arab and international scene, the representativeness of the PLO. The PLO alone, the letter asserted, was qualified to represent the Palestinian people:

1. It was the organization approved by the Palestinian people at their Jerusalem conference in the spring of 1964, since when it had devoted

itself to its command role and united all the Palestinian organizations.

2. At the second Arab Summit Conference in Alexandria (1964), the Arab states had recognized the legitimacy of the PLO and the fact that it represented the Palestinian people. This had been reaffirmed in Algiers in 1973. Moreover, the PLO now had offices in many friendly countries, both socialist and non-aligned.

3. There was no other Palestinian organization challenging the PLO or disputing it. This did not prevent the PNF from asking that the PLO be expanded, in other words, that the PNF play a greater role in its decision-making bodies:[8]

> Some people may not regard the present composition of the Organization as ensuring the desired representation. In our view the geographical dispersion of the Palestinian people, and the fact that a large part of our people are living under Israeli occupation, makes the desired representation impossible in the present circumstances. Nevertheless, we consider it to be the responsibility of the Organization, at the present stage, to seek in such ways as it considers feasible to expand the base of this representation so as to include more extensive sectors of the Palestinian popular masses and political forces.

The letter went on to deal with the problem of the attitude of Palestinians to the peace conference to be held in Geneva. While taking into account the military and other capacities of the Arab states, the Palestinians were not in a position, and were unlikely to be so for a long time, to attain their strategic goals. (Note that these were not defined.) But this should not discourage them: they had wider international support, Arab solidarity and the oil weapon; conversely, Israel was isolated. 'Therefore the peace conference will meet − if it does meet − in a situation that is negative as far as Israel is concerned.' Israel therefore would put obstacles in the way of its being held, and attempt to divide the Arabs and prevent the PLO participating in it. This required co-ordination with Egypt and Syria. Moreover, 'the alternative to participation by the PLO in the projected conference on the Middle East is the regime in Amman'. And this regime was opposed to the rights of the Palestinians and was co-ordinating its action with Israel and the United States to prevent the PLO representing the Palestinians at the conference. Israel feared this participation because:

1. Such participation was contrary to the idea that the West Bank and Gaza were abandoned territories which Israel was entitled to administer to the same degree as Egypt and Jordan.

2. The emergence of a Palestinian state would oblige Israel to define its geographical frontiers. There was no such definition in its constitution and this gave it absolute freedom of settlement.

3. Definition of the frontiers would interfere with the way in which Israel dealt with its internal problems by distracting attention by constant

aggression against its neighbours (1956, 1967, and so on).

4. The ingathering of the Palestine people to their land and the recognition of their right to self-determination would lead to their calling on the United Nations to implement its successive resolutions since 1947, and this could only be at the expense of the Zionist usurpation of Arab territory.

5. The building by the Palestinian people of its own state would enable the Arab states to devote themselves to their internal problems, and to solve them by using the resources that, for 25 years, had been used to repel Israeli aggression. This would create additional difficulties for imperialism and Zionism. In addition, Israel's return to the 1967 frontiers (which would only be secured by coercion and pressure) would ruin expansionist Zionist plans, undermine the credibility of Zionism and lead to a reduction in immigration into Israel, as well as in the financial aid and moral enthusiasm evoked by the 1967 victory. Finally, this would considerably worsen the internal crisis in Israel.

This statement clearly set out the immediate objective: to go to Geneva in order to secure the creation of a Palestinian state in the West Bank and Gaza. *This is a decisive point.* Especially since the letter spoke of Israel's defining frontiers, which constituted a *de facto* recognition of Israel by the Palestinians. It is true that the statement contained no renunciation of the strategic objectives. The belief remained that the crisis in Israel was developing, and that it might lead to its collapse, but military means of securing it were ruled out. The Palestinian people's other demands (in particular the right of return) would be raised at the United Nations.

Several other letters and statements from the PNF were published in the months that followed; their goal was to reaffirm support for both the PLO and a realistic attitude. Thus the statement of 21 December 1973[9] called for a positive attitude to the possibilities opened up by the October war. So did the declaration of January 1974[10] and that of February 1974, [11] which, in addition, indicated support for the first Israeli–Egyptian disengagement agreement (17 January 1974) and hence for the peace process, at a time when this peace process was the focus of violent opposition from a number of fedayeen organizations.

The PLO Decision-Making Centres

While it is true that the impact of the Palestinians in the occupied territories grew in 1973–74, decisions were still taken in Beirut. It was there that the PLO leaders had their headquarters; it was there that the armed forces of the Palestinian Resistance were concentrated; and it was there that the decisive questions were settled.

What were these decision-making bodies? The main one was, in theory, the Palestine National Council, the PNC. This is a sort of parliament, whose membership is changed every three years, by agreement among the various fedayeen organizations. The last session before the October war, the eleventh, was held in Cairo from 6 to 12 January 1973. There were then 180 seats. These were divided up as follows: 85 for the guerrilla organizations (including 33 for Fatah, 12 for Sa'iqa, 12 for the PFLP, 8 for the PDFLP, 8 for the ALF, 3 for the PFLP-GC, the rest for a number of small organizations and 6 for the PLA), and 95 for independents and representatives of various mass organizations (students, trade unions, writers, women, and so on). Most representatives of the mass organizations and a large number of independents were close to one or other of the guerrilla organizations. There were very few exceptions: the few representatives of the occupied territories, often personalities who had been expelled; the three or four representatives of the Jordanian Communist Party. This does not mean that the PNC was simply a rubber-stamp body; the length of its sessions and the lively debates which took place there suggest the opposite. Nevertheless, the real decision-making centres were to be found in the guerrilla organizations. The executive committee was made up of ten individuals, each of whom headed a working department of the PLO.

The members elected by the eleventh PNC were:

> Yasser Arafat: Fatah; chairman of the executive committee.
> Muhammad Yusif al-Najjar: Fatah; political department (international relations).
> Zuhair Mohsen: Sa'iqa; military department.
> Yasser Abd al-Rabbo: PDFLP; national affairs.
> Ahmad al-Yamani: PFLP; popular organizations.
> Abd al-Wahhab Kayyali: ALF; cultural affairs.
> Yusif Sayeah: independent; finance.
> Kamal Nassar: independent; information and guidance.
> Hamed Abu Sitteh: independent; occupied territories.
> Muhammad Zohdi al-Nashashibi: independent; general secretariat.

It will be recalled that al-Najjar and Nassar were killed in the Israeli raid of April 1973.

In principle, the executive committee was the supreme body of the PLO between sessions of the PNC. Every decision had to be ratified by it. But in the period between the October war and the twelfth PNC, its role was somewhat marginal, for a number of reasons: it was weakened by the loss of two of its most important members; the PNF and the PFLP-GC were not represented in it; and the 'unified departments' (military, information, and so on) had little meaning, since the fedayeen organizations had retained very considerable independence in most areas, especially the military one.

The eleventh PNC created a central council to ensure that PNC decisions were implemented. It included the members of the executive committee and some 20 other members: 4 representatives of Fatah, 2 each for the PFLP,

Sa'iqa, PDFLP, ALF, 6 for the professional unions and 5 independents (including several representatives of the PNF from October 1973 onwards). Meetings were held, in theory, once every three months. The central council was broader and more representative than the executive committee and was to play an important role in the discussions of 1973–74.

It was predominantly in each of the Palestinian organizations, and the relations of force that developed between them, that the future of the Palestinian Resistance was decided. We shall see this more clearly when we study the concrete process through which the decision was taken to set up a 'national authority'. But, first, we must examine the positions of the main organizations.

The PDFLP: Resolute Support for a 'National Authority'

The PDFLP was undeniably a small organization: it had only 8 representatives on the PNC as against 33 for Fatah and 12 for the PFLP. But it played an important role. It was a very 'ideological' organization; since 1971 it had purged itself,[12] eliminating leftist elements; the leadership had acquired considerable homogeneity and in its secretary-general, Hawatmeh, had a respected and influential figure. The Front had a weekly newspaper *al-Hurriya*, published jointly with the Lebanese Communist Action Organization (LCAO), whose quality attracted not only Palestinian but also Arab intellectuals. The Front also had numerous contacts in the Arab world with the PDRY, Algeria, Syria, and so on, and also, especially after 1973, with the socialist countries.

These factors, combined with its stand in favour of a national authority in the West Bank and Gaza, in the summer of 1973, placed the PDFLP in a vanguard position which stood out all the more because the other organizations, including Fatah, were holding back.

At the beginning of November 1973, with the war scarcely over, there was a meeting of an enlarged session of the central committee of the PDFLP. Its purpose was to study the consequences of the war and the position of the Palestinian Resistance now faced with new objectives.[13] The communiqué's analysis of the results of the October war was positive, although somewhat nuanced: the battle joined with the war was continuing in spite of the cease-fire; with the support of the US, Israel was trying very hard to restore the situation. Arab forces must be mobilized, together with maximum international support, first and foremost among the socialist countries. In this situation:

> the outcome of the October war raises forcefully today the question of guaranteeing the permanent national rights and the vital interests of the Palestinian people, in the face of imperialist, Zionist and reactionary manoeuvres.[14]

The communiqué went on to denounce attempts to liquidate the Palestinian Resistance as the sole representative of the Palestinian people. This would be a major blow to the struggle to reconquer their land and build 'a democratic state in the whole of Palestine'.[15] One of the essential questions at the time was the struggle for the right of the Palestinian Resistance to be the sole authentic representative of the Palestinian people. In this framework, it was the task of the Palestinian Resistance to lead the struggle in the occupied territories to put an end to the occupation and impose self-determination.

These very explicit theses did not mark any advance on those of the summer of 1973. It was not until Hawatmeh's speech to the Arab University in Beirut, on 6 December 1973, that new details appeared.[16] After recalling the battle waged by the PLO at the Arab Summit in Algiers, the secretary-general of the PDFLP stressed the pressures exerted by various forces for a settlement in the Middle East. The Palestinian Resistance, he said:

> faces a choice: negative opposition which aids the American–Zionist–Hashemite plan — and revolutionary opposition, positive opposition to assert itself as a partner in the fight and enter the struggle . . .[17] [This last position] makes it possible to enter the struggle in all its forms, and, with our arms, to assert the independent presence of our people in every part of its land from which Israeli forces withdraw, whether as a result of force, the threat of force or a settlement imposed by the forces active in the area. We will not permit the return of any Palestinian land to King Hussein, nor annexation by Israel; we must build an independent Palestinian national authority.[18]

This authority would have three advantages: it would preserve the independence of the Palestinian people; it would enable it to play a role in the Palestinian Resistance and the Arab liberation movement; and it would constitute a revolutionary base to continue the struggle.

Hawatmeh went on to draw a parallel between those who had rejected an authority in Jordan in 1970 (i.e. Fatah) and those who rejected an authority in the liberated territories. He added that there was no question of recognizing Israel and that the strategic objective remained the democratic state.

Thus the PDFLP clearly took a position in favour of a 'national authority' in any liberated part of Palestinian territory. By implication, this meant the West Bank and Gaza. This moreover was what Hawatmeh stated in Moscow at the end of November 1973: according to the PDFLP leader, both the USSR and the PLO 'reaffirmed the absolute right of the Palestinian people in the West Bank of Jordan and the Gaza Strip to determine their own future'.[19] He confirmed this point in an interview, saying that in the present relations of force:

> we must struggle to drive the Zionist occupier out of the Arab and Palestinian lands occupied in 1967 and give our people the possibility

to determine its own future independently and establish a national authority in every part of Palestinian soil from which the occupier has been driven out, without making any concession of principle to the enemy Zionist state.[20]

The PDFLP was the first organization to accept the idea of a national authority and it threw itself wholeheartedly into the ideological debate with its opponents in the Rejection Front. A speech by Hawatmeh on the occasion of the fifth anniversary of the Front, on 24 February 1974, enables us to see the various aspects of the controversy. To the Arab nationalists who rejected the very idea of a special entity for the Palestinians, he replied:

> Yes, we are Arabs; but we are, at the same time, Palestinians. Just as every Arab people has a full right to an independent national existence, so the Palestinian people too has a full right to an independent national existence.[21]

To those who put forward slogans such as 'The whole of Palestine at once' or 'Palestinian territories liberated from occupation are to go to the regime of King Hussein', the secretary-general of the PDFLP asserted:

> Our answer to these currents of thought is: They shall not succeed in directing [*sic*; diverting] the attention of the revolution from its objectives at this stage. Our people, our revolutionary bases and all the vanguard of the revolution know well that they must submit a pragmatic programme which puts the Palestinian people as a whole, the revolution as a whole and the movement for Arab national liberation against the American–Israeli–Hashemite solution of surrender and liquidation.[22]

This solution, a national authority, required new defeats to be inflicted on the enemy, and a change in the balance of power. But these new defeats also depended on the capacity to advance 'intermediate' slogans. In reply to arguments as to the economic viability of the West Bank and Gaza, Hawatmeh said:

1. Even if our territory was a desert, it would still be our land. Moreover, if this argument of non-viability had been accepted, half the countries in Africa and the majority of Asian countries would not have achieved independence.
2. The occupied territories have great potential.

Finally, Hawatmeh refuted the argument of those who saw in a national authority the risk of a division between Palestinians in the occupied territories and those outside. On the contrary, he said, this new authority would provide a support base for the struggle of all Palestinians.

From this point the debate broadened. At the beginning of February 1974 three organizations, Fatah, Sa'iqa and the PDFLP, presented a joint document in favour of a 'national authority'. From then on the PDFLP was no longer alone in the front line with the PNF. It had played a role in crystallizing the essential elements of the debate, and enabling Fatah not to become too involved so that a compromise solution could later be reached which would maintain the unity of the Palestinian Resistance. But this vanguard position of the PDFLP did not mean that it supported all initiatives directed towards a political settlement. It was more distrustful than Fatah of the Egyptian regime and condemned the first Egypt–Israel disengagement agreement.[23] The PDFLP even appeared to accuse Fatah of having illusions about the peace process and its chances of success in the short term.[24]

Fatah: Unite the PLO

Fatah was the most powerful and best organized of all the Palestinian organizations. Its armed forces were greatly superior to those of the other organizations. It dominated most of the mass organizations, as well as the apparatus of the PLO. It was, of course, formally in a minority within the executive committee and the PNC, but many of the 'independents' were really in its camp. In addition, it had woven a solid web of alliances with most Arab countries and with other Palestinian organizations (Sa'iqa and the PDFLP in particular). Finally, it had a united leading group and a leader who was undisputed on the Palestinian level, and, increasingly, on the international level.

It was thus essentially within Fatah that the continuing debate unfolded. Very soon after the October war, it seems, the central committee of Fatah declared itself in favour of the idea of a Palestinian state in any liberated part of the territory. It even, as we have seen, encouraged the PNF to take vanguard positions. This is not surprising. Long before 1967 Fatah had supported the idea of a revolutionary authority in the West Bank and Gaza (see Part One, p. 24). Although the Kaddoumi report on such a state had been rejected in 1967:

> yet for all that the Fatah leadership was still bent on getting the phased policy . . . In order to move forward, towards the interconfessional democratic society of which we used to dream, we had to establish our own state, even in an inch of Palestine. This idea gained more ground at the 'base' of the movement after King Hussein made public his proposal for a United Arab Kingdom on 15 March 1972.[25]

Yet Fatah's first text, adopted on 4 November 1973, was not very clear as to the immediate objectives. The statement[26] referred to ongoing consultations within the organization and the need to continue them. It then set out the five basic points of Fatah's position:

1. The strategic objective was liberation and the building of a democratic state in the whole of Palestine.

2. The present situation must be studied objectively and the Palestinian people must be consulted, 'within and outside the occupied homeland, as well as our Arab brothers and our friends in the world, so that our decision may be in harmony with these consultations'.

3. The October war had had some positive effects and others that had not yet been determined. 'Mobilization of all Arab and Palestinian official and popular efforts' would be necessary; in these circumstances Fatah condemned the issuing of unilateral statements 'that are not based on a true and responsible appraisal of the seriousness of the current situation'.

4. It was important not to oppose the Palestinian Revolution's allies in the world.

5. Every decision must be based on the following principles:

a) emanate from Palestinian national interest and preserve legitimate and historic rights;

b) continue the political and armed struggle:

c) preserve the rights already achieved through the struggle;

d) preserve the unity of the Palestinian Resistance.

Why was there no clear formulation in this statement of the slogan of a national authority in every part of liberated Palestine, when the central committee of Fatah was, at that time, already agreed on this intermediate objective? The essential reason is given in the statement itself: the problem of Palestinian unity, and at two levels. In the first place, there was the unity of Fatah itself. While the central committee was united, the same could not be said of the rest of the organization. Some leaders were not insensitive to the rejectionist arguments.[27] It must be remembered that Fatah had little ideological homogeneity and that it counted among its members people on both the extreme left and the extreme right. Secondly, there was the unity of the Palestinian Resistance. In Part One, we have already explained the decisive importance for the PLO of maintaining its unity. Because of its key position in the organization, Fatah felt that it had a unifying mission which was all the more necessary because it had at all costs to avoid a split which would weaken the PLO's credibility, both at the level of the Arab world and internationally. In this situation, Fatah preferred to see the PDFLP and PNF move to the forefront — with its tacit approval — and retain for itself a possible future role as broker.

This did not prevent Fatah from waging a major ideological struggle against extremist tendencies. It did so, first, by insisting that the West Bank and Gaza must not be returned to King Hussein. 'This is the touchstone of our political activity today',[28] declared Abu Iyad in late November 1973. He added, a few weeks later, that these territories must be transformed into bases for the struggle, without in any way compromising 'our historic rights'.[29] In January 1974 he declared:

So far as the occupied territories are concerned, we have said two things ... no return to the regime of King Hussein to govern our people. And, at the same time, we have stated that this part of the land of Palestine does not represent the whole of our national recognized right in Palestine.[30]

In the same interview, he stressed the need for the PLO to present a 'transitional action programme' and recalled that it was because it had failed to do so that the government of the whole of Palestine had disappeared in 1948. In this statement, the Palestinian leader asserted that, after two months of discussions, it was time to reach a decision. Another argument used by Fatah during this period was that of the position taken by the allies of the Palestinian Resistance, on the one hand, the patriotic Arab regimes which had launched the October war, and on the other the USSR. We shall return to this point.

In early January 1974 Fatah publicly took a position in favour of a 'national authority'. But it did so in a way that was very defensive as to the theses of the Rejection Front. 'We are not against the setting up of an independent national authority, but on three conditions: no peace, no recognition [of Israel], no abandonment of our historic rights',[31] declared Abu Saleh, a member of the Fatah central committee, on 7 January 1974. In my opinion, this must be seen as the result not only of the campaign by the forces of the Rejection Front, but also of the growing suspicion of American initiatives — particularly Kissinger's — at a time when the Geneva Conference had just held an inaugural session that was, in the event, also to be its last.

On the Geneva Conference, Fatah's political position did not change much. On 26 October 1973 Sadat suggested to the Palestinians that they take part in the peace conference; the following day, the leadership of Fatah decided not to reply 'until we received a formal invitation'.[32] Arafat expressed the same position in an interview with the Egyptian newspaper *al-Ahram* on 28 November 1973. We have not, he said, spelled out our position on the Geneva Conference. 'The good of our cause requires that we should speak last.'[33] But these positions, which were both advanced (compared to the rejectionist forces) and modest (if we look at the PNF theses), did not prevent the Fatah leadership — or at least Arafat — from attempting a policy of making overtures on the international scene.

Hammami's Articles: Fatah's Double-Talk?

Arafat sent 'signals' both to the Western powers and to Israel: he was attempting to convince them of his desire to reach a peaceful solution. It was a mode of political action that is difficult to grasp because it rested on the action of individuals, in particular Said Hammami and, later, Dr Sartawi. In both cases, we are dealing with figures who were prominent in Fatah, but were not in the front ranks. They were not mandated for these initiatives by either the PLO or the leadership of Fatah, but were responsible directly to Arafat himself. They had real room to manoeuvre and an autonomy that was full of risks. They were given the task of exploring new possibilities that were ahead of their own organizations and of the consciousness of the Palestinian masses. It was an uncomfortable, even dangerous, position: Said Hammami was to pay for it with his life in 1978 and Sartawi in 1983. But they were assured of Arafat's support.

Hammami had joined Fatah in 1967; he had taken part in several military actions and represented the PLO in Lebanon after Black September. During the period we are examining, he was the PLO representative in London and was kept in this post until his assassination by killers belonging to the Abu Nidal group operating out of Iraq. As for Sartawi (at least in the period 1973-77)., he remained a member of the revolutionary committee of Fatah and enjoyed Arafat's support, notably at the thirteenth PNC. (We shall meet him again in Part Five.)

The proposals formulated by Hammami were very attractive, but they raise a question that cannot be avoided. Was it double-talk? In other words, were the PLO and Arafat saying one thing aimed at world (and particularly Western) public opinion, and another aimed at the Palestinian people? I do not think so. But the PLO did not want to take unilateral initiatives for peace; and this was because of the very circumstances of the decision-making process in the organization, and the need to maintain a broad consensus until a detailed solution was proposed to the Palestinian Resistance. We shall return later to this question in detail. Nevertheless, for the leadership group, and Arafat in particular, ways to a solution had to be explored; a clear formulation had to be given to PLO texts that were often ambiguous. The reactions of the US and Israel had to be sounded out. While it may be observed that Hammami's formulations and proposals were never officially taken up by PLO bodies, it was because they never evoked the slightest interest on the part of the Israeli leaders. They were trial balloons that showed a real desire to compromise, but had few tangible consequences.[34] It was difficult for Arafat to try to get them adopted by the PLO (and thus run the risk of a split) if there was no reciprocity. To do this, the PLO would have had to develop a different type of strategy, a strategy towards the Israeli masses similar to that adopted by the Vietnamese in the United States but in a situation where the Palestinian Resistance did not constitute a real military threat to Israel. But that is another question . . .

The texts of the proposals, published in London in the autumn of 1973, were nevertheless remarkable. Hammami's first article appeared in *The Times* on 16 November.[35] In it he spelled out the principles that could help towards peace efforts:

1. The right of the Palestinians to participate in any forthcoming peace conference . . , on an equal basis with the other parties, must be acknowledged by the international community.

2. Representatives of the Palestinian people, both those living in exile

and those still living under Israeli occupation . . , should be invited to participate in any peace conference.

3. The recognition of the inalienable rights of the Palestinian people, in particular their right of self-determination in accordance with the Charter of the United Nations, constitutes an indispensable element in any lasting settlement in the Middle East.

This must also be acknowledged by the international community.

> Many Palestinians believe that a Palestinian state on the Gaza Strip and the West Bank, including Al Hammah region, is a necessary part of any peace package. Such a Palestinian state would lead to the emptying and closing down of the refugee camps, thereby drawing out the poison at the heart of Arab–Israeli enmity.

It must be remembered that these theses were published at a time when Fatah had made no pronouncement either on the Geneva Conference or on a national authority, and even less on the question of removing 'the poison at the heart of Arab-Israeli enmity'.

Hammami's theses were spelled out in another article published in *The Times* on the eve of the opening of the Geneva Conference and significantly entitled, 'Making the First Move towards Peace in Palestine'.

> As a result of the 1948 war a new map of the Middle East was drawn, with a new state making its appearance and a new nation emerging. It seems that the October war could similarly create a new map of the Middle East with a new state of Palestine joining the comity of nations.

After this bold parallel, Hammami defined the two basic features of the conflict:

> 1. The Palestinian Arabs and the Israeli Jews were and still are the principal parties to the conflict. The clash of their interests and aspirations has formed the background of the entire conflict.
> 2. Consequently, these two parties – and only these two parties – can lay the foundations for a peaceful future in the Middle East.

Hammami went on to spell out the attitude of his people towards a democratic state:

> We, the Palestinians, have no reason to change our belief that a binational secular state consisting of all Palestine, in which all Palestinian Arabs and all Israeli Jews can live together democratically, is ultimately the only just and stable solution for the conflict. But we know that ultimate solutions are by their nature long-term aims to be worked for,

rather than the intial position to start from. We are well aware of the fact that a state in partnership can be constructed only if and when the two parties genuinely want it and are ready to work for it. Past decades of enmity do not provide a good ground for an immediate realization of a state in partnership. [And the author added:] I believe that the first step towards that should be a mutual recognition for the two respective parties. The Israeli Jews and the Palestinian Arabs should recognize one another as peoples, with all the rights to which a people is entitled. This recognition should be followed by the realization of the Palestinian Arab entity through a Palestinian state, an independent fully-fledged member of the United Nations.

Hammami then recalled the three points on which the PLO was not ready to compromise:

1. The Palestinians form only a single people, wherever they live.
2. The PLO is their sole representative.
3. The PLO seeks a solution for all Palestinians.

He went on:

Once these principles are accepted by the United Nations and the great powers . . . I am sure the Palestinian leadership would accept an invitation to the peace conference. The Palestinian leadership knows how hard a task it is to convince a people who had been cruelly wronged as we were to make the first step towards reconciliation for the sake of a just peace that would satisfy all parties.

He concluded:

Thus far, and no further, can we go. It is now up to the world.[36]

This article does not call for much comment. Without rejecting the idea of a democratic state as a long-term objective (conceived as a binational state), the whole argument turns on the recognition of two nationalities with the same rights to self-determination: the problem is to reconcile these rights.

The Rejectionist Forces

At the beginning of November 1973 the various Palestinian organizations that were later to come together in the 'Palestinian Front of Forces Rejecting Capitulationist Settlements' (better known as the Rejection Front) took up a position against any attempt at a settlement. On 2 November the PFLP-GC condemned capitulationist solutions and proposals for a Palestinian state.[37]

At the beginning of November the ALF denounced attempts at a settlement, acceptance of Resolution 242, participation in the Geneva Conference and the establishment of a Palestinian state.[38] During the same period, the PFLP declared that 'acceptance of a settlement, in whatever form', would be a betrayal of the undertakings made by all fractions in the Palestinian Resistance. It added that it did not oppose:

> the establishment of a revolutionary authority on the soil of Palestine, or part of it, liberated by force of arms. There is a great difference between that and the establishment of a Palestinian state through negotiations whose basic point, speaking historically, will be the recognition of the Zionist entity and its acceptance in the heart of the Arab nation.[39]

Of all these organizations, the PFLP had the greatest impact on the Palestinian stage. It had effective armed forces, a solid base of support in many refugee camps — especially in Lebanon and Gaza — and a charismatic leader, George Habash. It had limited but firm support in the Arab world, particularly in Iraq and Libya but also in Algeria and the PDRY. Its leading group at times appeared not to be very homogeneous; since its third congress, in March 1972, at which the PFLP had decided to suspend its operations outside Palestine, one wing led by Wadi Haddad had gone over into opposition while remaining within the organization. The strength of the PFLP (compared to other organizations, such as the ALF and PFLP-GC) made it the backbone of opposition within the PLO. Its high degree of 'ideologization' made it the theoretician and leading spokesman of this tendency.

In a working paper addressed to the leadership of the PLO on 8 November 1973, the PFLP spelled out its positions:[40] the most important result of the October war was that American imperialism had become aware of the dangers threatening its interests in the region and was seeking a solution based on Resolution 242. What was new and dangerous for the Palestinian people was that some voices were being raised to call on the PLO to take part in the peace conference on the basis of this resolution. But all fractions of the PLO had rejected Resolution 242, which envisaged not only the evacuation of the territories occupied in 1967, but also Israel's right to exist. Hence the PLO's participation in the conference would signify its acceptance of this last point; and it was illusory to think that a signed agreement could later be called into question; imperialism would impose its conditions: 'demilitarized areas, international presence, recognition [of Israel], economic co-operation, etc.' The achievement of tactical objectives would then come into conflict with the strategic objectives. Those who claimed that the choice lay between a Palestinian state in the West Bank and Gaza and the return of the occupied territories to Jordan were forgetting another way, continuation of the revolutionary struggle [sic]. The document ended with a clear rejection of Resolution 242 and 'participation by the PLO in a conference convened on this basis'. The whole text was thus focused on the PLO's eventual participation in a peace conference; it touched only in passing on the question of a state in part of Palestine.

A month later, George Habash, in a long speech to a public meeting, summed up his organization's stand on the proposal for a state.[41] He argued that it would not be possible to establish a national authority to continue the struggle against Israel. For who would set the limits of this authority? Those who headed it? No, this would be done by the concrete realities in which this state had been born:

> Have we realized that this state will be squeezed between Israel on the one side and the reactionary Jordanian regime on the other? Have we realized that this state would be the result of an Arab and international gift? This solution will be the 'final solution' to the Middle East problem.

To this argument, which all in all was logical and drew on the contradictions in the thinking of Fatah and the PDFLP, was added the idea that the Palestinian masses were not concerned about the establishment of a state and that it was not economically viable.

> Have we thought about the area of this state, and the contradiction that will arise between it and the Palestinian masses whose vital problems will not be solved through this way? This state will be 6,000 km^2, 22.5% of the surface of Palestine. And the rest of our people? An essential contradiction will exist between the state and the Palestinian masses from the 1948 areas whose vital questions will not be solved by this state. Have we thought about the economic resources of such a state?

The only path to self-determination, he added, was the path of a democratic Palestinian state. And our Arab non-aligned and socialist allies could not do otherwise than recognize the PLO as the sole representative of the Palestinian people, which therefore had the right to express its opinion on self-determination and to say that neither Resolution 242 nor the Geneva Conference would enable it to implement this right.

Finally, in reply to a question, Habash asserted that the enemy did not reject a Palestinian state. Naturally, Israel was opposed to such a state, but the principal enemy was the United States. And the United States was ready to accept a Palestinian state and even that the Palestinian Resistance take part in the negotiations! Here we see the completely imaginary notion of an American 'plot' to create a Palestinian mini-state surfacing again.

The PFLP affirmed on several occasions that it did not reject the idea of a revolutionary authority. Habash repeated several times that what had to be taken into account was 'the great difference between the liberation of part of the soil of Palestine through struggle with the creation of a revolutionary authority and its liberation, not through struggle, but through renunciation of the other part of this soil'.[42] We might note that this argument contradicted the one developed above on economic viability.

These rejectionist positions found an echo in some of the mass organizations of the PLO, especially in intellectual circles. Thus at the end of November 1973 the General Union of Palestinian Writers and Journalists condemned attempts at a peaceful solution and the Geneva Conference.[43] According to Mury, the General Union of Palestinian Students also published a communiqué condemning the mini-state and Geneva.[44]

What impact did the various lines being put forward have on the Palestinian masses? This is difficult to estimate, but I can agree with Abu Iyad, when he writes about the refugees living in Tel Zaatar — who rejected a 'national authority' — that their rejection was motivated by the fact that they came:

> from the part of Palestine that became Israel in 1948, [and] they considered themselves foreigners in the West Bank! They didn't feel they were even concerned with mini-state proposals. The Rejection Front had thus found fertile ground for its 'maximalist' theses.[45]

He added however that the audience for this rejection extended:

> to other strata of the population, and curiously enough to the rich or comfortable Palestinians in the diaspora, especially those established in countries far from the battlefield. Taking no physical risk, living in ideal social conditions, lacking for nothing, they could afford the luxury of intransigence without having to fear eternal exile.[46]

It must be recognized that this attitude was also present among a number of intellectuals, and even activists close to the PLO. While the Palestinians 'inside' were largely won over to the theses of the realists, the situation elsewhere was more complex. It also explains the length of the debates within the PLO which ended, according to Abu Iyad, in a victory among the masses of the realist theses.

11. External Factors and Palestinian Decision-Making

Arab Factors

The PLO, as an integral part of the Arab world, lies at the heart of the conflicts and struggles cutting through it. It is not my intention here to go back in detail over the complex relationships between Arab and Palestinian reality.[47] But it is important to see that the Arab context broadly favoured the realistic trend in the PLO during 1973-74.

Iraq and, to a lesser extent, Libya,[48] which stood by diehard positions and support for the Rejection Front, were isolated. This isolation was such that these two countries refused to participate in the sixth Arab Summit in Algiers, held from 26 to 28 November 1973. The general atmosphere favoured a move towards a political solution and an overall settlement. This was the avowed aim of Cairo but it was also that of Damascus and virtually all Arab capitals. The PLO knew that it could not, even if it wanted to, oppose it. On the other hand, it had acquired sufficient weight to insist that Palestinian reality be taken into account. And it was to this task that it devoted itself, while being fully aware that 'Arab recognition' — and international recognition more generally — had a price: greater moderation, and acceptance of the principle of a political settlement.

At the sixth Arab Summit, the PLO won official recognition. In secret decisions,[49] which however soon became public knowledge, the highest body of the Arab world — after fixing the temporary objective as the liberation of territories occupied in 1967, including Arab Jerusalem — asserted the need to see the rights of the Palestinian people restored 'in the manner decided by the PLO in its capacity as the sole representative of the Palestinian people'. This point was accepted despite the reservations of the Jordanian representative. This gave the PLO not only recognition, but also — theoretically — a right of veto over any solution. Without the agreement of Jordan, however, this document risked having only limited practical effect. Throughout 1974, until the Rabat Summit which was held in October, a sword of Damocles was thus suspended over the heads of the Palestinian leaders, the more so as the Hashemite ruler had not abandoned his claims.

The Impact of the Hashemite Position

Immediately after the October war, and despite the loss of prestige resulting from his not having participated in it, King Hussein attempted to take advantage of the prospects of settlement that were opening up to defend his claims to the West Bank. On the occasion of Kissinger's visit to Jordan, the Amman government presented a memorandum summing up its stand.[50] It demanded the return of the West Bank and Jerusalem to Jordan; and it accepted the participation of a Palestinian delegation in the peace negotiations, while asserting that it did not recognize 'the right of any Palestinian whosoever to represent all Palestinians' and that the role of this delegation must be 'limited to the defence of the rights of the Palestinian people excluding the West Bank and Gaza'.

The document went on to deal with the problem of a state in the West Bank and Gaza. Hussein would not allow this question to appear in an agreement with Israel. But he agreed, after the return of the West Bank to Jordanian sovereignty, to grant 'the people of the West Bank, for the second time,[51] the right to decide their future'. There would be three options: a separate Palestinian government; implementation of the proposal for a United Arab Kingdom; and maintenance of the Hashemite regime such as it had been before 1967. These proposals differed little from those presented by the King just before the war. He also maintained his designs on Gaza, since, a few days later, he asserted the need to unify all Palestinian lands.[52]

After the Algiers Summit, the King stepped up his pressure at the international level. He denied the PLO's right to represent all Palestinians. 'And why should this body [the PLO] arrogate to itself the sole right to represent the Palestinian people, when we have refrained from having such claims, out of respect for the will of this people which has not yet been expressed?'[53]

He proclaimed his commitment to Arab unity.

> How do you explain why the Arab nation, which aspires to unity, should be so lamentably divided into tiny economically unviable states? Those who say they are, or claim to be, the architects of this unity are the very ones who have decided, in Algiers, to separate what geography and history have united: the two banks of the Jordan.[54]

Finally, he threatened not to go to Geneva:

> if the position has changed after the Algiers Summit and now is to turn the West Bank and the Gaza Strip into a Palestinian state, as it is said .., then we shall not go to the peace conference; let those who have become the representatives of the Palestinian people go there .., it is a decision of our brothers in the Arab states, and let them take the responsibility for it.[55]

This threat was serious for, since conditions were not yet ripe for the participation of the PLO, there was a likelihood of creating a 'vacuum' over sovereignty over the West Bank.

At the same time, the King launched a campaign among his supporters and the population in the West Bank. Already in September 1973, on the eve of the war, he had ordered the release from prison of 750 people, and amnestied 2,500 others who had been gaoled after the events of 1970-71.[56] After October the newspaper *al-Quds* and Shaikh al-Ja'bari waged an active campaign in favour of the King. His supporters were promised posts in the future United Arab Kingdom.[57] But this was all without much success. Economic and social change had undermined the influence of the pro-Jordanians; the Algiers Summit had strengthened the authority of the PLO. By developing an active struggle against the occupier based on realistic positions, the PNF became the decisive force in the occupied territories.[58]

It was against this background that the King made his speech of 1 May 1974. He asserted that Jordan had recognized the PLO ever since 1964 and that the PLO must go to Geneva to discuss the Palestinian problem, but not the West Bank and Gaza. He added, however:

> We shall also respect the collective Arab will if it is the wish of the Arab countries and their leaders to create a new situation in which the Palestine Liberation Organization is made fully responsible for discussing, striving and working for the recovery of the occupied Arab territories, including the West Bank and Jerusalem, and the recovery of Palestinian rights . . . We shall . . . regard it [such a decision] as absolving us of our responsibilities.[59]

Despite the retreat in the Jordanian position, which was underlined by the PLO,[60] it would be wrong to see in it an abandonment of traditional positions. It was, after all, a type of blackmail that the Jordanian Prime Minister spelled out a few days later:[61] if it was to be the PLO that spoke for the Palestinians and the occupied territories, he said in substance, this would prolong the occupation since the Israelis would not talk with the PLO. If he spoke for the Palestinians, however, he could secure the withdrawal of the Israelis and then he would come to an agreement about the future of the occupied territories. This argument was somewhat similar to that developed by King Hussein after the 1982 Lebanese war. But he was then to do it more carefully and more discretely. Until the Rabat Arab Summit, the King waged a long fight to secure recognition by the Arab states of his right to 'look after' the occupied territories.

In conclusion, it must be emphasized that Hussein's position helped the moderate current in the PLO. In fact, as many leaders of Fatah stressed, while the PLO was not laying claim to the West Bank and Gaza, Jordan was. There was thus a simple choice, both for the leaders of the Palestinian Resistance and for the population of the occupied territories — all the more so as some governments, such as that of Egypt, seemed hesitant about total support for the PLO. There was a subtle balance at work: if the PLO did not agree to take part in the negotiating game — as it had done over the Rogers Plan — it risked the withdrawal of all recognition. For organizations such as the PFLP, whose goal was revolution in the Arab world, this, of course, had no great importance. The Rejection Front, moreover, placed great emphasis on the risks involved to the revolutionary character of the PLO if the organization gained Arab and international recognition. For Fatah, on the other hand, only joint action with the existing regimes in the Arab world could lead to a successful conclusion: that was the only realistic path. This was explained by Abu Iyad:

> The October war against Israel was waged by patriotic regimes. It is true that, in their confrontation with Israel, these regimes set limits to their actions. But neither by outbidding them nor by fighting them will we be able to get them to strengthen their patriotic tendencies and limit the concessions they are ready to make to secure a settlement. Progress, even if only partial progress, in this direction will only be made through brotherly discussions. If we had not adopted this attitude, we would not have been able to achieve the success we won at the Algiers Summit, and the PLO would not have been recognized as the sole legitimate representative of the Palestinian people.[62]

For the PLO as for the Arab states, it was thus clear that the price for Arab recognition was moderation. The whole of 1974 was marked by this reality, in particular in the context of a forthcoming Arab Summit and the convening of the Geneva Conference.

In this overall picture, Syria remained a special case. While engaged, like Egypt, in negotiations for a political solution, it was somewhat more hesitant. The negotiations being carried on by Damascus with Washington to secure the partial withdrawal of Israeli troops from the Syrian front were only concluded on the eve of the twelfth PNC. They were marked by ups and downs and the war of attrition in the Golan Heights. In addition, Damascus would have nothing to do with the Geneva Conference. The Palestinian leaders had to take all these facts into account, the more so as — whether directly, or through Sa'iqa — Hafez al-Assad repeatedly reminded the PLO of how much it owed him. As Shafiq al-Hut, a historic leader of the PLO, said:

> There is no separate Palestinian position. This is the nature of the struggle. We cannot contradict the Syrian position at present . . . Perhaps I do not approve of the Syrian position, but I cannot fight it.[63]

The Palestinian Resistance was to pay dearly for having forgotten this harsh truth in 1976 and again in 1983.

In this context, a word should be said about Sa'iqa. Sa'iqa was under the thumb of the Syrian government and enabled that government to bring pressure to bear on the PLO. One can sense the 'unionist' designs of

Damascus piercing through behind its various positions. Thus, in a statement issued on 22 December 1973, Sa'iqa declared that the future of the occupied territories must be decided among Arabs after Israel's withdrawal.[64] The close subordination also appears in its refusal to go to Geneva, announced the day after the Syrian decision,[65] and in the support given to a *rapprochement* between the PLO and Jordan when relations between Damascus and Amman were being normalized.[66]

In conclusion, it must be stressed that, among the Arab factors affecting decisions, there were the PLO's 'popular' alliances, particularly in Lebanon. As we have seen, Lebanon was the last land of refuge for the PLO; its military presence there was vital for its political autonomy, and its alliance with the Lebanese National Movement was a decisive condition for it to be able to stand up to the Lebanese state, the army and the Phalange. In this context, the leaders of the Lebanese Progressive Forces had a not insignificant influence on the discussions in the PLO, and this influence was predominantly in favour of moderation.[67]

International Factors: The Role of the USSR

Changes at the international level and the growing support for the Palestinian viewpoint promoted the PLO's integration into international diplomacy and, by the same token, its realism. The UN had undergone a marked evolution from the recognition of the rights of the Palestinian people in 1969, to recognition of its right to self-determination in 1970 and of its right to struggle in 1971. On the eve of the 1973 war, the summit of the Non-Aligned Movement had recognized the PLO as the sole representative of the Palestinian people.[68] Black Africa, where the Israeli presence was very strong,[69] had switched sides. Western Europe itself, hit by the oil embargo, was rethinking its position.

All this constituted so many assets that the leadership of the PLO sought to exploit them and capitalize on them. In order to do so, it was absolutely necessary to put forward a new image of its struggle — and this is what it was to devote itself to during the run-up to the twelfth PNC.

It was the USSR that weighed heavily and directly on the debate in the PLO. It was the USSR that, while the 1973 war was still not over, pressed the PLO to define clear positions with a view to a settlement. Its influence on the discussions preparing for the twelfth PNC is generally recognized. Following many other 'realistic' leaders, Abu Iyad wrote:

> The Palestinian revolution is not occurring in an international vacuum. We have friends in the world, first and foremost the Soviet Union and the other socialist countries. Not knowing who one's friends are is not a political attitude. If the USSR is our friend, we must keep its friendship and strengthen it, and, to do that, maintain the dialogue with it and take account of its viewpoint and its positions. But no dialogue is possible if we start by saying no. How can we hope one day to win

Palestine if we are incapable of keeping and strengthening our friendships?[70]

The Rejection Front was hitting the right target when it did not miss a chance to attack the USSR. The time had long passed when the Soviet Union would meet Arafat secretly (in 1968), at Nasser's pressing insistence. The time had passed for criticisms of 'adventurism', although the USSR remained very firm in its condemnation of terrorism and aeroplane hijackings. The USSR received Arafat in February 1970, again in October 1971 and again in July 1972. The first deliveries of Soviet weapons to the PLO arrived towards the end of 1972.[71] The deterioration of Soviet-Egyptian relations with the expulsion of Soviet military advisers from Egypt in July 1972, and the PLO's concern at the changes Sadat was undergoing, created a wide area of understanding. It should be observed that this *rapprochement* was occurring to the detriment of relations between the PLO (or at least Fatah) and the People's Republic of China.[72] On the eve of the October war, both political and military relations between the two sides were very good. Soviet influence in Syria, Iraq and even in Egypt made the USSR a most desirable ally for the PLO. In addition, the international weight of the 'land of the Soviets' constituted a major diplomatic support. The Palestinian leaders had observed with satisfaction that at the Brezhnev-Nixon summit, the final communiqué stressed the need 'to take into due account the legitimate interests of the Palestinian people'.[73] In the middle of a period of *détente*, receiving the support of the USSR was also, for the Palestinian leaders, a means of making contact with the United States.

12. The Decision-Making Process and the Preparations for the Twelfth PNC

'Speak Last'

Even before the October war had ended, the Palestinians were already confronted with its political consequences. On 26 October 1973 Sadat suggested that the Palestinians should participate in the Geneva Peace Conference.[74] At about the same time, the Soviet ambassador in Beirut, Sarvar Azimov, handed a memorandum to the Palestinian leaders.[75] This called on 'the representatives of the Resistance to adopt a realistic and constructive attitude which consists in claiming the recovery of the territories lost in 1967'.[76] The memorandum pressed the Resistance to agree to participate in the Geneva Conference which, it continued, would not be a simple matter, given the opposition of the United States, Jordan and Israel. The USSR would nevertheless support the Palestinian Resistance if that was what it wanted.

These requests caught the Palestinian Resistance unprepared: Zuhair Mohsen, for example, replied in an interview given on 5 November 1973:

> The Resistance at present has no specific proposal. It was logical that the great powers themselves should have put forward a proposal; this would have been discussed by the Palestinian leadership, and accepted, amended or rejected.[77]

But the recent meetings between Brezhnev and Nixon[78] had not agreed on the bases of a solution to the Palestinian question, nor by whom the Palestinians would be represented. Mohsen added that 'the whole burden has fallen on the Palestinians, and the PLO in particular', who must themselves settle what they want. This represented a

> real deadlock, for if we ask to rule the Gaza Strip and the West Bank that will mean that we abandon our historic rights to the rest of the land of Palestine ... If the Palestinian Resistance says that it is not concerned by Security Council resolutions and this solution, then it officially abandons the West Bank and Gaza to the Jordanian regime.

This attitude seems typical; when questioned about the peace conference on 28 November, Arafat himself stated that the PLO had not yet spelled out its position. 'For the good of our cause we should speak last.'[79] He added that the executive committee had taken the decision not to reply to this question.

This position, expressed almost 'naively', sums up very well the difficulties encountered by the PLO. If it was so difficult to fix a position — or rather to make a proposal, to be 'the first to speak' — that was because of the very nature of the PLO. Could the PLO, divided as it was by several currents, take the risk of seeing its unity broken — and thus throwing open the question of its representativeness — to make a concrete proposal when it did not know whether it would be accepted by the US and Israel? Could it take a decision which would set it against the Arab states and which ran the risk of harming their interests? In short, could it make concessions without being certain of the *quid pro quos*? The PLO leadership was ready to take the risks, but they had to be 'reasonable' risks. And how were they to be defined? This was precisely the subject of the discussions which now got under way.

The Tripartite Fatah — PDFLP — Sa'iqa Working Paper

After a lengthy preliminary debate and the reaffirmation of the positions of the various forces, and after the opening of the Geneva Conference and the first disengagement agreement between Israel and Egypt, a new phase of the internal debate within the PLO opened at the beginning of February 1974. On 8 February Fatah, the PDFLP and Sa'iqa adopted a 'working paper' that they submitted to the central council of the PLO[80] and not to the executive committee which did not play any real role in the debate. The essential points of this document were as follows. The general strategic aim was:

> the liberation of Palestine from Zionist colonialism, the establishment of a democratic Palestinian state in the whole of the Palestinian land, the return of all Palestinian nationals to their homeland, and their exercise of their right to self-determination and complete national sovereignty.

After stressing the need to continue the armed struggle against Israel and to strengthen the determination of the Arab states against the United States and Zionism, the document set out the three immediate aims of Palestinian policy:

> A. To put an end to the occupation and force the enemy to withdraw unconditionally from the West Bank and Gaza sector without making any political concessions to him in return. This demand represents only a part of the minimal programme of the Palestinian people's demands and legitimate rights at this stage.

B. To refuse the return of Hashemite authority over any Palestinian territory from which occupation has receded.

C. To wrest back under PLO leadership the Palestinian people's legitimate and just right to self-determination, national independence and complete sovereignty in the Palestinian land whose liberation has been completed.

The three organizations went on to assert the need 'to seek to rally all the Palestinian forces, factions and masses around this programme through constant dialogue among all the groups and on all levels'. There had to be agreement on the following points:

1. Commitment to the general strategic objective.

2. Commitment to continue the armed struggle and struggle by various other methods.

3. Struggle to defeat occupation, to prevent the return of Hashemite authority over Palestinian territory and to insist on our people's right to self-determination and national sovereignty over their land.

4. Demand that the Arab countries support all forms of Palestinian struggle and maintain the conflict with the Zionist entity until our people's objectives are fully realized.

5. Appeal to the friendly states to support the Palestinian struggle, to maintain their break of diplomatic and economic relations with it [the state of Israel] and to emphasize this stand by withdrawing recognition [of Israel].

6. The continued refusal of Security Council Resolution no. 242 which does not meet the Palestinian people's minimum demands and legitimate rights, which denies the existence of the Palestinian people and their political rights, and which considers the problem of our people as a problem of refugees while it is actually the problem of a people who have been expelled from their land.[81]

The PLO central council discussed this document at length during February.[82] The session lasted several days, interrupted by Arafat's visit to Lahore for the second Islamic Conference, at which the PLO was recognized as the sole representative of the Palestinian people.[83]

At the same time, the three parties signatory to the document reached agreement on:

contacts with friendly Arab and international forces (in particular Egypt, Syria and the Soviet Union), to reach a joint agreement between them and the Palestinian people; and we declare that what the working paper demands represents the minimum rights of the Palestinian people.[84]

The central council's meeting ended without results and the debate continued. The Fatah leaders, and Arafat in particular, were fully involved in the debate. They were anxious to obtain an agreement on the idea of a 'national authority', but they were also trying to win over their opponents. They therefore responded to all the arguments which accused them of betraying the revolution and wishing to give up the armed struggle. In an interview with the Lebanese newspaper *al-Safir*, at the end of March 1974, Arafat laid down the principles guiding his action:

1. Continuation of the armed struggle.
2. No concession on our historic rights.
3. No reconciliation.
4. No negotiations.[85]

On 1 April he spelled out this stand,[86] by saying that it was necessary to: continue the armed struggle; reject any concession on the historic rights of the Palestinian people; refuse recognition and peace [*sulh*]; support the right of the Palestinian people to self-determination and its right to return; assert the sovereignty of the Palestinian people over every liberated piece of land from which the enemy had been driven out.

It is useful here to quote an argument that often recurred in Fatah's explanations. It rested on the history of the Palestinian people. Speaking of the experiences of 1936 and 1948, Abu Iyad said:

> We must read history so as to extract lessons for ourselves. What were the mistakes of our previous leaders? . . . Their mistake was adhering to our people's historical rights without adopting stage-by-stage programs of struggle under the obtaining conditions.[87]

This was to be a leitmotiv running through the debate. Some even went so far as to compare the way in which the Zionists had conducted their plan and the inability of the Palestinians to do the same.[88]

Thus it was not a matter of ending the struggle but of taking into account the reality of the relations of force. Khalid al-Hassan, then a member of the Fatah central committee, declared:

> If a Palestinian state is established today, it will not be established over the whole of the land of Palestine. It is by continuing the struggle that the establishment of a state over the whole of Palestine will be made possible.[89]

On the question of Geneva, Fatah's response was unchanging: we have not been invited; we are awaiting an invitation before we announce our decision. This attitude was encouraged by the fact that Sa'iqa had spoken out against Geneva since Syria was not participating in it.

There was real internal opposition within Fatah.[90] This can be seen from an interview with Abu Hatem, a member of the Fatah revolutionary council, in the spring of 1974:

> Fatah is against any compromise. It sees the only solution as recognition of a democratic Palestinian state in the whole of its territory. In the short term, we are not against the establishment of a revolutionary authority over any part of our territory liberated by force of arms. There is no question of recognizing a rump state, resulting from negotiations with the enemy. [And he added] Faced with all the offensives [of imperialism], it would be impossible for Fatah to think in narrow terms of the establishment of a Palestinian entity.[91]

In fact, Abu Hatem, as well as several other members of the Fatah revolutionary council, were opposed to the plan. There seems to have existed a gap between the Fatah central committee, which was unanimous in favour of a 'national authority', and middle-level activists who were much more divided. As Abu Hatem pointed out to me,[92] no Fatah congress had endorsed the slogan of a 'mini-state', not even the fourth Congress which was held in 1980.

Sa'iqa's attitude in the debate was somewhat passive. Sa'iqa was affected above all by the stiffening of Syria's military presence on the Golan Heights and the fighting around Mount Hermon which went on throughout April 1974. It was also the time of the Kissinger initiatives to secure a disengagement agreement on the Syrian front. This situation made Sa'iqa an organization 'apart' in the Fatah–PDFLP–Sa'iqa front. 'We differentiate ourselves', said Mohsen, 'from the two Palestinian currents, the one that wants to take part in the political solution and the one that condemns this solution verbally but does nothing to prevent it.'[93] He rejected any solution in the framework of the existing relations of force, and added that if there were a political solution, that would mean:

> that the United States is really inclined to put pressure on Israel and oblige it to evacuate the occupied territories. At that time, the solution will become a reality, or, more precisely, an inevitable catastrophe. It will then be necessary for us to draw up a programme to deal with that catastrophe.

He ended by saying that the national authority must not be the result of concessions! It sounded like the line of the rejectionists. And yet, Sa'iqa had signed the 'working paper'; and it was to approve the twelfth PNC's resolution. But this, of course, was only to be voted after the disengagement on the Syrian front.

Hawatmeh's Interview with *Yedioth Aharonot*

The PDFLP stepped up its participation in the debate in a spectacular fashion.

Its secretary-general agreed to publish an interview in a leading Israeli daily, *Yedioth Aharonot*, on 22 March 1974. The interview was granted to an American journalist, Paul Jacobs,[94] who had no hesitation in describing it as a historic event:

> 1. Because, for the first time, a Palestinian leader of this importance no longer demands the destruction of the state of Israel as a pre-condition for a dialogue and even an agreement between Israelis and Palestinians.
> 2. Because, for the first time, a Palestinian PLO leader makes a distinction not only between the Israeli government and the Israeli people but also right-wing and left-wing Zionists.
> 3. Because Hawatmeh agreed that his statement be published first in an Israeli paper.[95]

Hawatmeh himself, in an introduction to the French translation which appeared in the Beirut newspaper *Le Jour*, explained his approach:

> I thought it would be useful to the Israeli people — all sectors of opinion and at all levels — to take note of the Palestinian–Israeli–Zionist struggle from the revolutionary Palestinian point of view... This interview provides an opportunity to inform Israeli society of the Palestinian viewpoint, and to refute all the tendentious interpretations put about by official propaganda seeking to show that the Palestinian revolution's only aim is to drive the Jews into the sea... I do not see why we should accept that Arab reactionaries should start a dialogue with the most extremist Israeli circles and forbid progressive forces to do the same with progressive Israeli forces. It is true that such a dialogue constitutes a threat to both Zionism and Arab reaction.

In the interview, Hawatmeh declared:

> But we do not foresee a quick solution; we know that achieving real peace will take a long time. But we also know that certainly an essential factor to help in arriving at a real solution will be the acquisition by the Palestinians of some of their national rights, at a later stage.
> Heading the list of those rights are the rights of the Palestinian people in the West Bank and Gaza to form a national independent state and that of the Palestinian refugees to return to the homes taken from them in the past period... The implementation of these rights will open the way to a democratic dialogue between democratic and progressive Palestinians and their Israeli counterparts, allowing both forces to search for a radical democratic solution to the problem, based on the establishment of a democratic Palestinian state.[96]

This calls for two observations. First, Hawatmeh reaffirmed, very clearly, the objective of the present phase, and thus placed himself in the 'realistic' school of thought. The second is that — following Hammami — he was sketching out a subtle dialectic between the short-term aim and the long-term aim (the democratic state). The door was not closed on a peaceful evolution — after the establishment of a Palestinian state.

The other high point of the interview — but this time much more ambiguous — concerned relations with progressive Israeli forces. Hawatmeh asserted that:

> even enlightened Zionist personalities like Ben Aharon and Eliav,[97] who recognize the existence of the Palestinian people and part of its national rights, are working in the interests of the future of Israelis a thousand times more than Golda Meir and people like her.

He still denied that the Israelis were a nation.

> From a scientific point of view it is false to speak of an Israeli 'nationality' because the Israelis have not, according to scientific concepts [*sic*], evolved as a nationality . . . The Israelis lack the following features to constitute a nation: a common language, a common history continuing uninterruptedly over several centuries and a common psychology expressed in common traditions and customs.

These 'constituent' elements serving to define a nation were taken directly from a text of Stalin's which, for over 30 years, had formed the basis of Communist thinking on the national question.

Thus, while maintaining his stand on the non-existence of an Israeli people, Hawatmeh seemed to accept a dialogue with Zionist forces that recognized the existence of a Palestinian people, as well as some of its national rights. But the PDFLP did not hold to this stand. Not only did it come out against a dialogue with the Israeli left, but, on 17 April 1974, Hawatmeh set out in an interview what he meant by the Israeli left.[98] The forces of the left, he said, were made up of small organizations like the Revolutionary Communist Organization and Matzpen. The majority of the Arab population in Israel was in Rakah, the Israeli Communist Party, 'not because it adopts a radical leftist position towards the state of Israel', but because it enabled them to struggle against Zionist expansionism.

> With these forces we can struggle together. But as regards the existence of a Zionist left, we can say that the only relations between the left and Zionism are relations of permanent warfare. For that reason, there is nothing that could be called the Zionist left.

Thus, while initial reactions in Israel to Hawatmeh's interview were favourable,[99] its impact in the end was very limited. The Maalot operation, and its justification by Hawatmeh himself,[100] wiped out any possibility of a dialogue emerging from this interview. This was recognized by the PDFLP leader when he said: 'I have been disappointed by the reactions to my interview with *Yedioth Aharonot* . . . When the peaceful approach collapses, all that is left is to intensify the armed struggle.'[101]

One cannot but be surprised at such a lack of coherence, and at seeing the opportunity arising from a bold initiative ruined in this way. For if the secretary-general of the PDFLP saw the interview as the beginning of an attempt at dialogue with the Israelis — the vast majority of whom remained hostile to Palestinian national rights — how could it be imagined that striking results could be reached in such a short time? In fact, Hawatmeh ran foul of the contradictions in his own thinking and in that of a large part of the Palestinian Resistance. What was the point of embarking on a dialogue with the Israelis when they were not even considered to be a people, and were denied the right to an elementary national aspiration (a denial that was in any event altogether theoretical since the Israelis themselves expressed this aspiration vigorously, even violently)? What too was the point of rejecting any discussion with Zionists? It meant reducing the dialogue to its most basic expression. The identification (all too common in Palestinian thought) of Nazism and Zionism, in addition to its being tactless, outrageous and even insulting, encapsulates a great inability to analyse the reality and contradictions of Israel. To divide Israel into Zionist and non-Zionist meant driving into the camp of the Israeli leaders all those for whom Zionism meant no more than their attachment to the Jewish state. It meant rejecting the more fruitful distinction between those who accepted the right of the Palestinians to a state and those who rejected it. It was to Fatah's credit — and above all to that of Arafat — that it attempted, with the difficulties that we shall see, to set out on this road.

Finally, we may observe that the interview had a great impact on the Palestinian scene. It certainly contributed to the continuing debate and aroused the great ire of the diehards; the General Union of Palestinian Writers and Journalists went so far as to accuse the leader of the PDFLP of advocating 'coexistence with the Zionist occupier and officially recognizing Israel'.[102]

The Rejection Front and the 'Relaunching' of the Armed Struggle

Beyond the debate, which was pursued vigorously, the rejectionist organizations relaunched spectacular military actions. The first of them was carried out by the PFLP-GC, one of whose commando groups occupied a building in Kiryat Shmoneh on 11 April 1974, seized a number of hostages and demanded the freeing of many Palestinian political prisoners. After some talking, the Israeli army took the building by storm. The result was 21 dead, including 3 fedayeen, and many wounded. This operation was of course not the first since the end of the October war, but by virtue of its spectacular nature and the number of civilian victims, it tended to restore the PLO's 'terrorist' image. In a communiqué issued on this operation, the PFLP-GC declared that it:

> rejects any defeatist solution of the Palestinian problem, rejects the establishment of a Palestinian mini-state and reaffirms that it will continue the revolutionary struggle until the total liberation of Palestine . . . We have launched an operation against Kiryat Shmoneh, the capital of Upper Galilee, situated within the 1948 borders, to underline that our liberation struggle is not limited to the West Bank and Gaza.[103]

More than a year later, Abu Abbas, a member of the politbureau of the PFLP-GC explained the impact of the 'suicide operations' that his organization had begun with Kiryat Shmoneh.[104] They had a political importance in the climate of demobilization brought about by the attempts by the PLO to take part in political solutions, and they had three aims: to rekindle the revolutionary spirit; to put a halt to attempts by the Israeli army to assure the security of the country, and to inflict maximum losses on the Israelis; and to make the voice of the rejectionists heard and put a halt to the temptation to seek a peaceful settlement.

While this operation annoyed the PLO leadership, the PLO nevertheless took responsibility for it. A release from the PLO news agency Wafa asserted that:

> operations launched in occupied Palestine are the ones that have the greatest impact on the enemy and worry it most . . . this operation also shows that pursuit of the struggle in conformity with the strategy of the Palestinian revolution will tilt the scales more and more in favour of the revolution.[105]

In order to understand this reaction, two factors must be taken into account. The first is the reactions of Palestinians themselves, whether in the camps or in the occupied territories. Thus a young Palestinian in Nablus told the correspondent of *Le Monde*:

> Of course, the fedayeen operation was murderous and the PFLP-GC was trying to annoy Yasser Arafat. But no one in Nablus can forget that a year ago Kamal Nasser and his two companions were assassinated in Beirut by Elazar's men. Yes, I am not afraid to say so, everyone here is rejoicing over Kiryat Shmoneh.

The second factor is the weight of the myth of the armed struggle in the ideology of the PLO. It was on the basis of this myth that Fatah was formed and supplanted its rivals in the years 1965–68. And that remained so, despite the fact that operations in Israel and the occupied territories — according to the PLO's own figures — fell from 2,390 in 1969 to 326 in 1972, 637 in 1973 and 396 in 1974.[106]

Even if one could denounce, as the magazine *Israël et Palestine* did, *de facto* complicity between the authors of Kiryat Shmoneh and the Israeli extremists who used this incident to reject any dialogue with the PLO,[107] this observation does not exhaust the problem. Palestinian extremism has deep roots, both at the popular level and in ideology, a fact which made the Kiryat Shmoneh operation a 'success' for its authors. It should moreover be observed that the next operation of the same type was carried out by the PDFLP at Maalot in May 1974: it ended in the death of 3 fedayeen and 16 Israelis, including many secondary school children. The PDFLP, however, was not seriously suspected of wanting to sabotage eventual peace negotiations.

This problem of the armed struggle contains an inexhaustible subject for debate. Of course, the armed struggle had played a major role in the Palestinian national renaissance in the 1960s. It had enabled the PLO to be an active factor in the Middle East crisis. In Lebanon, it had been a condition for the autonomy of the Palestinian Resistance. And, from the point of view of principle, the right to armed resistance against foreign occupation is an internationally recognized right. But it might well be asked, especially after the October war, whether there was not a need to rethink the problem – at the very least, by spelling out in detail the aims of this 'armed struggle'. Acceptance of operations of the Kiryat Shmoneh type – whose effectiveness against the Israeli war machine was zero and which helped to unite the Israeli people around its leaders – shows that the leaders of the PLO lacked sufficient political courage to tackle this problem. They thus gave the organizations in the Rejection Front considerable room for manoeuvre and the Israeli leaders an excuse – a convincing one in the eyes of their public opinion – to refuse any negotiation over Palestine.

Agreement

The PLO central council had been unable to reach agreement on the tripartite 'working paper'. The PFLP and the ALF both asked for time to think and, a few days later, the PFLP put forward another programme that rejected the idea of an intermediate stage.[108] This document took up the traditional ideas of the PFLP by denouncing the convergent pressures by the US, the USSR and the Arab countries for a settlement of the conflict. But there was a possiblity of foiling it by strengthening the Palestinian struggle through fusing with the Arab peoples, and the Jordanian people in particular. What was needed was:

> to struggle resolutely and seriously to bring about the failure of the Geneva conference – convened on the basis of UN Resolution no. 242 – or any other conference based on the same resolution. To frustrate all the capitulationist settlements aimed at the cause of our people and [aimed] at diminishing the cause by submitting proposals for the

establishment of a Palestinian authority or state in a part of Palestine, and to resist these proposals with armed struggle and the political struggle by the masses that is associated with it.

In response to the proposals for a national authority, the PFLP then proposed 'to impose the sovereignty of the Palestinian people over all Palestinian territory so that from it our people may continue its struggle, armed actions and mass political struggle for the liberation of the other parts'. It went on to denounce any national authority which might emerge as a result of a political settlement based on Resolutions 242 and 338.

Faced with the impasse in which it found itself, the PLO central council decided to set up a committee of national dialogue under the chairmanship of Arafat. It included the secretaries-general of the PDFLP, the PFLP, Sa'iqa, the ALF, the PFLP-GC and a representative of the PNF. The PNF was thus participating on the same basis as the armed organizations and this committee brought together 'those who count in the PLO'. Fundamental questions would be resolved and disputes settled at this level.

The committee of seven met in May 1974.[109] The press reported new Soviet assurances following the meeting between Arafat and Gromyko in Damascus in early May that supposedly made the position of the PFLP more flexible. In addition, negotiations on the disengagement agreement between Israel and Syria were well advanced. Despite the obstacles arising from the Maalot operation on 15 May, the agreement was signed before the end of the month. After a meeting lasting several days, the seven reached a measure of agreement. This was announced but not published. Mohsen says that unanimity was reached on the need to establish 'a Palestinian national authority' in the West Bank and Gaza, but that there was no agreement on the criteria that would enable this or that authority to be described as 'national'. He added that, with the exception of a number of individuals (the Communists?), all the participants opposed Resolution 242.[110]

The agreement did not settle the problems, indeed far from it. In reply to a statement by Kaddoumi, asserting that unanimous agreement had been reached among all the organizations to establish a national authority over every inch of liberated Palestinian territory, the PFLP, PFLP-GC and ALF published a joint statement on 21 May.[111] This stated: what had happened at the summit must remain secret; Kaddoumi had not brought up the rejection of Resolution 242 and the Geneva Conference, but there was agreement on this rejection; the three organizations reserved their right to express their opinion at the next session of the PNC and to publish the agreement of the seven.

The PNC was able to meet, although pressures continued from supporters of total rejection. One example was a memorandum issued in Baghdad on 29 May[112] and signed by, among others, several former members of the executive committee and by Yahya Hamuda, Shuqairy's successor as head of the PLO. This statement categorically rejected political solutions, upheld the validity of the National Charter and called on the PLO to take clear stands.

The Twelfth PNC (June 1974)

The twelfth PNC opened in Cairo on 1 June 1974, attended by 187 delegates, 7 more than at the previous session (all the new ones were independents). The opening came a few hours after the announcement of the success of the Kissinger mission and the Israeli–Syrian disengagement agreement, which was immediately condemned by the PFLP.[113] The main discussions bore on the interpretation of the 'ten-point programme' agreed upon by the Palestinian leaders. These attempts at clarification came above all from rejectionist organizations which tried to give the narrowest possible interpretation of the agreement.

As the PFLP–GC representative stressed, there were indeed two tendencies in the Palestinian Resistance. One hoped for a political settlement which would allow the establishment of a national authority in the West Bank and Gaza; the other wanted to stand by the National Charter and the PLO's political programme, arguing that any political settlement could only result in a non-national authority.[114] In the same speech, the PFLP–GC asked that the debate be kept open. The ten-point programme was a proposal to be debated and several points in it required clarification:

1. The rejection of Resolution 242. Some were now talking of amending this rejection; but did the resolution trouble people only because it described the Palestinians as refugees or because it implied the recognition of Israel?
2. Could a political settlement lead to a national authority? No, it could not. Behind the call for all forms of struggle, some saw acceptance of a settlement. This point must be clarified.
3. The door must be closed on the Geneva Conference and the principle of any negotiation with the enemy rejected.
4. Jordan must again be clearly condemned.

The PFLP, for its part, accepted the ten-point programme, but subject to the following clarifications:[115] rejection of Resolution 242 in all its forms; refusal to take part in the Geneva Conference; the Palestinian Resistance could not be a party to negotiations leading to a settlement and hence its own liquidation; 'the national authority for which we are all struggling is a real national authority, which cannot arise from the measures currently being undertaken, but only from our armed struggle, and our political struggle based on it'; the Jordanian regime was a traitor regime and it was necessary to struggle to establish a national democratic regime in Jordan.

The ALF went even further: it proposed to rule out 'in any circumstances whatsoever' any presence at Geneva.[116]

After lengthy discussions and numerous clarifications, the programme was adopted by an overwhelming majority, with only four members voting against. One of them was a member of Fatah, another of the PFLP, the third was a former Ba'thist and the fourth an independent.[117] Perhaps this diversity is a sign that the divisions not only went between organizations but also cut through them. The text adopted,[118] known as the ten-point programme, was in fact entitled 'phased [*marhali*] political programme', which is quite significant, since the PLO had previously rejected any policy based on a phased policy. The preamble referred to the National Charter, the eleventh PNC and the right of the Palestinian people 'to return to and determine their fate on all their national soil'.

> Point 1: We confirm the earlier PLO position regarding Resolution 242, which ignores the national rights of our people and deals with our people's cause as a refugee problem. Therefore we refuse to have anything to do with this resolution at any level, Arab or international, including the Geneva Conference.

This point reflects very well the contradictions running through the PNC, but it is noteworthy that the opposition to Resolution 242 was not motivated by the fact that it implied recognition of Israel. As for the Geneva Conference, the refusal to take part was not absolute, but rested on the fact that it was convened on the basis of Resolution 242. This point was indeed taken up by the press. Thus the Lebanese magazine *L'Orient — Le Jour* stressed that:

> circles close to the PNC are concerned to point out that the PLO specifically motivates its refusal to send a delegation to Geneva by reference to Resolution 242. The Resistance, it is stated in these same circles, would like to see this resolution amended or would even be satisfied with an international accord on the interpretation of the UN text involving the United States and the USSR.[119]

> Point 2: The PLO will struggle by every means — the foremost of which is armed struggle — to liberate Palestinian land and to establish the people's national, independent and fighting authority on every part of Palestinian land that is liberated. This requires a major change in the balance of power in favour of our people and its struggle.

This was the central idea. For the first time in their history, the PLO and the Palestinian people had set themselves an intermediate goal which was not the liberation of the whole of Palestine. We may also note that the phrase 'liberation of Palestine', which is at the centre of the National Charter, was totally absent from this text. It had been replaced by 'liberation of Palestinian land', a phrase which can, as Hourani notes,[120] mean two different things: from the Palestinian point of view, the whole of Palestine; from the point of view of international legality, the territories of the West Bank and Gaza.

> Point 3: the PLO will struggle against any plan for the establishment of a Palestinian entity [*kiyan*] the price of which is recognition [of

Israel], conciliation [*sulh*], secure borders and renunciation of the national rights of our people, and its right to return and self-determination on its national soil.[121]

In his analysis of the ten-point programme, of which I have made much use, Hourani puts forward an ingenious explanation of this point. He asserts that the proposal for an entity can be accepted if all the actions (recognition, conciliation, and so on) do not happen *at the same time*. This explanation is interesting because it shows that the text left the Palestinian leadership plenty of room for manoeuvre.

> Point 4: Any step towards the liberation is a step towards the realization of the PLO's strategy of establishing a democratic Palestinian state, in conformity with the resolutions of the previous PNCs.

This point calls for two observations. First, it identified the strategy of the PLO with a democratic state: but mention of a state is not to be found in the Charter. Moreover, nothing was said about the means of achieving a democratic state. In an excellent analysis of the two currents within the PLO,[122] Muslih says, referring to Shafiq al-Hut:

> Some here even talked about the need to convert the Palestinian and Israeli means of fighting into peaceful ones which may ultimately result in the peaceful establishment of a democratic secular state in Palestine.

This idea was gaining ground in the Palestinian Resistance. Thus a Lebanese politician declared:

> A fraction of the Resistance may see this mini-state as a springboard for pursuing the struggle . . . which could take a new form: political and social. A secular state on the borders of Israel could act as a ferment and an example for it.[123]

This was talking about what might happen *after* the establishment of a Palestinian state. This was an idea that several PLO leaders were to elaborate later, even referring to the problem of Germany and the existence of two German states.

Points 5, 6 and 7 referred, respectively, to the establishment of a national authority in Jordan, unity between the two peoples, the Arab liberation movement and Palestinian national unity. Point 8 referred to the need to continue the struggle for the sake of 'completing the liberation of all Palestinian territory and as a step along the road to comprehensive Arab unity'. Point 9 affirmed the need for solidarity with the socialist countries and progressive and liberation forces. Point 10 said: 'In the light of this programme, the leadership of the revolution will determine the tactics which will serve and make possible the negotiation of these objectives.'

At the end of the programme, a phrase was added asserting the need to call an extraordinary meeting of the PNC should a new situation arise affecting the destiny and future of the Palestinian people, which tended to limit the significance of Point 10. This last phrase was variously interpreted.[124] To some, it concerned an eventual invitation to Geneva, to others (including Fatah) it was related to the need to respond to concrete proposals involving the establishment of a national authority.

Despite the addition of this phrase, Point 10 was very important in that it left the leadership (concretely, the Fatah–PDFLP–Sa'iqa alliance) ample room for manoeuvre. Equipped with real power, a programme envisaging the establishment of a national authority (despite the ambiguities) and unanimous agreement, the PLO thus equipped itself with the possibility of responding to possible future political and diplomatic approaches.

Some questions remain, however. Was the time not ripe for the leadership of the Palestinian Resistance to go farther in the acceptance of a compromise solution to the Middle East crisis? – as, at another time, the Zionist movement had done by accepting the Partition Plan in 1947. Besides the constraints peculiar to the PLO, we should simply note that the choice was never put to the Resistance during the period 1973--77 (nor indeed after). No plan backed by the great powers and the UN was ever put before it. It is very unlikely that, in a purely diplomatic framework, more concessions would have brought about a change in either the US or the Israeli government. But would this not have been a means of winning wider support among international and Israeli public opinion? The question remains open.

The new executive committee elected at the twelfth PNC enhanced the power and autonomy of Yasser Arafat. The executive committee comprised 14 members:

Yasser Arafat: Fatah; chairman.
Farouq Kaddoumi: Fatah; political department.
Zuhair Mohsen: Sa'iqa; military department.
Yasser Abd al-Rabbo: PDFLP; information.
Ahmad al-Yamani: PFLP; popular organizations.
Abd al-Wahhab Kayyali: ALF; without portfolio.
Talal Naji: PFLP–GC; culture and education.
Muhammad Zohdi al-Nashashibi: independent; secretary-general.
Abd al-Aziz Wagih: independent; assistant for the popular organizations.
Hamed Abu Sitteh: independent; occupied territories.
Abd al-Jawad Salah: PNF; assistant for the occupied territories.
Walid Kamhawi: PNF; Palestine National Fund (finance).
Abd al-Mohsen Abu Mayzar: PNF; national affairs spokesman of the PLO.
Elias Khoury: independent; no definite responsibilities.

The PFLP-GC entered the executive committee; this was the only change involving the fedayeen organizations. The number of independents rose from three to seven. Yusif Sayegh, who had identified himself with the rejectionists, was removed. Representatives of the occupied territories, on the other hand, were numerous in the new executive committee; this was a victory for the 'realists'. By virtue of its make-up and its broadened membership, the executive committee was to take on a new weight in the life of the PLO, of which it was, in principle, the next highest body after the PNC.

By way of conclusion we can attempt to assess the decision-making process in the PLO. First of all, it must be stressed that it was democratic. This is not a value judgement. It took more than eight months to reach a decision on a 'national authority', and achieve the widest possible agreement. It was vital − for both internal and external reasons − to achieve the widest possible consensus. A mere majority decision would risk both leading to a split in the PLO and a confrontation between it and some Arab countries.

The second aspect, linked to the first, is thus the need to compromise. No organization within the PLO, even the largest, could impose its viewpoint. This did not have only positive consequences, but reflected another aspect of the reality of the PLO, the low level of integration of the organizations. Each had retained its own organizational, political and military autonomy. Thus an agreement did not so much involve going through the established organs of the PLO as reaching a compromise between the various fedayeen organizations, to which now had to be added the PNF. However, the PLO remained a unifying symbol and a formidable quasi-state administrative machine, and it was difficult for any organization to run the risk of a 'split'.

External factors played more heavily on the PLO than on any comparable liberation organization. The PLO had no 'liberated zones' and was subject to pressure from the Arab states; it was hence dependent on the outside world, both politically and militarily. In an Arab environment that was increasingly divided, it was difficult for the PLO to find its own way. Given these circumstances, it is easier to understand why the PLO always sought 'to speak last' or, as the report by the executive committee to the twelfth PNC put it, to retain 'control of the initiative in our hands and not to show our trump cards to the enemy'.[125] This explains the relative passivity of the PLO and the difficulty it had in taking political initiatives. The PLO reacted to external approaches. It did not act; it reacted.

One major reservation must be made to this analysis, however. The leadership of Fatah − and Arafat in particular − demonstrated a considerable capacity for initiative throughout the period 1973-77. By authorizing Hammami to publish his articles in *The Times*, by opening up the dialogue with Zionist forces and by formulating a new stand on the question of Israeli–Palestinian relations, Fatah and Arafat were doing something new, were acting, and attempting to get out of the impasse. The relative lack of success of these attempts was due to many factors, among which must not be forgotten the total, seamless intransigence of the two main political forces in Israel.

Notes to Part 4

1. *Le Monde*, 21–22 October 1973.
2. *Le Monde Diplomatique*, December 1973.
3. A.M. Lesch, *Political Perceptions of the Palestinians in the West Bank and the Gaza Strip*, Washington, D.C., The Middle East Institute, 1980, p. 56; see the text of the communiqué in *Al-Wathaiq al-'arabiya al-filastinya 1973* [Palestine Arab Documents], Beirut, Institute for Palestine Studies, p. 504. (Henceforth cited as *PAD* with the year of reference.
4. *PAD 1973*, p. 504.
5. F. Hourani, *Al-fikr al-siyasi al-filastini 1964–1974* [Palestinian political thought], Beirut, PLO Research Centre, 1980.
6. Ibid., pp. 187–8.
7. The letter was published by *al-Nahar*, a Lebanese daily, on 17 December 1973. An English translation appeared in the *Journal of Palestine Studies* (henceforth *JPS*), Beirut, no. 11, Spring 1974, pp. 187–91.
8. Ibid.
9. *PAD 1973*, p. 539.
10. *PAD 1974*, pp. 29–32.
11. Ibid., pp. 34–5.
12. Interview with Abu Adnan (Abd al-Karim Hamad), member of the politbureau of the PDFLP, Paris, December 1981.
13. See the final communiqué of the meeting, *PAD 1973*, pp. 430–2.
14. Ibid.
15. Ibid.
16. Ibid., pp. 506–8.
17. Ibid., p. 507.
18. Ibid.
19. Quoted by H.S.H. Behbehani, *China's Foreign Policy in the Arab World, 1955–1975*, London, Kegan Paul International, 1981, p. 116.
20. *PAD 1973*, p. 539.
21. *International Documents on Palestine 1974*, Beirut, Institute for Palestine Studies, pp. 410–11. (Henceforth cited as *IDP* with the year of reference.)
22. Ibid.
23. *PAD 1974*, pp. 25–6.
24. Interview with Abu Adnan, December 1981.
25. Abu Iyad, *My Home, My Land: A Narrative of the Palestinian Struggle*, New York, Times Books, 1981, pp. 139–40.
26. *PAD 1973*, p. 423.
27. Hourani, *Al-fikr al-siyasi*, pp. 194–5.
28. *PAD 1973*, pp. 469–72.
29. Ibid., pp. 520–2.
30. *PAD 1974*, pp. 19–21.
31. Ibid., pp. 5–6.
32. Abu Iyad, *My Home, My Land*, p. 132.
33. *PAD 1973*, pp. 472–5.
34. But they did have an impact on some forces inside Israel. We shall come back to this question when we deal with the problem of Israeli–Palestinian contacts.

35. *IDP 1973*, pp. 517–19.
36. *The Times*, 17 December 1973.
37. *PAD 1973*, pp. 421–2.
38. *Al-kitab al-sanawi lil-qadiya al-filastiniya 1968* [Annual Survey of the Palestine Question], Beirut, Institute for Palestine Studies, p. 19. (Henceforth cited as *ASPQ* with the year of reference.)
39. Ibid., pp. 18–19.
40. *PAD 1973*, pp. 445–7.
41. Ibid., pp. 528–33.
42. *PAD 1974*, pp. 41–3.
43. *PAD 1973*, pp. 458–9.
44. *Le Monde*, 13 February 1974.
45. Abu Iyad, *My Home, My Land*, p. 143.
46. Ibid.
47. See Quandt *et al.*, *The Politics of Palestinian Nationalism*, University of California Press, 1973; and W.W. Kazziha, *Palestine in the Arab Dilemma*, London, Croom Helm, 1979.
48. On the more nuanced position of Libya, see Abu Iyad, *My Home, My Land*, p. 131, or Jalloud's statement to *L'Orient-Le jour*, 17 May 1975.
49. *PAD 1973*, pp. 478–80.
50. Ibid., pp. 420–1.
51. Probably a reference to the 'consultation' of the inhabitants of the West Bank — with the elections of April 1950 — after which King Abdallah formally annexed the West Bank.
52. *PAD 1973*, pp. 424–5.
53. Interview with *Le Monde*, 11 December 1973.
54. Ibid.
55. *PAD 1973*, pp. 493–6.
56. Lesch, *Political Perceptions*, p. 56.
57. *Le Monde*, 30 November 1973.
58. Lesch, *Political Perceptions*, pp. 57–8.
59. *IDP 1974*, p. 434.
60. Ibid., p. 436.
61. Ibid., pp. 436–8.
62. *Le Monde*, 20–21 January 1974.
63. *Palestinian Leaders Discuss the New Challenges for the Resistance*, Beirut, PLO Research Centre, 1974, p. 74.
64. *PAD 1973*, pp. 540–1.
65. Ibid.
66. Ibid, pp. 543–7.
67. See the very interesting contribution by the Lebanese Communist leader K. Mroue to *Shu'un Filastiniya*, no. 31, March 1974, on a state in the West Bank and Gaza and the transitional stages in each revolutionary struggle.
68. *IDP 1973*, pp. 273–6.
69. *L'Afrique Noire et le Moyen-Orient*, Paris, Documentation Française, Problèmes Politiques et Sociaux, no. 139–40.
70. *Le Monde*, 20–21 January 1976.
71. Galia Golan, *The Soviet Union and the PLO*, London, International Institute for Strategic Studies, Adelphi Papers no. 131, 1976.
72. Behbehani, *China's Foreign Policy*, pp. 102–96.

73. *IDP 1973*, pp. 259-60. On the discussions on the Middle East which took place during this summit, see H. Kissinger, *Les années orageuses*, Paris, Fayard, 1982, Vol. I, pp. 345-50.

74. Abu Iyad, *My Home, My Land*, p. 129.

75. *Israël et Palestine*, no. 2, 25-26 January 1974; *Le Monde* 1 and 6 November 1973.

76. *Le Monde*, 6 November 1973.

77. *PAD 1973*, pp. 425-8.

78. The meeting between Nixon and Brezhnev in June 1973; the final communiqué said that a settlement 'should take into due account the legitimate interests of the Palestinian people'. See *IDP 1973*, pp. 259-60.

79. *PAD 1973*, pp. 472-5.

80. *Le Monde*, 13 February 1974.

81. Published by *al-Nahar*, 10 March 1974, and reprinted in A.Y. Yodfat and Y. Arnon-Ohanna, *PLO Strategy and Tactics*, London, Croom Helm, 1981, pp. 167-9.

82. *Le Monde*, 16 and 23 February 1974.

83. *PAD 1974*, p. 60.

84. Ibid., pp. 86-7.

85. Ibid., pp. 93-5.

86. Ibid., pp. 99-100.

87. *Palestinian Leaders*, pp. 68-9.

88. Ibid., p. 31.

89. *PAD 1974*, pp. 104-8.

90. See report and denials in *Le Monde*, 28-29 December 1973.

91. *Nouvelle Revue Socialiste*, no. 5, 1974.

92. Interview with Abu Hatem (Muhammad Abu Mayzar), Beirut, May 1982.

93. *PAD 1974*, pp. 102-4.

94. The best translation in French is that published in *Le Figaro*, 22 March 1974; the Arabic text was published in the PDFLP's weekly, *al-Hurriya*, 1 April 1974; it is available in *PAD 1974*, pp. 100-2, and in English in *New Outlook*, 17 March 1973, pp. 65-7.

95. Statement to *Le Nouvel Observateur*, 25 March 1974.

96. All the quotations are taken from the version published by *New Outlook*.

97. Former Histadrut secretary-general and former Labour Party secretary general, respectively.

98. *PAD 1974*, pp. 127-30.

99. *Le Monde*, 24-25 March 1974.

100. See interview with Hawatmeh in *Le Figaro*, 17 May 1974.

101. Quoted by P. Rondot, 'Résistance Palestinienne, Conférence de Genève et "refus arab"', *Politique Etrangère*, no. 3, 1974.

102. *Le Monde*, 24-25 March 1974.

103. Ibid., 14-15 April 1974.

104. *PAD 1975*, pp. 322-6.

105. *Le Monde*, 13 April 1974.

106. *Fiches du Monde Arabe*, Palestiniens Fiche IP6 (13 March 1981).

107. *Israël et Palestine*, no. 4, May 1974.

108. See the text in Yodfat and Arnon-Ohanna, *PLO*, pp. 169-72.

109. See *L'Orient–Le Jour*, 9, 10, 11, 12 and 13 May 1974.
110. Ibid., 13 May 1974.
111. *PAD 1974*, p. 171.
112. Ibid., pp. 173–4.
113. Ibid., p. 194.
114. *PAD 1974*, pp. 197–9.
115. Ibid., pp. 194–5.
116. *L'Orient–Le Jour*, 9 June 1974.
117. Hourani, *Al-fikr al-siyasi*, p. 247, note 209.
118. See the text in R. Hamid (ed.), *Muqararat al-majlis al-watani al-filastini 1964-1974* [Resolutions of the PNCs 1964–1974], Beirut, PLO Research Centre, 1975, pp. 247–8, and in Yodfat and Arnon-Ohanna, *PLO*, pp. 173–4.
119. *L'Orient–Le Jour*, 3 June 1974.
120. Hourani, *Al-fikr al-siyasi*, p. 209.
121. Contrary to the translation which appeared in *Maghreb-Machrek*, no. 64, it does not say 'the whole of its national territory'.
122. M.Y. Muslih, 'Moderates and Rejectionists within the Palestine Liberation Organization', *Middle East Journal*, no. 30 (2), spring 1976, pp. 127–40.
123. Quoted by Philippe Rondot, 'La Révolution palestinienne au seuil de 1974', *Défense Nationale*, pp. 73–84.
124. See Hourani, *Al-fikr al-siyasi*, p. 216.
125. Quoted by Hourani in ibid., pp. 200–1.

Part V:
Towards a Palestinian State?
(1974-1977)

13. Confirmation of the PLO's Stand and International Recognition

Yasser Arafat's success at the twelfth PNC constituted a turning-point in Palestinian political thought. But as with every major change, the ten-point programme, as we have seen, contained many ambiguities. It remained marked by all that had happened in the previous period.

The three years that followed — up to the holding of the thirteenth PNC and Sadat's visit to Jerusalem — enabled the PLO to assert more clearly the new political line on two major questions. First, on the Palestinian state. The formula of a 'national authority' was in fact ambiguous; it was half-way between a 'liberated zone' and a state. Even for the leaders of Fatah, things were far from clear. 'We have never proposed the establishment of a Palestinian state. We are proposing the establishment of a national authority',[1] declared Abu Iyad a few weeks after the twelfth PNC had ended. The issue was a real one; even though the Palestinian leaders had never posed the problem in legal terms, accepting the establishment of a state in part of Palestine meant undertaking to respect international law and the UN Charter (on the principle of effectiveness in international law). It thus meant *de facto* acceptance of the existence of the state of Israel. The consequences were not the same if it was a matter of a 'Palestinian national authority' whose international status had never been defined.

The second question was that of a political solution and the Geneva conference. In spite of the difficulties, and the civil war in Lebanon, the readiness of the PLO to negotiate was more and more affirmed. This readiness was made easier by the two major successes won by the PLO on the international level. The first came at the Arab Summit in Rabat, in October 1974. Despite last-minute Jordanian efforts,[2] and despite a very skilful speech by the King,[3] the Arab Summit — this time unanimously — pronounced in favour of the PLO. The resolution was unambiguous:

1. To assert the Palestinian people's right to return to its homeland and determine its own fate . . .
2. To assert the Palestinian people's right to establish its own independent national authority under the leadership of the PLO — the sole legitimate representative of the Palestinian people — in all liberated Palestinian territory. And the Arab countries will assist this authority

> when it is established in all fields and on all levels.[4]

King Hussein had no choice but to accept this decision which, moreover, greatly strengthened the realistic stand taken by the chairman of the PLO. Eric Rouleau gave this explanation of this historic summit:

> In my opinion, the decision by the Arab Heads of State was dictated by at least three political considerations:
> a) The passivity of King Hussein during the October war had finally discredited him in the eyes of the Palestinians. The Arab Heads of State felt that he was no longer in a position to negotiate a settlement in Geneva that would be sufficiently credible to be lasting.
> b) Any peace agreement reached with Israel would necessarily involve concessions, which would risk endangering the position of those who consented to them. The Arab Heads of State had no wish to take on such a heavy burden without the approval, vital in their eyes, of those most concerned, the Palestinians. And since the fedayeen organizations could in no way be suspected of complaisance towards the Jewish state, why not bring them to the negotiating table and have them associate themselves with a global settlement that would, one day or another, be reached?
> c) The Arab Heads of State knew, even before the October war, that some PLO leaders were ready to contemplate a compromise.[5]

The other great success was Arafat's participation in the UN General Assembly in November 1974. On 14 October the General Assembly had adopted, by 105 votes to 4 with 20 abstentions, a resolution inviting the PLO to participate in its work on the Palestinian question.[6] Arafat was given a triumphal welcome in New York, while the population of the West Bank and Gaza demonstrated, for several days, its support for the PLO. Two resolutions of great significance were adopted. The first, Resolution 3236, recognized:

> the inalienable rights of the Palestinian people, including:
> a) The right to self-determination without external interference;
> b) The right to national independence and sovereignty.

It stated that the Palestinian people 'is a principal party in the establishment of a just and desirable peace in the Middle East'. Resolution 3237 invited the PLO to participate 'in the sessions and the work of the General Assembly in the capacity of observer'.[7]

It was against this favourable regional and international background that the PLO affirmed its readiness to negotiate. It did so above all through delegations to the socialist states. On 30 July 1974 Arafat went to Moscow, invited for the first time by the Soviet government. Despite the PFLP's refusal to take part in the delegation and the extremely violent attacks by organizations in the Rejection Front, the visit was a success. The USSR recognized the PLO as the sole representative of the Palestinian people and agreed to the opening of a PLO office in Moscow. Of greater significance, however, was the PLO's agreeing to the inclusion of the following phrase in the communiqué:

> the Soviet side affirmed the support of the Soviet Union for the participation of the PLO in the Geneva Conference, on the condition of equal rights for the participating sides.[8]

Without actually adopting the phrase directly as its own, the PLO nevertheless thus made a gesture of great political significance.

The next visit to the Soviet capital took place between 25 and 30 November 1974. It occurred just after the Brezhnev–Ford summit in Vladivostok, at the end of which mention had been made of the 'legitimate interests of all the peoples of the area, including the Palestinian people'.[9] Arafat met Brezhnev for the first time. In the communiqué issued at the end of this meeting, Soviet support for the Geneva Conference was again mentioned.[10]

A few weeks later, in an interview with the newspaper *Le Monde*, Arafat denounced the aim of reactionary and imperialist forces 'to torpedo the Geneva Conference, to conduct "step by step" negotiations outside of any international control'.[11] This was a backhand way of stressing the interest the Palestinians had in Geneva!

But the most spectacular manifestation, although once again indirect, took place in February 1975. In a major speech, Brezhnev said that it was necessary to convene the Geneva Conference with the participation of the representatives of the Palestinian people and that all peoples — including the Israeli people — were interested in peace.[12] In a letter addressed to the Soviet leader, Arafat thanked him for the support he was giving the Palestinian people in this statement.[13]

In the weeks that followed, the PLO made a direct appeal for the holding of the peace conference. On the occasion of a visit by Kaddoumi to Bulgaria:

> the two parties call for an early meeting of the Geneva Conference, so as to discuss and iron out all aspects of the Middle East crisis and in particular the Palestinian problem, on the basis of Resolution 3236 adopted by the 29th session of UN General Assembly on 22 November 1974. They consider that participation by the PLO with full rights in the Geneva Conference is an essential condition for its success.[14]

It can be observed that this formulation indicates unambiguously the readiness of the PLO to sit at the same table as the Israeli government.

This stand was confirmed when Arafat visited Moscow again in May 1975.[15] Once again in August, the Palestinian leader declared that the PLO was ready 'to participate in any meeting, any international conference convened to respond to the aspirations of the Palestinian people, such as they have been laid down in UN General Assembly Resolution 3236', adding, 'This is the only condition we make.'[16]

Thus, a year after the twelfth PNC, the 'majority' of the PLO had asserted its readiness to participate in the Geneva Conference on the basis of Resolution 3236, which recognized the national rights of the Palestinian people. It even took a step forward by accepting, once again implicitly, the draft resolution submitted to the Security Council in January 1976. According to UN Secretary-General Kurt Waldheim, the debate thus joined had brought out 'the two major elements of the Middle East problem: the Palestinian dimension and the reaffirmation of the right of all states in the region to live in peace within secure and recognized borders'.[17] The draft resolution was rejected, however, following an American veto that Kaddoumi publicly regretted.[18] Arafat himself stressed the importance of this debate, the fact that it had nullified Resolutions 242 and 338, and the fact that the PLO had not opposed the new resolution. This was at the thirteenth PNC.[19]

The move from acceptance of a 'national authority' to that of an independent state is harder to grasp. In several statements made before the twelfth PNC, Palestinian leaders had spoken indiscriminately of a state or a national authority. But no official text had yet endorsed this fact. Several factors were to operate in this direction. First, the stand taken by the USSR, which in November 1974[20] pronounced in favour of the establishment of a Palestinian state. Next, several Palestinian organizations declared themselves in favour of a state. The first to do so was the PDFLP, which issued a political programme at the end of 1975.[21] In it, it was stated:

> The October war has brought about a relative balance in the relations of force in the region and created the objective possibility of developing the struggle with a view to forcing the enemy into complete withdrawal from occupied Arab and Palestinian lands and seizing the right to self-determination and national independence of the Palestinian people in the framework of an independent and sovereign national state.[22]

On their side, the Communists came out in favour of the right to self-determination of the Palestinian people, in all freedom, 'including the establishment of an independent national state in the whole of the territory from which the Zionist occupation forces withdraw'[23]

In February 1976 *al-Watan*, the organ of the Palestinian Communist Organization in the West Bank (a branch of the Jordanian Communist Party formed in July 1976), called on the PLO, in an editorial, to abandon the slogan of the establishment of a Palestinian state in the whole of Palestine. This stand, it said, was incomprehensible after 25 years of war between 'the two components of the population living in Palestine'.[24] On the contrary, all efforts must be concentrated on the right of the Palestinian people to set up an independent state and the right of refugees to return to their homes. This stand was reiterated in July 1976 in a joint communiqué of the Jordanian and Israeli Communist Parties which asserted the right of the

Palestinians to 'an independent state in the West Bank — including Arab Jerusalem — and Gaza, and the right of refugees to return, in conformity with the resolutions of the UN'.[25]

This general evolution, which was underlined by the contacts between Israelis and Palestinians and the various activities of the 'free-shooters' in Fatah, could not fail to concern the rejectionist forces which were gradually sliding into total opposition.

14. The Rejection Front: Towards a Split?

> This unanimity [achieved at the twelfth PNC] was unfortunately short-lived. No sooner had the meeting ended than the polemics and the out-bidding broke out within the various organizatons, and the most radical elements criticized their comrades for having given their endorsement to a 'liquidationist' text. Of course, the extremists won out over the moderates, as always happens in such debates. Except for Fatah, the PDFLP and Sa'iqa — all of which had homogeneous leadership groups — all the other groupings reversed their stands and launched a campaign against the mini-state.[26]

This is how Abu Iyad described the atmosphere in the PLO immediately after the twelfth PNC. A few weeks after the PNC, the central committee of the PFLP met and adopted a very hard-line document, entitled communiqué no. 1.[27] The document first spelled out the PFLP's interpretation of the ten-point programme:

1) Rejection of Resolution 242, even if amended.
2) Refusal to participate in the Geneva Conference.
3) Refusal to participate in compromise negotiations.
4) A national authority will not be achieved by the present manoeuvring, but by armed struggle and political struggle based on it.
5) Rejection of any co-ordination with the King of Jordan. Need to establish a democratic national regime in Jordan.

The communiqué went on to denounce the pressure being put on the PLO to co-ordinate its action with the Jordanian regime and participate in the Geneva Conference on the basis of Resolution 338. The Palestinian masses would not forget, it added, the statements made 'after the National Council, by the leader of an organization which participates in the executive committee and which has set out its conditions for participating in the Geneva Conference' (Hawatmeh?). Nor would they forget the person who set out his conditions for co-ordinating his action with King Hussein.[28] Then followed a very strong attack on those in the occupied territories who 'claim to represent the Arabs', but who had never believed in the armed struggle (a clear reference to the Communists). The statement ended with a threat to the leaders of the PLO.

Such vehemence is surprising coming so soon after the twelfth PNC had ended with complete agreement. Two factors were at work in this rapid change. On the one hand, the political process was speeding up, as the prospect of a settlement drew nearer. On the other hand, the agreement on the ten-point programme was based on a misunderstanding.[29] According to the PFLP, the text on which the seven had reached agreement contained explicitly, in point 2, rejection of peace and recognition, but also of *negotiation*. This term had disappeared, however, from the text submitted to the twelfth PNC. Neither Habash nor several leading PFLP figures had participated in the Cairo meeting; the result was a misunderstanding and a feeling in the PFLP that it had been the victim of a 'dirty trick'.

Whatever the truth of the matter, the PFLP's opposition came to be asserted more and more forcefully. On 20 July 1974 communiqué no. 2 appeared,[30] denouncing attempts to induce the Palestinian Resistance to participate in the proposals for liquidationist settlements, whether in the Geneva framework or outside it. Its view was that the PLO leadership had to be prevented from participating in these solutions. A few days later, a *rapprochement* got under way between the PFLP, the PFLP-GC and the ALF, which appealed jointly to the executive committee of the PLO.[31] The PFLP distanced itself from the ten-point programme and Habash declared:

> It is not possible for a real . . . and lasting national unity to be established on the basis of the ten-point programme . . . National unity can be built on only one political line: rejection by the PLO clearly . . . of all proposed forms of settlement.[32]

If the PLO participated in Geneva, he added, the PFLP would walk out of the PLO. In this context, the PFLP condemned Arafat's visit to Moscow at the end of July 1974, after refusing to participate in the delegation.[33]

In fact, as Abu Ali Mustapha, the present assistant secretary-general of the PFLP, explained to me,[34] the essential difference bore on whether or not there was a possibility of reaching a settlement. For Fatah, there were two possible settlements in the region, one imperialist, the other national. For the PFLP there was only one, an imperialist settlement, and any move towards it was an act of treason. No one therefore should be surprised by the PFLP communiqué on 26 September announcing its withdrawal from the executive committee:

> The PFLP announces its withdrawal from the executive committee of the PLO so that it may not be held responsible for the historical deviation in which the leadership of the organization has become involved; and so that it may continue to struggle in the ranks of the masses to correct this deviation, to express the will of the masses and to impose

the sound revolutionary political line on the leaderships that have become mere appendages of the reactionary and surrenderist regimes.[35]

After asserting that 'the liquidationist imperialist settlement . . . [would result in] the spread of American influence . . , the confirmation of the legitimacy "of Israel", its future and its security', the PFLP accused the PLO leadership of being actively involved in this solution. The twelfth PNC had been only a manoeuvre to create the impression that a political settlement was being rejected. Faced with this situation, however, the PFLP announced that it was remaining in the PNC and the mass organizations, in other words, it was not leaving the PLO.

The PFLP was followed in its opposition by the ALF, the PFLP-GC and a small organization, the Front of Palestinian Popular Struggle (FPPS), which together formed a Central Council of the Rejection Front.[36] All the political activities of the PLO were denounced as being part of attempts at a settlement. The Rejection Front condemned the Rabat Summit[37] and the PFLP condemned Arafat's journey to the UN General Assembly.[38] The PLO's invitation to the Security Council in January 1976 did not find favour in their eyes either.[39]

For the Rejection Front, any call for a national authority was, under existing conditions, suspect. The PFLP denounced those who sought to suppress the Palestinian cause 'with proposals for a Palestinian entity or state in a part of Palestine'.[40] Habash himself stated:

> there is no place, in the framework of a settlement, for the establishment of any Palestinian authority on Palestinian land, unless it is linked to reactionary forces in the region, recognizes the existence of Israel and has good relations with all reactionary and imperialist forces in the region.[41]

It was in this same speech that the leader of the PFLP denounced the municipalities that had just been elected in the West Bank!

If a balance sheet is drawn up of the activities of the Rejection Front, one cannot but be struck by how little impact it had during the period following the twelfth PNC. This was not only because of its political and ideological heterogeneity, but also because of the absurd machinery in which it had become enmeshed. There can be little doubt that the condemnation of Arafat's journey to the UN — at a time when everywhere, and particularly in the occupied territories, the Palestinian people was hailing this enormous political victory — or the condemnation of the municipal elections in the West Bank — when 80% of the population had voted for pro-PLO lists and the municipal councils were becoming one of the bases of resistance to the occupation — did nothing to increase the audience and prestige of the Rejection Front. The fact that it did not break away and leave the PLO, despite its denunciations of the PLO leaders' betrayal, shows also that it was aware of its limits. On the other hand, the very existence of the Front made the PLO leadership look 'realistic' and moderate.

That of course did not mean that the 'rejectionist' attitude, deeply rooted in Palestinian political thought, had disappeared. It existed, even within Fatah. But so long as the prospect of a political settlement remained, its impact was reduced.

15. The Question of a Palestinian Government-in-Exile

The problem of the proclamation of a Palestinian government-in-exile remained, for the Palestinian movement, a stock item on the agenda. In 1984 it had still not been settled, even though periodic rumours announced its imminent proclamation. During his official visit to the USSR in October 1981, when the opening of a Palestinian 'embassy' in Moscow was announced, Arafat replied as follows to a question about a Palestinian government:

> The solution of this problem lies with the Palestinian leadership. If, at some point in our struggle, we reach the conclusion that the establishment of this government will help our movement, we shall do so. The more so as the PLO leadership is fully capable of implementing this task. I would like to recall that at present the PLO is a full member of the Arab League and the Islamic Conference Organization. It enjoys observer status at the UN and the Organization of African Unity. At the same time, the PLO is an active member of the Non-Aligned Movement. However, I repeat, the question of the establishment of a government will be settled only by the Palestinian leadership.[42]

According to Shafiq al-Hut, this reflects the rather inglorious experience of the first Palestinian government. On 23 September 1948 the Arab Higher Committee, meeting in Gaza, proclaimed the formation of an 'Arab Government for the whole of Palestine'. Ahmad Hilmi Pasha was to be its Prime Minister. Supported at first by the Arab League (except for King Abdallah), it had, in fact, no power. The annexation of the West Bank by the new Kingdom of Jordan, and the compromises worked out by the Arab League on this question, consigned Hilmi Pasha's government to the scrap-heap of history.[43]

The issue resurfaced at the time of the polemics about 'a Palestinian entity' in the 1960s. But it was above all after the Six-Day war and the recognition of the Palestinian movement that the problem was again raised so strongly that Arafat in person asserted, in April 1970, that 'we are not acting to establish any form of government whatsoever'.[44]

The debate took off again in September 1972. In a speech to the central committee of the Arab Socialist Union on the second anniversary of the death of Nasser, President Sadat made the following proposal:

> I think that the time has come for our Palestinian brothers to form their entity [*kiyan*]. I want to announce in your presence that we here in Egypt will welcome and recognize that entity when the people of Palestine and the Resistance take the necessary measures to establish their provisional government. Exactly what happened in Algeria has happened, is happening, today, in Palestine.[45]

The Jordanian government's reaction was immediate and hostile,[46] the PLO's more embarrassed; the executive committee appeared divided, even though a majority pronounced itself, in the prevailing circumstances, against the proposal.[47] The communiqué issued at the end of the meeting devoted to this subject is indicative:

> The executive committee of the PLO, at its meeting on 1 October 1972, studied the present political situation of the Palestinian question and our people's armed struggle. It decided that it was necessary to develop the Palestinian personality, support the Palestinian entity [*kiyan*], represented by the PLO, develop its institutions, support its National Charter and increase its effectiveness in the struggle against imperialism and international Zionism.[48]

Despite the vagueness of this statement, it seems that one of the points around which the debate had raged was the affirmation of 'the Palestinian personality'. The executive committee, whatever position it might adopt on the provisional government, wanted there to be no ambiguity on this point. The Palestinian refusal was not to be confused with the Jordanian refusal.

On 7 October 1972 a PLO delegation led by Khalid al-Fahum, chairman of the PNC, who was not one of the key leaders of the PLO, met President Sadat. At the end of the meeting, a communiqué was issued in which the President explained his position: he denounced imperialist and Zionist attacks; asserted that the Palestinian people alone could decide its future; and confirmed his attachment to the unity of the Resistance.[49] A few days later, in response to a question on the Palestinian rejection of a provisional government, Khalid al-Hassan declared:

> President Sadat did not make this proposal for us to accept or reject it; he put forward the idea of a provisional government, and then confirmed that the Palestinian people and the Palestinian Resistance have the responsibility of discussing this idea . . . [and that the Palestinian people] has the right to decide its stand. And we agreed on the strengthening of the PLO which has similarities to a provisional government.[50]

The incident with Egypt was closed on this ambiguous formulation, but the debate remained open.

We can already try to draw up a balance sheet of the way in which the various organizations reacted.

> The reaction from the Commando leadership was varied, but generally hostile . . . The Popular Front for the Liberation of Palestine quickly rejected the idea, calling it 'an attempt to involve the resistance in capitulationist settlements' . . . Fatah's response was similar, but slower and more cautious. A split had developed within this organization over the advisability of opting for a sort of government-in-exile scheme at least a year prior to President al-Sadat's speech.[51]

What were the arguments adduced? For Fatah, there is available a long article, written in rather bad French, entitled 'Le gouvernement de l'exil [sic] et la solution politique' [The government-in-exile and the political solution].[52] This text, which attempted to clarify the position of the Palestinians towards Sadat's proposals, can be summarized as follows: the question of a Palestinian government-in-exile had already been raised twice, first after the killings in Jordan in September 1970. Recognition of such a government by numerous Third World countries would have meant withdrawing recognition of the Jordanian government as representing the Palestinians. Then, after the proposal for a United Arab Kingdom: would not the proclamation of government have killed this proposal? But this was not the way Palestinians analysed it. Their analysis:

> does not reject the idea out of hand, but opposes above all the timing of its implementation. The formation of a provisional government is certainly a decisive stage in the history of every revolution, but this government will only be effective to the extent that the revolution has attained a certain strength which is indispensable to it to secure victory in the event of negotiations.[53]

If this proposal came too early, added the author, either it would be ineffective, or it would lead us to negotiations in which our opponents would impose their conditions. In the prevailing circumstances, the formation of such a government was directly linked to the establishment of a Palestinian state in the framework of an overall solution. And this was rejected by the PLO. Linking the question of a government to the question of a state, the author then examined the positions of the United States, Israel and Jordan. He saw in the first 'those most active in favour of a Palestinian state'. After developing these points at length, the author asserted that the only solution lay in continuing the struggle [sic].

After the October war, the debate took off again. According to convergent testimony, the issue of the formation of a government was not put on the agenda of either the twelfth or the thirteenth PNC.[54] For Arafat, the proclamation of this government was linked to a political solution: it was not an end but a means.

> If a government really bring us possibilities of establishing a national authority in our land, we shall form it at once. If the proclamation of a government is a condition for cutting through the knots and securing a land, we shall not be found wanting.[55]

In other words, if it was necessary to form a government in order to get to Geneva, the PLO would do so. The proclamation of a government thus constituted one of the factors in the negotiations underway with the United States by some Arab leaders and the PLO to move towards a settlement.[56] So long as the negotiations had not been concluded, it was unlikely that the PLO would announce the creation of this government. This is what Arafat told the thirteenth PNC. After recalling that Jalloud, the Libyan Vice-President, had in his presence in 1975 proposed the formation of a government-in-exile, he added:

> I have always said one thing, my brothers: if a government is in our people's interest, then we will do it tomorrow; until then I see no interest in it. If there was an interest, then I would not let you leave this meeting without having taken such a decision.[57]

As Shafiq al-Hut said in 1981, 'the provisional Palestinian government cannot be formed before we are sure that it will not remain provisional and will not spend all its life in exile'.[58]

The only organization to come out officially in favour of such a government was the PDFLP. Indeed it was Hawatmeh who, in a speech in February 1975, officially asked the PLO to do so.[59] But this idea does not appear to have become a war-cry of the PDFLP. It was missing from its 1975 political programme and, in February 1977, the same Hawatmeh condemned the idea of a provisional government.[60]

16. The Economic Viability of a Palestinian State

The debate on the establishment of a Palestinian state in the West Bank and Gaza, and the acceptance by the PLO leadership of this objective, led to a plethora of studies on the 'economic viability' of such a state. It is of course true that the main debate was not at this level and Arafat could state in response to criticism from the PFLP:

> Since when did a homeland constitute a commercial operation? Whether it be poor or rich, the land of our ancestors is dear to us and we are struggling to recover it. That goes without saying for any committed patriot. Amilcar Cabral is building an independent state in Guinea-Bissau, one of the smallest and poorest states on the planet. It is the same with the South Yemenis who have established their republic despite the wretched circumstances of their country.[61]

Nevertheless this issue is not without interest. For example, determining the capacity of the future state to absorb refugees is a point which could strengthen — or weaken — the supporters of a political solution. If the future state could absorb a large number of refugees, that would create the conditions in which animosities and irridentism could be reduced and hence promote the stability of a political settlement.

The issue of 'economic viability' is less obvious than it appears, however. As one of the best studies of the occupied territories stated:

> To ask, 'Could a West Bank–Gaza Strip state be viable?' is to pose the wrong question. For this, as for other territory about which the question might be asked, the answer is neither 'Yes' nor 'No'. The only realistic answer is 'Only if'.[62]

Detailed economic studies of the occupied territories[63] were followed by studies analysing the viability of a state in these territories. The pioneering study remains that by Ward, Peretz and Wilson.[64] Although updated in 1977, it suffers from the use of statistics that were overtaken by the changes in the West Bank and Gaza. The most comprehensive, and the most stimulating, study is that carried out jointly by an Israeli Mapam leader, Haim Darin-

Drabkin, and a Palestinian university teacher, Elias Tuma.[65] The starting-point is defined in this way:

> Assuming the policy makers have agreed on a solution, will the resulting State of Palestine be economically viable? What minimum conditions must be met for it to survive and prosper? What size population can it support? What boundaries should it have, and what period of time must elapse before the full potential and viability of such a state can be realized?[66]

The response is that a state established in the West Bank and Gaza (the two territories being linked by a motorway) could be viable, but that viability 'must be achieved. It is not inherent in the prospective state, but it is achievable.'[67]

Without going into their argument in detail, we may note that the authors suppose significant, but not excessive, economic aid for five years. The United Nations Relief Works Agency (UNRWA) would provide \$150 million a year, the Arab states about \$400 million and Israel \$600 million; additional foreign aid would be \$500 million in the first year and \$200 million thereafter. All these figures are given using 1975 prices.[68] By comparison, we may note that US aid to Israel was \$2.5 billion in 1974, \$650 million in 1975 and \$2.2 billion in 1976.

The most interesting point is the capacity of the new state to absorb extra people. The working hypothesis is that the state could absorb (still on the basis of 1975 figures), in addition to the 680,000 residents of the West Bank and 430,000 in Gaza, 390,000 refugees, 812,000 residents of Arab countries and 50,000 Israeli Arabs. This would bring the number of inhabitants of the new state up to about 2.4 million.[69] This capacity, which is much greater than might have been imagined, would give a political settlement a degree of stability, especially as the authors conclude: 'We estimate that the State of Palestine can support far more than the two and a half million people expected in the first few years.'[70]

As to the relations between the future state and its neighbours, the authors specify:

> A State of Palestine would be more likely to achieve its confidence of dentity and economic viability if it stays independent and refrains from integration with its neighbours. Integration with Israel and/or Jordan carries the risk of economic imperialism by one party or another, and a threat to the confidence of identity of the new State of Palestine. After the state had achivied viability, large-scale integration with other economies may be considered.[71]

Another researcher reaches more or less the same conclusion.[72] The author, who is somewhat sympathetic to the Israeli position, accepts Israeli statistics uncritically, and limits his study to the West Bank, but concludes his book, despite everything, with various possible scenarios:

> In summary, federation with Israel may work economically, but it will not work politically. Federation with Jordan may work politically, but it will not work economically. Neither solution meets our viability criterion. Of the three possible settlements, there is, in my opinion, only one that can be considered both economically and politically feasible: a Palestinian region.[73]

To end this chapter, I shall draw attention to the development over the last few years of studies by Palestinian researchers who take into account not only economic problems but also social structures (municipalities, charitable societies, education, housing, and so on) that exist in the West Bank and Gaza, and that the Palestinian state will inherit.[74] Some of these studies have been carried out in the occupied territories themselves, at the University of Bir Zeit and around the Arab Thought Forum which has held several congresses since 1981. At these congresses, several dozen papers have been presented on the municipalities, the trade unions, the various industries (tobacco, cement, petrochemicals, and so on), water policy, electricity policy, health policy, agriculture and stock-breeding.[75]

17. Israeli-Palestinian Talks

We have already seen the circumstances under which a dialogue had begun between the PDFLP and some small leftist Israeli organizations, as well as the way in which Fatah paraded the participation of a handful of Israeli Jews in its struggle. The fact remains, however, that during the period 1967–73 contacts between Israelis and Palestinians were so few as to be almost non-existent. The sole exception was the solid and profound link established between the Israeli Communist Party and large fractions of the population in the occupied territories, particularly militants of the Jordanian Communist Party. Rakah's resolutely anti-annexationist stand and its courageous defence of human rights in the occupied territories gave the Israeli Communists considerable prestige.

During the same period, contacts between Arabs and Israelis did take place. The Egyptian left — notably K. Mohiedin — played a key role, particularly in the preparation and proceedings of the International Conference for Peace and Justice in the Middle East held in Bologna from 11 to 13 May 1973. This conference brought together representatives from dozens of countries in Europe, Africa and Asia. Seven Arab countries were represented including Egypt, Syria and Iraq. The Palestinian delegates who were to have participated — with the formal approval of Arafat — were prevented from doing so by events in Lebanon.[76] The Israeli delegation included, in addition to the Israeli Communist Party, several small Zionist groups such as that of Uri Avneri and several independent figures, including Nathan Yalin Mor, the former leader of the Stern Gang. The Bologna conference was undeniably a first. But the October war was to bring the problem of contacts between Israelis and Palestinians to the forefront. The importance of these contacts, especially in so far as concerns the subject of this book, lies in two facts;

First, the dialogue with Israeli democratic forces amounted, for the Palestinians, to recognizing — step by step — the national reality of Israel. It was no longer a matter of seeing them join the PLO's struggle; it was a matter of hammering out jointly the principles of an understanding. It was a decisive step towards recognition of the binational reality existing in Palestine. Secondly, during these discussions, the Palestinian leaders were led to refine their ideas and to make proposals which were way ahead of the PLO's but which reflected the views of Arafat.

After Hammami's articles in 1973, which set out the bases of an agreement, the first dramatic initiative was Hawatmeh's interview. But it very rapidly aborted, as we have seen above, because of the deadly military operations undertaken by the PDFLP after its publication and also because of its political bases. What the PDFLP was looking for — and this despite certain ambiguities to be found in Hawatmeh's interview — was a dialogue with anti-Zionist forces. This had the effect of reducing the discussions to contacts between the PLO and the Israeli Communist Party. In these circumstances, it is not surprising that the PDFLP condemned the Israeli–Palestinian contacts of 1976. Hawatmeh declared:

> These meetings were held between second-level figures in Fatah on the one side, and Zionist representatives belonging to the Israel–Palestine Committee [in fact the Israel–Palestine Peace Council] on the other. The PLO was unaware of them and had not given its approval. These contacts have no real political value. At most they have a tactical or propaganda meaning. Only meetings between delegates of the PLO and members of Israeli and anti-Zionist movements could set out the path to peace.[77]

The boldest initiatives came from the central core of Fatah. In September 1974 an attempt was made to arrange a meeting between Hammami and Aharon Yariv, the Israeli Minister of Information, who had made statements sympathetic to a dialogue with the PLO;[78] but the latter was forced to resign. At the end of the same year, Hammami tried to organize a meeting between Arafat and Nahum Goldmann, the president of the World Zionist Organization.[79] The proposal collapsed because Yitzhak Rabin, then Israeli Prime Minister, objected to it. On 3 May 1975 an international conference on the Middle East was held in Paris, attended by over 100 participants from some 30 countries. The Palestinians were represented by A. Hourani, general secretary of the Palestine Peace and Solidarity Committee, and Ezzedine Kallak, the PLO representative in Paris. The Israelis were represented by T. Toubi, the assistant secretary-general of the Israeli Communist Party, and Nathan Yalin Mor. During the conference, which voted in favour of UN Resolutions 338 and 3236, Hourani declared:

> We are extremely grateful for the struggle waged by democratic forces in Israel, alongside us, for the right of the Palestinian people to self-determination to be recognized and implemented.[80]

But this presence, side by side, was still not really a proper dialogue. This was to develop during 1976 and the best description that we have of it is the lecture given by Henri Curiel, the main organizer of these meetings.[81] He first explains the circumstances in which the Palestinians agreed to these meetings. It was:

The Palestinians who had to be convinced and it was their agreement that had to be secured. It was given . . . in June 1976. This was just at the beginning of the conflict in Lebanon. It looked as if the so-called Islamic–progressive camp which included the Palestinians was going to come out on top. It was only somewhat later that we realized that this imminent victory was the factor that had led the Palestinian leaders to commit themselves. If they won, it would be possible to get the whole Palestinian Resistance to agree to a basic turning-point in the policy of the PLO. It was not from the PLO but from Fatah and Yasser Arafat himself that the famous long-awaited 'green light' came to organize a Palestinian–Israeli meeting.[82]

The contacts were conducted on the one side by General Peled, Arie (Lova) Eliav, the former secretary-general of the Labour Party and a member of the Knesset, Meir Pa'is, a member of the Knesset, Uri Avneri, and Jacob Arnon, and on the other by Issam Sartawi and Abbri Jiryis, a brilliant intellectual who had made his mark with a book on the Israeli Arabs and in 1975 by non-conformist articles. The most striking feature of these contacts was the avowed 'Zionist' character of the Israeli participants. Curiel distinguishes two periods in these discussions. The first went from the end of July 1976 to the resignation of the Rabin government on 19 December 1976. A whole series of proposals was made by the Palestinian side and transmitted directly to Rabin; these were in fact indirect negotiations with Israel. They produced no result, given the intransigence of the Israeli Prime Minister.

It should be noted that in these talks, as General Peled said, the Palestinians:

> immediately accepted as a basis the manifesto of our council which affirms the sovereign right of the Jewish people to immigrate to and live in the state of Israel and which rejects any Palestinian territorial claims on Israel in its pre-Six Day War boundaries.[83]

The second period of these discussions went from December 1976 to May 1977. For the Palestinians, it was aimed, above all, at increasing the prestige of the Israel–Palestine Peace Council to which their Israeli opposite numbers belonged. With this in mind the Palestinians authorized the Israeli side to publish a communiqué outlining what had transpired at the meetings. It was not stricly speaking a joint statement. But the text nevertheless assumed considerable importance since it made the meetings official and affirmed that the Peace Council's manifesto was 'a suitable basis for the solution of the Israel-Palestinian conflict'.[84] It was also during this period, in February, that meetings were arranged between the Council and Presidents Senghor of Senegal and Houphouët-Boigny of the Ivory Coast. These contacts made possible new indirect negotiations between the PLO and Rabin; Arafat later confirmed this in a speech to the thirteenth PNC.[85]

Curiel provides a precise summation of these talks:

There was first of all a factor that is hard to measure but very noticeable; this is the mutual astonishment of those who were meeting each other. 'There are people opposite with whom we can talk', was the first and overwhelming observation of each of the two parties: this discovery seemed so important to them that the Israelis even published a notice about it in their press. And close personal bonds of friendship were created between the two parties.

These parties found a common basis for agreement; we have already mentioned it. It must be said that it corresponded to the positions generally agreed worldwide for the solution of the Arab–Israeli conflict in the Middle East.

Next, the parties to the 'talks' succeeded in convincing a growing number of their respective compatriots to share their feelings and positions and there is no doubt that the number of supporters of a peaceful and realistic solution, i.e. one acceptable to the other side, was growing among the two peoples. I have mentioned the sharp rise (from 5 to 30%) in those in Israel who now accept negotiations with the PLO. There are no figures available for the Palestinians, but I can assert that, at least among the leaders, the number is growing of those who support the solutions worked out during these 'talks'.

One cannot, for example, but attribute at least partly to what he had learned from the talks, the important declaration by Yasser Arafat, on 6 April 1977, to the *Chicago Daily News*: 'I am against terrorism wherever it may hapen [which means, even in Israel], Black September is a page of history that has been finally turned.'

Is it not surprising that such a declaration (of which I have photocopies available) should have aroused such little stir?

But it is at the international level that most progress has been made. First, among figures that have been more or less closely involved in the talks: I want to mention here first and foremost Pierre Mendès-France, whose role was considerable, the Austrian Chancellor Kreisky, Presidents Senghor and Houphouët-Boigny, of whom I have already spoken, etc. The very existence of these 'talks' and the bases on which they were conducted made many people feel that something had changed, at least among the Palestinians, that made possible the solution the whole world so wanted.

Apart from the figures I have already mentioned, leading figures who now consider themselves actively involved in the talks include people like Willy Brandt, current chairman of the Socialist International, Olof Palme, former Prime Minister of Sweden, George Ball, former American under-Secretary of State, and many others.

And I want to tell you that it is precisely this factor, the impact of the talks at the international level, that was the reason for Dr Sartawi's victory over his detractors in March in Cairo (at the thirteenth PNC).

To sum up, it may be said if the Paris talks did not in the end come to anything, they nevertheless had a great impact. In Israel, on the attitude of mind of the masses; among the Palestinians, at least among their leaders; at the international level, on several eminent figures who are particularly concerned about this problem.

The impact of these contacts is often played down or presented as the result of personal initiatives by members of the PLO. The various denials by Kaddoumi,[86] Fatah,[87] even Arafat himself,[88] would appear to confirm this. Yet, in my opinion, it is not so simple. These initiatives had received the personal support of Arafat, with all the impact that this gave them, but also the limitations due to the fact that they were never to be truly endorsed by the PLO. It was one of the main auvjects of discussion at the thirteenth PNC. Sartawi was at the centre of the attacks, both from members of the Rejection Front and from the Fatah–PDFLP–Sa'iqa coalition. It was Arafat himself who came to the defence of his adviser and had him applauded by the PNC.[89]

One of the 15 points of the final resolution of the thirteenth PNC (the 15-point programme) was devoted to this problem.

> The PNC affirms the significance of establishing relations and co-ordinating with the progressive and democratic Jewish forces inside and outside the occupied homeland, since those forces are struggling against Zionism as a doctrine and practice.[90]

This restriction of contacts to Israelis struggling against Zionism looks very much like a disavowal of the Paris talks. Yet Arafat gave his blessing to their continuation (as Curiel remarks):

> through a remarkable piece of exegesis. Israelis who accepted Israeli withdrawal from the occupied territories and the establishment of a Palestinian state in these territories . . . were not to be considered Zionists.[91]

The contacts were thus maintained, but they had not been endorsed by the PNC. They therefore had to remain secret and so lose some of their impact. For its part, the Rejection Front did not even accept this formulation, since it presupposed contacts with the Israeli Communist Party, which was fighting Zionism while accepting the existence of the state of Israel. The most dramatic consequence of the thirteenth PNC was to be the first official meeting between the PLO and the Israeli Communist Party on 3 and 4 May 1977 in Prague.[92]

18. Novel Arguments

Let us now look at the main arguments developed by the advocates of dialogue with the Israelis in 1975–77, in particular on the problem of the state of Israel and its coexistence with a Palestinian state.[93]

> I should like to outline [said Hammami] what might be the future of a Palestinian state established in a part of the Palestinian homeland, and if the leadership then decided to pursue an evolutionary strategy towards its ultimate goal of a 'state in partnership'.

After mentioning the need for the new state to devote itself to the task of economic development and the progressive 'ingathering' of the refugees, Hammami came to a third task:

> We would aim to open and maintain a continuous and developing dialogue with any elements within Israel who were prepared to meet and talk with Palestinians regarding the form of a mutually acceptable coexistence which might in time develop between the two peoples living in the country to which they both lay claim . . . Within reasonable limits . . . one need not even exclude the idea of allowing Israeli Jews to live in the Palestinian state . . . provided they accepted Palestinian citizenship and provided a corresponding concession were made to enable Palestinians to go and live in Israel.

It was only then that it would be possible:

> before long to work out a form of coexistence which will enable the two peoples to live together within a reunited Palestine, while maintaining through cantonal arrangements and a constitutional division of legislative and administrative powers the distinctive character of each.

For Jiryis, future relations and the problem of a democratic state were defined even more sharply:

> Our declared aim . . . is a single state in all of Palestine. I do believe in

it, theoretically. But practically, I am against it. I would not like to see a single state now in Palestine. The reasons are very simple, connected more with us than with the Israelis. On the West Bank and the Gaza Strip the people are almost of one social class, either agricultural workers or day labourers. Even if we had a single democratic state now, the Arabs would be of a lower class attached to the Israeli economy.

This argument was the same as some 'chauvinistic' opponents had used against the democratic state slogan in 1969–70. But it was now used with a completely different meaning. Jiryis added that in 10, 15, 20 or 25 years, the Palestinians might perhaps be in a position to talk about the problem of a single state, in a situation where, obviously, there would be no more war. Jiryis did not mince words on the problem of recognition of Israel:

> Eventually, there will be recognition. Otherwise, how can the Palestinian state be established? . . . But we cannot extend complete recognition to Israel now; no Palestinian can do it and be respected. [And he concluded:] To think that a Palestinian state could continue to fight Israel after it was established is simply a joke . . . Our people know that even if they say the fighting will go on, it simply cannot be.

For Sartawi, the idea of a democratic state became simply a stage in the evolution of Palestinian political thought. He did not take it up, even as a distant dream; on the contrary, he laid stress on the declarations of Palestinian Resistance leaders which looked towards recognition of the state of Israel.

On the subject of the guarantees that would make peace in the Middle East a lasting peace, Hammami developed a line of argument that was later to be taken up by Arafat. He did not deny guarantees for Israel, indeed quite the contrary:

> As far as we are concerned, we Palestinians are ready to accept and even to demand strongly that effective guarantees be given on condition that they not be intended only for the protection of Israel but also for the Palestinian state and the other Arab neighbours of Israel.

And he added that it would be Israel that would put obstacles in the way of accepting such a solution. The Jewish state would thus have to lose its Zionist character or else resume its role as aggressor.

Hammami, remaining attached to the strategic objective, resolved the contradiction between this fact and the maintenance of a Jewish state in this way:

> Allow me to draw your attention to the fact that the situation has been seen many times before where a government, a country or a people come into being in a situation that they do not like . . . Such would be

our position faced with the present state of Israel if an agreement was reached in Geneva based on Resolution 242, which gave birth to a certain form of Palestinian national entity. The world must not expect us to approve the maintenance of the existing Zionist state. But we recognize that we shall have to live alongside it until such time as, *insh'allah*, a better basis for coexistence between our people and the Jewish people established in our land appears.

Above and beyond differences of appreciation, these three texts were at one on two essential points: recognition of the existence of an Israeli people; and *de facto* recognition of this people's right to have a state for a given time, it being possible to build the remoter future only with the agreement of both peoples. It should be observed too that none of these three texts accepted the idea of an official and formal recognition of Israel without anything in return.

I have drawn attention to these stands because they reflected the enormous distance travelled by Palestinian intellectuals and leaders since 1967. Without being dominant in the PLO, they nevertheless constituted a sign of the 'change in mentality'. If they remained vague on some aspects and not officially endorsed, this was because they constituted trial balloons sent up for the Israelis and the Americans; for them to be clarified would no doubt have required that they receive a wider response.

19. For a Palestinian State: The Thirteenth PNC

The PLO Central Council (December 1976)

During the greater part of 1975 and 1976 the PLO was involved in the Lebanese conflict. The civil war and the Syrian intervention considerably weakened the Palestinian Resistance even though, in the end, it managed to survive and maintain its political autonomy.[94] But if the conflict in Lebanon took up most of the PLO's activity it did not prevent either the launching of the Israeli–Palestinian contacts or the evolution of the PLO's political thought.

Proof of this came at the meeting of the PLO central council in Damascus from 12 to 14 December 1976. This meeting sealed the reconciliation between the Palestinian Resistance and the Ba'thist regime. A secret report by the DFLP deals with this important meeting.[95] It was held in the presence of 38 of the 42 members, the representatives of the Rejection Front having boycotted the meeting. There were three items on the agenda: Palestinian–Syrian relations; the Palestinian stand on a political solution to the Middle East crisis; and the Palestinian stand on the opportuneness of a meeting of the PNC. It was more than two years since the PNC had met.

On the problem that concerns us here — the Palestinian attitude to a political solution — the same text refers to three positions during the central council meeting: the 'defeatist' position that wanted to tie the PLO to the Arab regimes and urged the Palestinian Resistance to establish 'balanced' relations with imperialism; the 'spontaneous-mechanistic' position that wanted to confront imperialist designs on the basis of the National Charter; and the 'national revolutionary [position] represented by the DFLP and Fatah' which took account of the PLO's international successes and the development of the struggle in the occupied territories. This last position meant in particular the struggle for the PLO to be treated as the sole representative of the Palestinian people and for the establishment of an independent state.

It was the last position that carried the day. The final communiqué took note of it:

The Council has noted that the liquidation of the Israeli presence in the occupied territories and the recognition of our people's national rights, especially its right to return, to self-determination and to the establishment of an independent state on its national soil, were questions on which the international community was now unanimous, except for the Zionist enemy and its ally, the United States of America.[96]

Thus, for the first time, a text issuing from an official organ of the PLO made mention of an independent state that would not necessarily be established in the whole of Palestine. It had taken the PLO almost ten years to reach that position.

The DFLP's text also gives an interesting insight into the Syrian position. Dealing with the meeting between the central council and President Hafez al-Assad that had taken place on 13 December, the DFLP stressed that the Syrian Ba'th had not so far taken a stand supporting the establishment of an independent Palestinian state. While President Assad had made some statements tending towards this,

these do not involve a stand based on principle but a tactical policy . . . The Syrian regime could thus modify its support for the establishment of an independent Palestinian state when it deems that the international situation allows it to do so.[97]

The Palestinians' mistrust of Syria was not due solely to the role played by Damascus in the attempt to crush the Palestinian Resistance in Lebanon. The *rapprochement* under way since 1974–75 between Jordan and Syria worried the PLO all the more because calls for Jordanian–Syrian–Palestinian federation were becoming more and more numerous. It was Zuhair Mohsen, the leader of Sa'iqa and the Syrians' man, who declared at the beginning of January 1977, in answer to a question about a Palestinian state and the tripartite confederation, that 'the problem today is to liberate the territories, afterwards we shall see'. 'The objective is liberation', he said,[98] taking up the old theses of the pan-Arab nationalists, which in this case was doing no more than acting as a cloak for Syrian ambitions.

It is doubtless because of this mistrust of the Damascus regime that Arafat accepted a *rapprochement* with the regime in Amman. Attempting to play off the contradictions between Arab countries, even two allies, was an activity at which the PLO leader was a past master. A PLO delegation therefore visited Amman in February 1977[99] and Arafat met King Hussein at the first Afro–Arab Summit just before the meeting of the PNC.[100]

The Communists' Position

It was also just before the opening of the thirteenth PNC that the Jordanian Communist Party and the steering committee of the Palestinian Communist Organization in the West Bank sent a long memorandum to the members of the Palestinian assembly.[101] This document stressed the need to clarify the PLO's political programme. Of course, the ten-point programme was a major and decisive step forward, but some of these points were subject to differing interpretations. There was, the Communists observed, almost complete agreement in the PLO on the establishment of an independent Palestinian state in the territories seized from the occupation, meaning those occupied by the enemy in June 1967. After listing the advantages of such a state, the Communists touched on two controversial questions.

First, the Geneva Conference. No one could claim in advance that the conference would be a success; it was a place of confrontation. But:

> it appears incomprehensible from the political point of view, especially at the international level, that the Palestinian Resistance should still hesitate to proclaim a clear and straightforward stand ... [in relation to this conference and that it] should continue to be a prisoner down to the present day of the waiting and vague formula on this subject contained in the ten-point programme.

The PLO must lead the fight to go to Geneva in an independent delegation. Thus, unlike other forces in the Resistance, the Communists did not emphasize the political basis of the conference. They thought, no doubt correctly, that a conference in which the PLO participated could not restrict itself to discussing the 'refugee' problem.

The second question was that of the democratic and progressive forces in Israel. These forces were, directly or indirectly, a source of support for the Palestinian people. This was particularly true of the Israeli Communist Party. And they concluded that strengthening the alliance with progressive forces inside Israel, in the struggle against Zionism and imperialist-Zionist aggression, was 'a just and necessary revolutionary task'.

This formulation contains both the need for an alliance between Israeli progressive forces and the Palestinian people — a need formulated with great clarity — and the restriction of this alliance to forces fighting Zionism, which considerably reduces the impact of the slogan.

The Thirteenth PNC (March 1977)

It was in these circumstances that the thirteenth session of the PNC opened in Cairo on 12 March 1977; it was to bear the name of Kamal Jumblatt, the leader of the Lebanese National Movement, who was assassinated by Syrian agents while the PNC was sitting. The number of members of the Council had risen from 187 to 289 and, despite pressures from Damascus, the balance of power within it had not altered. Fatah remained heavily dominant. Some 50 more figures from the occupied territories had also been invited, but the Israeli military governor would not allow any leader from inside the occupied territories to go to Cairo.

Besides the problem of contacts between Israelis and Palestinians, two issues dominated the proceedings: the issue of a state and the issue of the Geneva Conference.[102] On the former, the PNC reaffirmed the decisions of the central council's December meeting. Point 11 of the programme adopted (the '15-point programme') laid down:

> The PNC has decided to continue the struggle to regain the national rights of our people, in particular their rights of return, self-determination and establishing their independent national state on their national soil.

The change compared to the twelfth PNC is striking. At the same time we may note that the West Bank and Gaza are nowhere mentioned as the 'site' of the future state. In addition, point 9 specified that recovery of the inalienable national rights of the Palestinian people must be achieved 'without any conciliation [*sulh*] or recognition [of Israel]'.

On the Geneva Conference, the last point in the declaration confirmed:

> The PLO's rights to participate independently and on an equal footing in all the conferences and international forums concerned with the Palestine issue and the Arab–Zionist conflict, with a view to achieving our inalienable national rights as approved by the UN General Assembly in 1974, namely in Resolution 3236.

While the programme and the objectives were clarified — with some limits — the leadership's room for manoeuvre was increased. As the PFLP observed in its critique of the 15-point programme,[103] there was no longer any question of the PNC meeting in extraordinary session 'if a situation arises affecting the future of the Palestinian people'; but this is what had been decided at the twelfth PNC. If Arafat did not have the full powers that he wanted — notably the power to nominate the members of the executive committee[104] — the PLO leadership did have considerable room for manoeuvre. This was increased by the reintegration of the ALF and the PFLP–GC into the executive committee after they had accepted the PLO's programme. Only the PFLP remained excluded, although it had muted its attacks on the Palestinian state — which in fact it was to endorse a few months later — and was concentrating its attacks on the Geneva Conference.[105]

Thus, after a three-year struggle, it was the 'moderates' who had won in the PLO. By agreeing to participate in the peace process and endorse the idea of a Palestinian state, the PLO appeared to be taking its full place in an international settlement. This was particularly significant as the declarations of the new American President, Jimmy Carter, on 15 March 1977, recognizing the rights of the Palestinians to a 'homeland', gave grounds for expecting an American change of course.

But in the Middle East, changes occur very fast and only a few months separate victories from defeats. Menachem Begin's victory in Tel Aviv (1976) and President Sadat's visit to Jerusalem in November 1977 pushed the PLO away from the centre of the political scene in the Middle East and the Middle East away from the prospect of an overall settlement. The attack on Lebanon was already visible on the horizon.

Notes to Part 5

1. *Al-wathaiq al-'arabiya al-filastiniya 1974* [Palestine Arab Documents], Beirut, Institute for Palestine Studies, pp. 310–15. (Henceforth cited as *PAD* with the year of reference.)

2. See in particular the notorious Egyptian–Jordanian communiqué of 18 July 1974 which observed that 'the PLO is the legitimate representative of the Palestinians, except for those Palestinians residing in the Hashemite Kingdom of Jordan', in *PAD 1974*, p. 255; also in A.Y. Yodfat and Y. Arnon-Ohanna, *PLO Strategy and Tactics*, London, Croom Helm, 1981, p. 175. See the various Palestinian reactions in *PAD 1974*, pp. 256–72.

3. *PAD 1974*, pp. 414–18.

4. Ibid., pp. 420–1.

5. 'Le peuple palestinien: Histoire d'une conscience nationale', *Le Monde Diplomatique*, January 1975.

6. *Fiches du Monde Arabe* (henceforth *FMA*), Palestiniens Fiche IP 25, 2 September 1980.

7. *Les résolutions des Nations Unies sur la Palestine et le conflit israélo-arabe 1947–1974*, Beirut, Institute for Palestine Studies, 1976, 284 pp.

8. *PAD 1974*, pp. 285–6.

9. *International Documents on Palestine 1974*, Beirut, Institute for Palestine Studies, p. 360. (Henceforth cited as *IDP* with the year of reference.)

10. Ibid., pp. 465–6.

11. *Le Monde*, 7 January 1975.

12. *IDP, 1975*, p. 168.

13. *PAD 1975*, p. 47.

14. Ibid., pp. 129–30.

15. See joint communiqué in ibid., pp. 168–9.

16. *Le Monde*, 21–22 August 1975.

17. See *ONU Chronique*, UN Information Service, vol. XIII, no. 2, February 1976, for a full report of the debate.

18. *PAD 1976*, pp. 18–19.

19. Y. Arafat, *Khitab al-akh Abu Ammar fil-majlis al-watani al-filastini fi dawratihi al-thalitha ashr* [Speech by Y. Arafat to the thirteenth session of the PNC], n.p., 1977, p. 31.

20. *FMA* IP 8, 14 November 1974.

21. DFLP, *Programme politique du DFLP*, n.p., 1975.

22. Ibid., p. 18.

23. *Al-maham al-matruha amam al-hizb al-shiyu'i al-urduni fil-marhala al-rahina* [The tasks of the Jordanian Communist Party in the present stage], n.p., May 1974.

24. Quoted in *Les communistes et la question palestinenne*, n.p., n.d.

25. *PAD 1976*, pp. 154–6.
26. Abu Iyad, *My Home, My Land: A Narrative of the Palestinian Struggle*, New York, Times Books, 1981, p. 142.
27. *PAD 1974*, pp. 248–50.
28. Statement by Yasser Arafat in ibid., p. 240.
29. Interview with Abu Ali Mustapha, assistant secretary-general of the PFLP, Beirut, May 1982, and conversations with various Palestinian leaders.
30. *PAD 1974*, pp. 263–6.
31. Ibid., pp. 273–4.
32. Ibid., pp. 282–4.
33. Ibid.
34. Interview with Abu Ali Mustapha, May 1982,
35. *PAD 1974*, pp. 344–7.
36. X. Baron, *Les Palestiniens, un peuple*, Paris, le Sycomore, 1977, p.350.
37. *PAD 1974*, pp. 413–14.
38. Ibid., p. 451. G. Habash's interview with *Le Monde*, 6 February 1975.
39. Communiqué of the tenth session of the central council of the Rejection Front, in *IDP 1976*, pp. 355–6.
40. 8 March 1975, *PAD 1975*, pp. 75–7.
41. *PAD 1976*, pp. 122–4. Speech made on 1 May 1976.
42. *Les Nouvelles de Moscou*, 1 November 1981.
43. Baron, *Les Palestiniens*, pp. 78–9.
44. *PAD 1970*, p. 209.
45. *PAD 1972*, pp. 416–18.
46. Ibid., pp. 421–2, and *Le Monde*, 30 September 1972.
47. *Le Monde*, 30 September 1972.
48. *PAD 1972*, p. 424.
49. Ibid., pp. 431–2. See also Sadat's speech of 15 October 1972, ibid., pp. 440–5, in which he denied seeking to impose his idea of a government on the Palestinians.
50. Ibid., p. 445.
51. J.W. Amos II, *Palestinian Resistance: Organisation of a Nationalist Movement*, New York, Pergamon Press, 1980, pp. 38–9.
52. *Fath-Informations*, no. 18, 1 November 1972.
53. Ibid.
54. And this was despite the fact that on several occasions Palestinian leaders had announced that the question would be raised; see for example F. Kaddoumi, *PAD 1977*, pp. 66–70.
55. 8 November 1974, *PAD 1974*, pp. 434–5.
56. See for example the declarations by Z. Mohsen, 6 January 1975, *PAD 1975*, pp. 1–4.
57. Arafat, *Khitab*, p. 51.
58. Shafiq el-Hut, in *Shu'un Filastiniya*, April 1981.
59. *PAD 1975*, pp. 57–61.
60. *PAD 1977*, pp. 33–7.
61. *Le Monde*, 7 January 1975.
62. Brian Van Arkadie, *Benefit and Burdens: A Report on the West Bank and Gaza Strip Economies since 1967*, New York, Carnegie Endowment for International Peace, 1977, pp. 153–4.
63. See also Jamil Hilal, *Al-Dhaffa al-Gharbiya: al-tarib al-ijtima'i*

wal-iqtisadi 1948-1967 [The West Bank: Social and Economic Structure], Beirut, PLO Research Centre, 1974.

64. R.J. Ward, Don Peretz and E.M. Wilson, *The Palestinian State: A Rational Approach*, 2nd edn, New York, Kennikot Press, 1977 (1st edn 1970).

65. Elias H. Tuma and Haim Darin-Drabkin, *The Economic Case for Palestine*, London, Croom Helm, 1978.

66. Tuma and Darin-Drabkin, *Economic Case*, p. 13.

67. Ibid., p. 33.

68. Ibid., p. 95.

69. Ibid., p. 44.

70. Ibid., p. 115.

71. Ibid.

72. Vivian A. Bull, *The West Bank: Is It viable?*, London and Toronto, Lexington Books, 1975.

73. Ibid., p. 152.

74. Bichara Khader and Naim Khader, *Le peuple palestinien: ses potentialités humaines, économiques et scientifiques*, Louvain, Catholic University, 1980; Emile A. Nakleh, *The West Bank and Gaza: Towards the Making of a Palestinian State*, Washington, American Enterprise Institute, 1980.

75. *Arab Thought Forum*, Jerusalem.

76. *Le Monde*, 15 May 1973.

77. *Témoignage Chrétien*, 17 February 1977.

78. *Israël et Palestine*, no. 65, January 1978.

79. Ibid.

80. *Le Monde*, 7 May 1975.

81. H. Curiel, 'Conference au Grand Orient de France', 8 June 1977, mimeo. See also *Lettre d'israël et Palestine*, no. 7, and *Le Monde*, 11 January 1977.

82. Curiel, 'Conférence', pp. 7-8.

83. Interview with *Newsweek*, 6 December 1976.

84. *Le Monde*, 6 January 1977.

85. Arafat, *Khitab*, pp. 43-6.

86. *PAD 1977*, pp. 46 and 68.

87. Ibid., p. 47.

88. Ibid., pp. 53-6.

89. Arafat, *Khitab*, pp. 46-51. Extracts from this speech in English will be found in *Israël et Palestine*, April-May 1979, no. 74.

90. *PAD 1977*, pp. 96-8. See also Yodfat and Arnon-Ohanna, PLO, p. 198.

91. Curiel, 'Conférence', p. 63.

92. Baron, *Les Palestiniens*, p. 380.

93. The three texts used are: S. Hammami, 'A Palestinian Strategy for Peaceful Co-existence', *New Outlook*, vol. 18, no. 3, March-April 1975; interview with S. Jiryis, Beirut, June 1975, in IDP 1975, pp. 424-8; and I. Sartawi, speech to the symposium 'Peace in the Middle East', held in Washington, 12 February 1977, mimeo.

94. On the events in Lebanon and Syrian-Palestinian relations see W. Khalidi, *Conflict and Violence in Lebanon: Confrontation in the Middle East*, Cambridge, Mass., Harvard University, 1980; and A.I. Dawisha, *Syria*

and the Lebanese Crisis, London, Macmillan, 1980.

95. *Premier rapport sur les derniers développements de la situation dans notre région et perspective sur l'évolution future au Moyen-Orient*, 28 January 1977, mimeo.

96. Communiqué issued at the end of the Meeting of the Palestine Central Council (Damascus, 14 December 1976) in *Documents d'Actualité Internationale*, no. 6, 1977.

97. *Premier rapport*, pp. 15–16.

98. *PAD 1977*, pp. 2–5.

99. Ibid., pp. 62–3.

100. Ibid., p. 82.

101. See the text in French in *Les communistes et la question palestinienne.*

102. For the documents adopted or proposed to the PNC see *PAD 1977*, pp. 93–104. There is a good comparison between the 15-point programme and the Rejection Front proposals in Colin Legum (ed.), *Middle East Contemporary Survey 1976–77*, New York and London, Holmes and Meier, pp. 203–5. (Henceforth cited as *MECS*.)

103. *PAD 1977*, pp. 105–9.

104. *MECS*, pp. 184–5.

105. Ibid., p. 184.

Part VI:
From Camp David to Post-Beirut and Tripoli (1977-1984)

20. Palestinian 'Autonomy' or a Palestinian State?

Sadat's Visit to Jerusalem (19 November 1977)

When President Sadat deviated from the written text of his speech to the National Assembly in Cairo on 9 November 1977, no one yet knew that one small phrase would lead to peace between Israel and Egypt, as well as to a new war in Lebanon:

> You have heard me say that I am ready to go to the ends of the earth, if that means that any of my officers or men can be spared even a wound, let alone death . . . Israel will be astonished when they hear me say now that I am ready to go to their very home, to the Knesset itself, and discuss matters with them.[1]

Yasser Arafat, who was present, and whose name was mentioned several times by Sadat in laudatory terms, was quite taken aback. Like every other Arab leader, he was in the dark; he was of course aware that there had been secret contacts between Israeli and Egyptian leaders but he knew nothing of what had transpired.[2] While the Rejection Front immediately condemned Sadat's 'treason', and the DFLP did likewise,[3] Fatah remained silent. This was first because it was wondering about the meaning of this initiative; was it a mere propaganda exercise intended to demonstrate the intransigence of Begin's Likud which had just come to power? Then, when there could no longer be any doubt, Fatah concluded that Sadat must have secured concessions during secret negotiations with the Israelis. Thus Abu Iyad, following Sadat's journey to Jerusalem on television, said:

> Sadat had spent the entire day making conciliatory gestures towards his hosts, political gestures with far-reaching consequences which I still naively believed would be compensated by equivalent concessions.[4]

The last factor inclining Arafat to prudence was the 'waiting' attitude of the Arab states: Syria, like Saudi Arabia, waited until the last moment to condemn the visit. For its part Fatah, while refusing to describe Sadat as a 'traitor', did ask the Egyptian President to reverse his decision on 17

November;[5] on 18 November the executive committee of the PLO took a similar stand.[6] But it was only after the visit to Jerusalem that the danger became clear to the Palestinian leaders. The reaction of the population of the occupied territories was significant: it had always been in favour of 'moderation', but it condemned the visit unequivocally.[7] The speech by Kaddoumi to the UN General Assembly on 28 November summarized the reservations of the majority of the PLO:[8]

1. The visit had taken place without consulting any Arab leaders; it had thus led to divisions. Morocco approved Sadat's initiative whereas Jordan hesitated. And we have seen how much importance the PLO attached to Arab unity.
2. The visit implied recognition of Israel without anything in return: Begin's response to Sadat's speech to the Knesset was a categorical 'No'.
3. Sadat's presence in Jerusalem gave backing to the Israeli determination to make it their capital, contrary to all international decisions.

For all these reasons, according to Kaddoumi, the visit would have negative consequences. It risked making the Geneva Conference irrelevant, whereas in October 1977 the USSR and the US had agreed on the early convening of this conference which would bring the belligerents together under their co-chairmanship. Some problems remained outstanding, in particular that of how the Palestinians were to be represented. But Sadat's initiative strengthened the Israeli rejection of such a conference, to which Tel Aviv had always preferred 'direct contacts'; in addition, it freed the United States from having to exert pressure on Israel. Finally, it left the USSR outside the settlement and altered the balance of forces present to the benefit of the Israelis. Kaddoumi concluded that Sadat's initiative opened the way to separate settlements. Rarely has such an analysis been so prescient.

But another problem was preoccupying Arafat: the advantage that the Rejection Front could derive from such a situation. On 21 November the PFLP demanded that 'all the Resistance movements adopt a new political programme'.[9] Habash asserted that by supporting the Geneva Conference and Hammami's and Sartawi's initiatives the PLO leadership had prepared the way for Sadat.[10] In a letter from the Rejection Front to the PLO central council it was even written that it was the PLO that had 'given its blessing to his actions from the beginning'.[11]

The Fatah central committee was itself divided: some wanted to 'radicalize' the opposition to Sadat; the DFLP distanced itself from Arafat. This represented a questioning of the majority positions taken by the PLO at the thirteenth PNC. This debate went on all through 1978, which was one of the darkest years in the history of the Resistance.

The Rejection Front's offensive was first deployed in Tripoli at the beginning of December 1977, when the Steadfastness Front was formed. The heads of state of Libya, Syria, Algeria, and the PDYR were present as well as a representative of Iraq — who was to walk out of the meeting — and the PLO organizations. President Qadhafi of Libya attempted to impose Habash on the same footing as Arafat, and some lively exchanges took place.[12] Finally, the six Palestinian organizations present adopted a communiqué[13] which endorsed reunification but on much harsher terms: rejection of Resolutions 242 and 338 and any international conference based on these two resolutions; affirmation of the right of the Palestinian people to its state 'on any part of Palestinian land' but without peace (*sulh*), recognition or negotiations.

As Hawatmeh recognized, 'Sadat's cowardice and Israel's obstinate refusal to contemplate a compromise . . . are driving us ineluctably towards the positions of our opponents in the Rejection Front.'[14] But Arafat did everything he could to avoid this happening. Throughout the period leading up to the Camp David summit in September 1978[15] — marked in particular by the invasion of Lebanon in March 1978 — Arafat's strategy developed in several directions:

1. Maintain contact with Egypt in the hope that Sadat would reap the consequences of Begin's intransigence. A leading Palestinian personality, Said Kamel, continued to stay in Cairo despite the expulsion of the PLO representatives.

2. Strengthen the links between the PLO and the inhabitants of the occupied territories; Arafat's best ally turned out to be Begin himself, since his proposals for the 'self-government' of the inhabitants of the occupied territories failed to convince even the most 'moderate'. Having said this, Arafat was fully aware of the Hashemite Kingdom's influence in the West Bank, as of Cairo's in Gaza. There was a real danger that a section of the population — even if it were a minority (we have seen in Part Two how the influence of 'traditional' leadership had been eroded) — would accept a solution that excluded the PLO.

3. Try to maintain Arab unity, without getting locked into the Steadfastness Front. Arafat needed a counterweight to Syrian and Libyan pressure; he kept his lines open to Riyadh and endeavoured to open up a dialogue with Jordan.

4. On the international level, Arafat strengthened his relations with the USSR and the socialist countries while at the same time trying to initiate a dialogue with the United States. On several occasions he declared himself in favour of the American-Soviet declaration of 1 October 1977, accepted US and Soviet guarantees for the establishment of peace[16] and even tried — without success — to open up a dialogue with the Israeli Labour opposition.[17]

Nevertheless all Arafat's efforts must not be allowed to conceal the fact that during this period the PLO had lost the political and diplomatic initiatives. Israel, on the other hand, having succeeded in freezing the Egyptian front, turned its entire military effort in the direction of southern Lebanon. Using the excuse of a PLO raid on a bus on the road to Tel Aviv — an attack which once again raises the question of the Palestinian Resistance's military strategy — Israel invaded southern Lebanon in March 1978. This large-scale operation resulted in a new exodus of people, the arrival of UN forces (UNIFIL) in the south, and Israel's control of part of this region through Major Haddad's Christian militias.

Henceforth Tel Aviv concentrated all its efforts against the PLO in Lebanon and for four years devoted itself to wearing down the Resistance, and deepening Lebanese–Palestinian contradictions, before launching the 'final offensive' in June 1982. The passivity of the Arab states, whether 'moderates' or 'progressives', at the time of the 1978 invasion, had already shown Israel how little Arab solidarity meant.

During this period, the confrontation within Fatah and the PLO assumed a new dimension, fanned by divisions in the Arab world. Iraq, in particular, launched a war of extermination against moderate cadres in Fatah, with the assassination of Said Hammami in London in January 1978, of the PLO representative in Kuwait Ali Yassin in June, and of Ezzedine Kallak, the PLO representative in Paris, in August. Baghdad relied not only on the Fateh dissident Abu Nidal (the former PLO representative in the Iraqi capital who had rejected the conclusions of the twelfth and thirteenth PNCs), but also on the atmosphere of confrontation created by the Rejection Front towards anyone suspected of wanting a negotiated solution.[18] Over several months, from April to August 1978, confrontations arose between the majority of Fatah and its 'left wing' (Abu Saleh, Abu Daoud, Naji Alush) and some supporters of Abu Nidal.[19] For the first time on such a scale, 'the criticism of weapons replaced the weapon of criticism'. The danger of a war between Palestinians was all the greater because relations between Fatah and the other organizations in the PLO had become very strained. In a memorandum on 18 May,[20] the Rejection Front, joined by the DFLP, called for the convening of the PNC, with the purpose of ratifying the Tripoli document but also of forming a new leading body, made up of the secretaries-general of all Resistance organizations and independents, which alone would be empowered to express the stand of the PLO. The aim was clear; to prevent any movement towards a negotiated solution and to call into question the predominance of Fatah and Arafat.

But the holding and results of the Begin-Carter-Sadat summit were to transform the situation completely, in Arafat's favour.

From Camp David to the Treaty of Washington: What 'Autonomy' for the Palestinians?

At the end of the marathon summit between Sadat, Begin and Carter from 5 to 17 September 1978, the Camp David framework for peace agreements were signed.[21] Essentially, they concerned peace between Egypt and Israel and the future of the West Bank and Gaza. On the basis of the principles set out, parallel negotiations were to be conducted on each of the two points.

The first ended in the signing of a peace treaty between Egypt and Israel in Washington in March 1979.[22] This provided for the complete evacuation of

Sinai in stages over three years and its partial demilitarization; the dismantlement of Israeli settlements; and the normalization of relations between the two countries, in particular the exchange of ambassadors after the first stage of the withdrawal (planned for the beginning of 1980). This agreement was to be scrupulously respected; the only breach was to come from the UN's refusal to participate in a buffer force in Sinai. It was a multinational, essentially American, force that was to take on this task.

This indeed represented a total peace between the two countries and a separate peace, despite declarations by Egyptian leaders on the 'linkage' between negotiations on the future of the occupied territories and negotiations on relations between Egypt and the Jewish state. By signing the treaty of Washington, Cairo was deprived of the only trump card it could use to put pressure on Begin. The Israeli government used the ambiguities of the texts of the Camp David agreements on Gaza and the West Bank, and its power, to give away nothing on the second aspect of the negotiations.

As to this second point (the future of the West Bank and Gaza), the Camp David framework for peace agreements, confirmed by the treaty of Washington, envisaged a five-year transitional period during which 'full autonomy' would be granted to the inhabitants of the occupied territories. In addition, 'the Israeli military government and its civilian administration will be withdrawn as soon as a self-governing authority has been freely elected by the inhabitants of these areas'. To achieve this result, 'Egypt, Israel and Jordan will agree on the modalities for establishing the elected self-governing authority.' The Palestinians in the West Bank and Gaza would be able to be part of the delegations of Egypt or Jordan, on condition that all the parties (including Israel) agreed. As soon as the elections were held, some Israeli forces would withdraw from the occupied territories, and the rest would be redeployed.

Three years from the beginning of the transitional period (that is, from the election of the self-governing authority) negotiations would take place on the future of the occupied territories. Finally, the settlement would have to take account of 'the legitimate rights of the Palestinian people and their just requirements'. In a clarifying letter appended to the treaty, Carter spelled out to Begin that he had been informed that wherever 'Palestinians' or 'Palestinian people' were mentioned, the Israeli Prime Minister 'construes and understands [this] as "Palestinian Arabs"' (in short he rejected the notion of a people).

Key questions remained unsettled:[23] the refugee problem (their return being subject to agreement with Israel), the status of Jerusalem, the role of Jordan which had not been consulted,[24] and so on. Still more serious, the most basic question remained pending, the issue of a Palestinian state: could the proposed self-government lead, as some analysts at the time suggested, to self-determination? Certainly, the texts were ambiguous and various interpretations were always possible. But the Begin government's stand left no room for illusion: from the very beginning, Begin announced that he would claim sovereignty over the West Bank and Gaza at the end of the five-year transition period, and would refuse a return to the 1967 borders and the return of Arab Jerusalem, as well as any idea of a Palestinian state.

Moreover, the ambiguity over Israel's right to establish settlements in the occupied territories was resolved on the ground: from 1979 the government launched a settlement campaign on an unprecedented scale which aimed at altering the demographic characteristics of the West Bank (see below). Finally, the fact that Egypt had to wait three years for the evacuation of Sinai meant that it could no longer exert any pressure on Tel Aviv. All the Israelis then had to do was to impose their version of what autonomy meant:[25] the Israeli state would be responsible for internal security, all crown lands and water distribution; the settlers and settlements would come under its sole authority; it would also control the posts and telecommunications, exports and imports, travel to Arab countries, remittances of funds, and so on. It is thus not surprising that the negotiations on autonomy should have failed despite American efforts both before and after the death of President Sadat.

The most clear-cut opposition to the agreements came from the inhabitants of the occupied territories themselves. The announcement of the signing of the agreements was met with an uprising. On 1 October 1978 a national Congress attended by 150 West Bank figures and political representatives met 'officially to give Begin, Carter and Sadat a definite response: an absolute rejection and a formal condemnation of the Camp David agreements'.[26] On 20 October, a Congress of the same type met in Gaza and launched the same slogan, 'No to self-government, yes to the PLO'. In March 1979, during the Washington meeting, a new uprising engulfed the West Bank.[27] There was no room for any doubt about the feelings of the Palestinians inside the occupied territories.

The PLO, too, rejected the agreements absolutely and categorically,[28] whereas the Arab Summit, meeting in Baghdad in November 1978, marked a distinct evolution even though the summit rejected the results of Camp David. Striking a note of resolute optimism, the summit called for the evacuation of the territories occupied in 1967, including Jerusalem, and recognition of the Palestinians' right to a state: this meant *de facto* recognition of the state of Israel. The PLO was confirmed as the sole representative of the Palestinian people and considerable financial aid was allocated for the Palestinians and the front-line countries. The sanctions planned against Egypt were conditional: they would only be implemented in the event of a peace treaty being signed between Cairo and Tel Aviv. In April 1979, however, a distinct hardening of the whole of the Arab world was perceptible; the Arab countries broke their relations with Egypt, and decided on an economic boycott of Egypt and the transfer of the Arab League headquarters to Tunis. For Arafat the most important fact was the broad unity of the Arabs marked by the reconciliation between Damascus and Baghdad; the beginning of a *rapprochement* between the PLO and Jordan was one of the positive consequences.

It was against this background of unity restored and the growing isolation of Egypt that the fourteenth session of the PNC opened in Damascus in January 1979. The resolutions adopted confirmed the Palestinian Resistance's total opposition to the Camp David agreements and the unity of the PLO organizations.[29] The Rejection Front's hopes of 'destabilizing' Arafat turned out to be baseless. However, differences over the distribution of seats in the executive committee and over the management of the Arab Solidarity Fund cut short the work of the Council and led to the reappointment, unchanged, of the outgoing executive committee.

The debate on strategic options — especially a state — that had marked the thirteenth PNC had given way to opposition to Camp David. What was really happening was that the PLO was losing the political initiative; a peace process was underway from which it was excluded and so long as the United States, Egypt and Israel were 'caught up' in Camp David, it was essential for the PLO to preserve its unity and its international audience. Arafat tackled this successfully; but it was not until 1982 that an alternative to Camp David relaunched the strategic debate within the PLO.

The PLO's Diplomatic Counter-Offensive

After Camp David the most important, if not the most spectacular, aspect of Palestinian diplomacy was the drawing closer to Amman. The aim was to strengthen Jordan's opposition to Camp David as well as to strengthen the struggle in the occupied territories where King Hussein still retained some influence. The dialogue was not an easy one: on one side, Arafat was subjected to the PFLP's overbidding; on the other, King Hussein stubbornly refused to open up the Jordanian front to the Palestinian commandos, which was a *sine qua non* for a section of the Palestinian Resistance. It took several visits by Arafat to Jordan, at the end of 1978, to sort out the differences and enable the Jordanian — Palestinian committee to get down to the job of managing the $150 million fund allocated to the occupied territories by the Baghdad summit. This alliance survived the breach between Amman and Damascus in 1980 and the walk-out of all the Palestinian organizations except Fatah from the Jordanian-Palestinian committee. After the events in Beirut, this Jordanian-Palestinian co-ordination became one of the key factors in the future of the Middle East.

Western Europe was the second target of Arafat's diplomatic offensive, despite the rather postitive welcome it had given to the Camp David agreements. In July 1979 Arafat met Chancellor Kreisky and the chairman of the Socialist International Willy Brandt, in Vienna; he was later received in Lisbon, Ankara and Madrid. In the same year, the EEC for the first time recognized that the PLO was one of the 'parties concerned' by the settlement of the Middle East conflict; in June 1980 the Venice Declaration confirmed the EEC's stand. The PLO's breakthrough in Europe continued into 1982: PLO offices were opened in Finland and Ireland; Vienna raised the PLO's representation to ambassadorial level; Papandreou's Greece followed its example and Arafat was received in Athens. But there was one dark spot: the refusal of the EEC to recognize the PLO as the sole representative of the Palestinians, and one worry: the ambiguous stand of the new government of the left in Paris illustrated by President Mitterrand's visit to Israel in March 1982.

This breakthrough in Europe took place against an international background that was favourable to the PLO. Arafat was welcomed in New Delhi and Tokyo; in 1979, the PLO participated for the first time in the work of the UN Security Council; in 1981 the socialist states granted the PLO's representation diplomatic status.

These successes went hand-in-hand with the maintenance of 'realistic' stands. Without in any way modifying what the last PNC's resolutions had affirmed (from this point of view, the fifteenth PNC held in Damascus in the spring of 1980 brought nothing new), the PLO reiterated its readiness to negotiate, whether at the meeting between Arafat, Kreisky and Brandt[30] or in numerous statements by its chairman.[31] Arafat repeated again and again that the PLO's aim was not to destroy Israel but to establish an 'independent state in every inch of Palestinian land from which the Israelis withdraw', a formula which, significantly, had replaced that of the 'democratic state'.[32] Contact was maintained with the peace forces in Israel, at a colloquium in Rome in September 1979, and again in September 1980 through a meeting between Arafat and two Israeli deputies, the Communist T. Toubi and C. Bitton. However, the impact of the meetings with Zionist figures was reduced by the fact that the PLO refused to make them official (see Part Five).

Israel's growing isolation seemed to make little difference. Convinced of the extraordinary advantages gained from peace with Egypt, and assured of the total support of the United States which, after the fall of the Shah of Iran, was developing a strategy of direct intervention in the Middle East, the Israeli government stepped up the number of *faits accomplis*: in July 1980 Jerusalem was 'reunited' and confirmed as the capital of Israel; at the end of 1981 the Syrian Golan Heights were annexed, despite protests and international disapproval. But it was in the occupied territories that the full scale of this policy was seen.

Struggle in the Occupied Territories

From 1979 the West Bank and Gaza were to be the main focus of the Israeli-Palestinian confrontation. For the Begin government, settlement had to be stepped up, the influence of the PLO broken and 'autonomy' introduced. The Palestinians, on the other hand, felt they had to make the Camp David agreements collapse and keep open the chances of the establishment of an independent state.

The Palestinian national movement, organized around the mayors and municipalities elected in 1976, underwent considerable expansion.[33] The

Camp David agreements and the treaty of Washington provoked numerous and massive demonstrations. A committee of national guidance composed of West Bank mayors and leading figures orchestrated resistance to the occupation. Several dates mark the long struggle between the Israeli government and the national movement. At the end of 1979 the mayor of Nablus, Bassam Shakaa, was arrested and threatened with deportation. In April 1980 there was a popular uprising in the West Bank. In May and June 1980, after an attack that cost the lives of six Israeli settlers, the mayors of Hebron and Halhul were deported. Then three attacks were made simultaneously on Shakaa, who had to have both legs amputated, Karim Khalaf, the mayor of Ramallah, who lost a foot, and Ibrahim Tawil, the mayor of El Bireh, the only one to escape unharmed. In November 1980 there was a new uprising in the occupied territories. When, during the summer of 1981, the new Begin government took office and Ariel Sharon became Minister of Defence and thus responsible for the occupied territories, the political balance-sheet was largely favourable to the Palestinians.

The occupying power had been unable to break the influence of the PLO or to find an 'alternative' leadership capable of participating in negotations on self-government. From this point of view, the maintenance of the alliance between the PLO and King Hussein had undeniably had positive effects in the occupied territories.

Faced with this situation, the Begin government reacted, in the spring of 1982, by setting up a 'civil administration' in the occupied territories to replace the 'military administration' — the latter being synonymous with occupation. In fact the Tel Aviv government was taking a step further towards annexation. It wanted to 'normalize', in every sense of the word, the situation in the occupied territories. Menachem Milson, the head of the civil administration, did not conceal the purpose of his mission: for Israel to wage a decisive campaign against the PLO. Throughout March and April 1982 an insurrection on an unprecedented scale mobilized the Palestinian population of the occupied territories against the new 'administration'.

Some 30 young Palestinians were killed. The National Guidance Committee was dissolved, and a dozen mayors were removed, including Rashad Shawa, the 'moderate' mayor of Gaza. The main Palestinian leaders were put under house arrest. This offensive went hand-in-hand with the extension of the powers of the Village Leagues, set up by the Israelis, whose members were 'collaborators'. Despite the fact that they had little influence, they were given the powers previously enjoyed by the municipalities. They also acted as auxiliaries, not hesitating to break up demonstrations, alongside the settlers and the army. This no doubt was the sort of interlocutor that Begin was seeking in order to implement self-government.

At the end of this period of violent confrontations, it was clear that the Palestinians and the PLO had paid a heavy price: they had lost a vital base of support with the municipalities. Yet Begin had not succeeded in undermining the PLO's political influence and even less in promoting the emergence of a new leadership of 'collaborators'. And by invading Lebanon in June 1982, Begin was trying to liquidate the influence of the PLO in the occupied territories by liquidating it militarily in its sanctuary in Lebanon.

The fact was that the Palestinians in the occuped territories saw the PLO undeniably as *their* organization. This was shown by the 1976 elections and by various surveys carried out on the eve of the war in Lebanon,[34] although the forms of political organization and the balance of power were very different from what they were in Beirut; it was not without contradictions and some mistrust.

The PLO in Beirut had no wish to see installed a leadership of the occupied territories that was truly capable of carrying on the struggle. Most organizations — and Fatah in particular — lacked a centralized leadership in the occupied territories, which led to problems of co-ordination. The only political force that was organized and accustomed to clandestinity was the Communist Party. Originally organized in the Jordanian Communist Party and later in the Palestinian Communist Organization in the West Bank (still under the authority of the Jordanian Communist Party), the Communists had just, after a long internal debate within the Jordanian Communist Party and a party crisis, formed themselves into the Palestinian Communist Party at the beginning of 1982. As the only organization with a leadership inside the occupied territories, and being influential in the mass organizations and trade unions, the Palestinian Communist Party was a decisive force in the occupied territories whereas it was weak in Beirut. This situation fuelled Fatah's suspicions of the PNF[35] and all the unitary structures in the occupied territories in which the Communists played a major role.

Fatah even reached the point of precipitating a split in the trade union movement and directing PLO financial aid to 'reliable people'. This situation, which was already very harmful in the context of the upsurge of the national movement, risks becoming disastrous today, with the repression and the unprecedented extension of the settlement policy.

In Part Two we discussed Israeli settlement and confiscation of land. With the fall of the Labour government in 1977, a first stage came to an end.[36] Some 50 settlements had been established in the West Bank (including East Jerusalem); they had 3,500 to 4,000 residents, to whom must be added the 45–50,000 settled in Jerusalem. This post-1967 colonization (especially when compared to the Zionist colonization of the 1930s and 40s), was marked by the absence of ideological motivation; only fanatical supporters of Eretz Israel moved to the settlements (which are no more than fortified camps, with no real economic activity). Conversely, and for purely material reasons, many Israelis settled in the new buildings around Jerusalem. That did not prevent the Labour government confiscating lands and taking control of water supplies. But with the coming to power of the Likud, colonization was stepped up, basing itself on extreme right groups such as Gush Emunim. Today 25,000 settlers live in 'Judaea and Samaria' and 80,000 around Jerusalem. According to Jewish Agency figures,[37] between 1977 and 1982, 81 settlements were established in the West Bank and 9 in Gaza (as against 2 under the Labour government); this has been accompanied by the confiscation of 40–50% of the land in the West Bank and the construction of settlements on the outskirts of, or even in, Arab villages.

In 1985, the number of settlers in the West Bank reached 50,000. This total was achieved thanks to a building programme offering exceptionally attractive financial terms, aimed at that part of the Israeli population which finds it hard to get housing in Israel proper. Improvements to the road network, and the small distances, facilitate commuting between homes and places of work. This development has not been halted by the partial freeze on the construction of new settlements: expansion of existing settlements is sufficient to ensure a certain rate of growth in the Jewish population of 'Judea and Samaria'.

The Fahd Plan: a Missed Opportunity?

At a press conference in Riyadh on 7 August 1981 Crown Prince Fahd of Saudi Arabia put forward a plan which was to bear his name.[39] It included eight points which may be summarized thus: withdrawal by Israel from all territory occupied in 1967, including Arab Jerusalem; and a UN trusteeship over the West Bank and Gaza Strip for a transitional period not exceeding a few months, followed by the establishment of an independent Palestinian state with Jerusalem as its capital.

Point 7, the most controversial one, envisaged that 'all states in the region should be able to live in peace'. Finally, the implementation of the principles outlined would be guaranteed by the UN or member states of the UN. These proposals took up the relevant UN resolutions; they were not new, but the fact that the autonomy negotiations had got bogged down, the assassination of President Sadat on 6 October 1981 and the prospect of the total evacuation of Sinai on 26 April 1982 posed the 'post-Camp David' problem and put these proposals in the forefront of current affairs.

The Israeli raid on the nuclear power station in Iraq in June 1981, and the Israeli–Palestinian war on the Lebanese border during the summer, helped convince the Saudi leaders of the urgency of relaunching an Arab initiative. This was also, it seems, the opinion of Arafat, who is believed to have taken part in drawing up the plan. To understand fully what was at stake in the debate, it must be remembered that Begin rejected the plan outright — and was supported in doing so by a large section of the Labour Party — and that the American position was one that wanted to reduce it to a continuation of the Camp David process.

The debate took place in October and November 1981 in the run-up to the Arab Summit in Fez, at which the Saudis hoped to present their plan. The internal debate within the PLO was influenced by the stand of the Arab countries, which were generally favourable to the plan, with the exception of the states in the Steadfastness Front. This time the rejection movement was largely organized by Syria. Damascus's opposition was determined less by the content of the plan than by the context. Relations between the PLO and Syria — over which hovered the bitter memory of the Syrian intervention against the Palestinian Resistance in Lebanon in 1976 — had again deteriorated over the previous months: President Assad accused Arafat of promoting a plan on which he had not been consulted and which would tend to leave Syria outside a settlement.

Damascus therefore went all out against the Palestinian leader, and the pressures were stepped up. The dissident Abu Nidal, who had taken refuge in the Syrian capital (after a stay in Baghdad) increased attacks on Palestinian cadres deemed to be 'moderate'. The Palestinian organizations tributary to Damascus — with Sa'iqa in the lead — launched themselves into the debate, denouncing the illusions of those who were thinking 'of the possibility of establishing a Palestinian state in the West Bank and Gaza'.[40] The Rejection Front, which had in theory been disbanded, rejected a plan which recognized 'the Zionist entity' and in which it saw a repetition of Camp David. The argument of the DFLP — which since 1977 had moved away from Fatah and was hoping to become the left alternative to Arafat — was not much different. Hawatmeh's movement criticized the Fahd Plan for continuing Camp David under the patronage of Saudi Arabia, Egypt being — after Sadat's death — temporarily out of the picture. For the DFLP, moreover, this plan made no mention of the PLO and, above all, proposed the recognition of Israel with nothing in return.

Within Fatah itself, the plan met widespread hostility, whereas Arafat was making frequent favourable statements.[41] Opposition was expressed through the voice of Kaddoumi, head of the PLO political department, and hitherto very close to Arafat.[42] In his view, the circumstances were not propitious for a peaceful solution (but when had they been since 1967?). What was required was to alter the balance of power by bringing Egypt back into the Arab camp (for Kaddoumi, the Mubarak regime was only a 'transitional' regime). Finally, it must 'be clear to everybody that we, as Palestinians . . . , categorically reject [point 7]. This position is not negotiable.'

It was this point of view that prevailed in the executive committee, where Arafat found himself totally isolated.[43] The PLO went on to work very actively to make the Fahd Plan fail at the Fez Summit, whose proceedings were adjourned *sine die*.

Thus, once again, the PLO deemed that it was necessary to make haste slowly. We are ready to accept the plan, said Abu Iyad, on condition that the United States endorses it 'unreservedly';[44] put clearly, the PLO did not want to take any initiative and was waiting for its opponents to make 'a gesture'. Once again, the nature of the PLO as a 'reactive' organization was confirmed. And once again it was to pay for it very dearly.

The Israeli leaders, relieved by the failure of the Fahd Plan, made active preparations for the invasion of Lebanon; in early 1982 they were given the 'green light' by Washington. The stage was set for war and a new disaster for the Palestinians. Only Arafat, who saw the tragedy coming, stepped up his appeals for a plan that both the PLO and Begin had rejected.[45]

21. After Beirut

'Peace in Galilee'

At dawn on 6 June, exactly 15 years and one day after the 1967 war, Israeli tanks rolled into southern Lebanon. The declared aim was, as the name of the operation indicated, to restore 'peace in Galilee', and to remove the threat of 'Palestinian guns' hanging over northern Israel. In fact, this was an excuse: the Israeli–Lebanese border had been quite peaceful since the ceasefire reached between the PLO and Tel Aviv in July 1981. In a year the truce had been broken only twice after an Israeli attack. The true aim of the Begin government was threefold:

1) Destroy the Palestine Liberation Organization: that is, not merely to break the military potential of the PLO such as it had developed in southern Lebanon, but above all to dismantle the whole administrative and political apparatus established in Lebanon. Tel Aviv hoped, through this operation, to strike a decisive blow at the international standing of the PLO and weaken the resistance of the Palestinians in the West Bank and Gaza who had already been shaken by the confrontations of the Spring of 1982.

2) Block the whole peace process: the Israeli withdrawal from Sinai and its return to Egypt on 26 April 1982 brought the Palestinian question to the forefront. Plans had been put forward to replace the Camp David process, notably those of Prince Fahd, who had since become the ruler of Saudi Arabia. In addition, since Sadat's assassination, relations between Cairo and Tel Aviv had become strained. President Mubarak had not accepted the holding of a three-power summit meeting, with Begin and Reagan, on Palestinian 'self-government'. This situation made the Israeli government fear that strong pressure would be exerted on it to withdraw from the occupied territories. From this point of view therefore, the occupation of part of Lebanon has a double advantage. First, to give comfort to all those in the Arab world who think peace with Israel is impossible; and thus maintain the Jewish state in the state of permanent war that helps to unite the people and justify all annexations. Secondly, to make the territories occupied in Lebanon the subject of diplomatic talks over the next few years, which will allow the Israeli leaders during this time to step up the colonization of the

West Bank and Gaza and create irreversible *faits accomplis*.
3) Make Lebanon swing over to the Israeli side; for Begin, the aim of imposing a strong government capable of making peace with Israel in Beirut and designs on southern Lebanon and the waters of the Litani river was mixed up contradictarily with the partition of the country.

How the war went is well known. In eight days, Israeli troops, with Reagan's full support, were at the gates of Beirut, having met only sporadic and poorly organized resistance. The ceasefire, signed with Syria on 11 June, enabled Tashal to concentrate its force on Beirut. For three months, the joint Lebanese-Palestinian forces, under Arafat's personal leadership, resisted a deluge of fire and bombs. The PLO was not hoping to drive this formidable army back, but to resist being crushed and attempt to capitalize on international political and diplomatic support.

In mid-August, international pressure and the parallel interventions of the French and American governments led to a disengagement agreement under the supervision of a multinational force. On 21 August, the first Palestinian fighters left the Lebanese capital, followed by Yasser Arafat on 30 August; on 1 September the evacuation of Beirut by the PLO was complete.

A page of Palestinian history, opened in 1968–70, was turned. But, those who had believed that the presence of the Palestinians was the cause of the Lebanese crisis were to be quickly disappointed. Neither Amin Gemayel's election to the presidency — after his brother's assassination — nor the establishment of a Phalangist state, have settled the problems of Lebanon: confessional and political confrontations have become more numerous; and the country remains divided.

But there has been a major change in the situation of the 300,000 or 400,000 Palestinian civilians: left without protection, they are at the mercy of all the revenge-seekers, of every extraction, as was seen in the massacres of Sabra and Shatila.

The PLO After Beirut: A New Deal

At the end of the siege of Beirut, the PLO found itself in a radically new situation which was to make a profound impact on the internal debate: its whole strategy was being called into question, while the old behaviour remained, and the language of the various protagonists remained unchanged. Whether or not the PLO leadership was aware of it, the page opened after June 1967 had come to an end; another was beginning, whose contents would depend on the ability of the PLO to play the cards it had accumulated over 15 years.

After the disappearance of the Palestinian armed presence from southern Lebanon and Beirut, it was the very idea of 'armed struggle', one of the foundation 'myths' of the PLO after 1967, that was called into question. The battle of Karameh, in March 1968, had made possible the decisive development of the Palestinian Resistance by arousing the enthusiasm of the Arab masses and the massive enrolment of young Palestinians in the fedayeen organizations. Despite the loss of its Jordanian bases, in 1970-71, the PLO still had — in its various components — 25,000 to 30,000 men, mostly concentrated in Lebanon. While the effectiveness of this army against the Israeli war machine turned out to be very low after 1970, the presence of combatants on the 'enemy's' borders, the participation in the Lebanese civil war and the fight against the Phalangists had helped to keep up the mobilization and the mystique of the armed struggle.

The presence of these military forces made the PLO a necessary party to any settlement in Lebanon and gave it a degree of political autonomy. In 1982, all that disappeared: the bulk of the PLO's forces is scattered in nine Arab countries, far from the 'battlefield'; the few thousand men concentrated in the Bekaa valley are under Syrian control. This loss may well reduce its diplomatic weight and lessen the attraction it has for the younger generation of Palestinians, especially those in the camps.

But the Israeli invasion also destroyed the PLO's politico-administrative apparatus; for the Palestinian Resistance had concentrated a virtual state apparatus in Lebanon, with medical, social, administrative, craft and industrial sectors. Beirut had become a Palestinian centre, where leaders could meet, hold discussions and receive foreign visitors. From the point of view of the Palestinian struggle, this presence was not all positive; 'establishment' in the Lebanese capital assumed, for a section of the PLO bureaucracy, a permanent character; in Beirut one could 'wait' — wait for the total liberation of Palestine, wait for the 'Arab revolution' . But this did not make the departure from Beirut any less serious, and the PLO leaders, like their troops, had to disperse. Unable to establish himself in Damascus, where the Syrian grip was too strong, Arafat now has to commute between Tunis and the various Arab capitals. This dispersal may well hinder the political and diplomatic effectiveness of the PLO.

But an even more serious problem is that the Resistance leadership is now physically cut off from the bulk of the Palestinian people. Having evacuated Beirut — and all of southern Lebanon — the PLO has lost contact with the last major segment of the Palestinian people (300,000 to 400,000 people) who had previously provided it with many of its fighters and numerous cadres.

On the Arab level, the balance-sheet of the latest events is less negative: Arafat, haloed by his three-month-long resistance in Beirut, and faced with the inertia of the Arab states, has been able to have the PLO's position as the sole representative of the Palestinian people confirmed, and impose a consensus around the Fez plan (see below). His room for manoeuvre, first and foremost *vis-à-vis* the Arab regimes and Syria — has increased; the *rapprochement* with Jordan, and Egypt's return to the Arab stage, are the first signs of this.

On the international stage, Israel is increasingly isolated: Western public opinion was moved by the ferocity of the siege of Beirut but that was not translated into a decisive gain for the PLO: neither the United States – which still refuses to talk to the PLO – nor the West European countries – which still deny it formal recognition – have moved significantly.

In Israel itself, and for the first time during a war, a broad movement has developed against the government's policy; certainly, we are still a long way from having a dialogue with the PLO, and this first serious crack in the compact edifice of Israeli good conscience can only be widened if the Palestinian leadership knows how to exploit it.

This situation, which is a difficult one on the ground, is accompanied by an international balance of power, marked in the Middle East by a growth in the influence of the United States and the sidelining of the USSR.

After Beirut, Arafat's room for manoeuvre has thus been considerably narrowed at the very time when the urgency of the situation demands that he step up his initiatives and use all the trumps he still holds.

The Reagan Plan, the Fez Plan or Total Rejection

The debate got underway during the siege of Beirut, at a time when the question before the PLO was one of its survival, evacuation of the Lebanese capital and the political gains to be made from its long resistance. From this time, Arafat made more and more statements and 'openings'. He welcomed the statement by Mendès-France, Goldman and Klutznick calling for a political agreement between Israeli and Palestinian nationalisms, as 'a positive initiative towards a just and durable peace in the Middle East'. He accepted the Franco-Egyptian working paper, put forward at the UN, which called for mutual Israeli–Palestinian recognition. He gave a long interview to Uri Avneri who is not only a journalist but also an Israeli politician, and a Zionist.

Finally, around the UN resolutions Arafat adumbrated the concessions he thought would facilitate a dialogue with the United States. On 22 July, the Palestinian news agency Wafa published a long statement[46] in which it was said that the PLO accepted UN resolutions and particularly General Assembly Resolution 181, the notorious 1947 plan for the partition of Palestine into two states. On 25 July, in a document handed to the American congressman MacCluskey, Arafat affirmed that he 'accepts all the UN resolutions concerning the Palestinian question'. A long polemic ensued as to whether or not these included Resolution 242.

Arafat explained his position at length to the Israeli journalist Amnon Kapeliouk:

> In 1977, the Carter administration suggested to us that we accept this resolution. While making clear our reservations about this, we had accepted the proposal on three conditions: the opening of a dialogue between the United Nations [sic! in fact the United States] and the PLO; recognition of the rights of Palestinians to self-determination; and establishment of an independent Palestinian state. I hardly need to

say that the dialogue was broken off . . .

The same sequence of events was repeated in Beirut in 1982. Arafat's openings were met with American 'gestures', which themselves were supposed to lead the chairman of the PLO to 'clarify' his stand. But Washington did not move. The Palestinian initiative hung fire and the PLO left Beirut without even the beginning of a dialogue with Washington getting underway.

The debate within a traumatized PLO, which had just left Beirut, crystallized very rapidly around the various peace proposals. On 1 September 1982, in a long speech, President Reagan laid out the American options to achieve peace in the Middle East:

- Autonomy for the Palestinians in the West Bank and Gaza, as outlined in the Camp David agreements and for a limited period. In this context, the United States disapproves of the establishment of any new Israeli settlements in the occupied territories.
- At the end of the transitional period there can be neither the formation of an independent Palestinian state nor Israeli sovereignty over the occupied territories. The best form would be 'self-government by the Palestinians of the West Bank and Gaza in association with Jordan'.
- Resolution 242 must be applied to all fronts, including the West Bank and Gaza. Israel must therefore withdraw from the occupied territories in exchange for peace.
- The city of Jerusalem 'must remain undivided, but its final status should be decided through negotiations.'

These proposals, which are not a plan in the true meaning of the word, were made public a few days before the Arab summit in Fez. This summit, attended by all the Arab governments, except Egypt and Libya, in turn, on 9 September, adopted a plan which took up the main lines of the Saudi proposals of 1981, recognized the PLO as the 'sole and legitimate representative' of the Palestinian people and envisaged a Security Council guarantee of the implementation of the principles laid down. Point 7 envisaged: 'the drawing up by the Security Council of guarantees for peace for all the states of the region, including the independent Palestinian state.'

For the first time the Arab world as a whole – and the PLO – accepted in such a clear manner a formula guaranteeing the right of all the states of the region – and Israel – to peace. This precipitated a split in the Palestinian delegation, three members of which – Ahmed al Yamani, a member of the political bureau of the PFLP and a member of the executive committee of the PLO, Talal Naji, assistant secretary-general of the PFLP-GC and a member of the executive committee, and Nimr Saleh (Abu Saleh) a member of the central committee of Fatah – adopted the following communique:

> As members of the PLO delegation . . . we declare our rejection of Point 7 of the Summit resolution . . . The text in fact envisages that the Security Council guarantees peace among all the states of the

region, including the Palestinian state. We see this statement as a flagrant violation of the resolutions of the PNC and a concession to the enemy in exchange for illusory promises . . . We declare our total rejection of this point and proclaim that it in no way represents our position on the subject . . .

A few days later, four organizations, Sa'iqa, the PFLP, the PFLP-GC and the PPSF adopted a similar joint position. They were backed by Abu Saleh of Fatah. The debate was launched, and it bore on two particular points: 1) whether or not to accept point 7 of the Fez plan; 2) attitude to the Reagan plan, in particular to the need for a Jordanian–Palestinian *rapprochement*.

This debate was to overshadow all the rest, notably the one started in September-October on 'mutual recognition' between Israel and the PLO. The secretary-general of the DFLP had even let it be known that he would put down a motion at the PNC on this question.[47] In January 1983, Yasser Arafat explained that 'mutual recognition' was not a live issue since 'Begin himself has said, more than once, I do not need the Palestinian recognition of Israel'[48] and that this recognition would not lead to any change on the part of the Israeli government. In these circumstances, thought the Palestinian leaders, their acceptance of the principle of 'mutual recognition' would be a one-sided gesture.

Towards a Jordanian–Palestinian Confederation?

Arafat's reaction to the Reagan plan was cautious, and took account of the post-Beirut balance of forces. In an 'Address to the Nations of the World' at the end of November the PLO leader explained his stand:

> It is our right . . . to regard the plan declared by the US President Reagan . . . as not containing any new meaning as long as it is not accompanied by any practical steps to exert pressure on Begin's government which would then make it possible to say that it carries within it something new and credible.[49]

A similar stand was taken by the central council of the PLO meeting on 26 November, which

> . . . expressed the view that the Reagan plan does not fulfil the inalienable rights of our people under the leadership of the PLO because the Reagan plan ignores the right of self-determination for our Palestinian people and the establishment of an independent Palestinian state under PLO leadership.[50]

Starting from this carefully balanced position, Yasser Arafat went on to deploy intense activity directed towards Amman, with a dual goal: to prevent the Hashemite regime embarking on separate negotiations with the United States; and to attempt to initiate a dialogue with the United States and assess the extent of its commitment to the Begin government.

A play with three actors was under way: Arafat, Hussein and Reagan. The initial positions of the Palestinian leader were: yes to the establishment of a Jordanian-Palestinian confederation, but *after* the establishment of a Palestinian state; no to any delegation of power during the negotiations.[51]

No doubt the Palestinian leader saw this position as negotiable, but that would depend on Reagan's attitude. But Hussein's visit to Washington in January 1983 did not produce any new element. Arafat declared that, unlike the Jordanian monarch, who had informed him of the results, he was not optimistic.[52] He therefore stood by the two abovementioned great principles, the more so as he was the object of intense pressure, both internal and external. The Syrian government stepped up its attacks on the PLO leader and even questioned his legitimacy. They would not accept the *rapprochement* between the PLO and the Hashemite monarch (who supported Iraq), nor the autonomy of the Palestinian leadership. Qadhafi went one step ahead of them, accusing Arafat of treason, when he, Qadhafi, had not budged throughout the siege of Beirut, except to call on the Palestinian leaders to 'commit suicide'. These two Arab capitals manipulated most of the small organizations: Sa'iqa, PFLP-GC, PPSF, and so on. Only the ALF dissociated itself from them, reflecting the Arafat–Baghdad *rapprochement*.

The Sixteenth PNC: 14–21 February 1983

The sixteenth session of the Palestinian assembly, meeting six months after the Lebanon war, was held in Algiers: the choice of this capital symbolized the Palestinians' determination to escape from interference from certain quarters (especially from Syria) but also the removal of the PLO leadership from the 'battlefield'.

The run-up to the sixteenth PNC was quite similar to the one we studied in detail for the twelfth PNC; but with one major difference that few observers have noted. The leadership, of whatever tendency, decided not to adopt a new political programme (as had been done by the twelfth and thirteenth PNCs) but to content themselves with a 'political declaration' (as the fourteenth and fifteenth sessions had done) of a more limited import.

This decision may seem surprising after the turning-point of the PLO's departure from Beirut; but it is in the logic of what has prevailed in the Palestinian Resistance on various occasions. In 1974 and 1977, a prospect of peace appeared in the Middle East; the PLO, therefore, attempted to find a place in it by adopting a new programme and accepting the idea of a state in part of Palestine. In 1983, the situation was completely different: the balance of power was much less favourable to the Palestinian Resistance; the prospects of a settlement were very uncertain. The PLO, therefore, judged that it could not take a dramatic initiative — in the event, acceptance of the

> Reagan . . . as not containing any new meaning as long as ·it is not accompanied by any practical steps to exert pressure on Begin's government which would then make it possible to say that it carries within it something new and credible.[49]

A similar stand was taken by the central council of the PLO meeting on 26 November; it did not reject the Reagan plan out of hand, despite pressure from several Palestinian groups and Syria, but simply:

> . . . expressed the view that the Reagan plan does not fulfil the inalienable rights of our people under the leadership of the PLO because the Reagan plan ignores the right of self-determination for our Palestinian people and the establishment of an independent Palestinian state under PLO leadership.[50]

Starting from this carefully balanced position, Yasser Arafat went on to deploy intense activity directed towards Amman, with a dual goal: to prevent the Hashemite regime embarking on separate negotiations with the United States; and to attempt to initiate a dialogue with the United States and assess the extent of its commitment to the Begin government.

To this end, Arafat had several meetings with King Hussein; a Jordanian-Palestinian Higher Committee was set up to study the nature of the relations to be established between Jordanians and Palestinians. The most contradictory rumours were circulating: the PLO would accept sending King Hussein to the peace talks, it would agree to a federation, and so on. In fact, a play with three actors was under way: Arafat, Hussein and Reagan. The initial positions of the Palestinian leader were: yes to the establishment of a Jordanian-Palestinian confederation, but *after* the establishment of a Palestinian state; no to any delegation of power during the negotiations.[51]

No doubt the Palestinian leader saw this position as negotiable, but that would depend on Reagan's attitude. But Hussein's visit to Washington in January 1983 did not produce any new element. Arafat declared that, unlike the Jordanian monarch, who had informed him of the results, he was not optimistic.[52] He therefore stood by the two abovementioned great principles, the more so as he was the object of intense pressure, both internal and external. The Syrian government stepped up its attacks on the PLO leader and even questioned his legitimacy. They would not accept the *rapprochement* between the PLO and the Hashemite monarch (who supported Iraq), nor the autonomy of the Palestinian leadership. Qadhafi went one step ahead of them, accusing Arafat of treason, when he, Qadhafi, had not budged throughout the siege of Beirut, except to call on the Palestinian leaders to 'commit suicide'. These two Arab capitals manipulated most of the small organizations: Sa'iqa, PFLP-CG, FPPS, and so on. Only the ALF dissociated itself from them, reflecting the Arafat-Baghdad *rapprochement*. More worrying for Arafat was the behaviour of the PFLP and the DFLP: these two organizations had distanced themselves from Damascus and Tripoli — despite their differ-

Peace Council, made up of General Peled, Uri Avneri and Dr Arnon. Thus, after several years of unofficial meetings, the chairman of the PLO publicly endorsed the contacts with the Israeli, even Zionist, peace movement. The Tunis meeting was the target of concentrated fire: from Syria to the PFLP and from Libya to the DFLP. The change of atmosphere on this issue was, nevertheless, perceptible throughout the PNC session: reading of a message from the Israeli Communist Party, presence of an Israeli journalist, Amnon Kapeliouk, speeches by delegates making favourable mention of the contacts, including one by Abu Iyad speaking for Fatah. However, the text adopted on this issue — in the name of the sacred principle of unity — was sufficiently ambiguous for each camp to find in it what it wanted. It can be summed up by saying that the PNC did not disavow Arafat and did not veto further contacts, but it did not give them a decisive impetus either.

The true leitmotif of the Council was the affirmation of 'national unity' and the 'independence of Palestinian decision-making' *vis-à-vis* the Arab regimes. And the three main fedayeen organizations, Fatah, PFLP and DFLP agreed — while retaining numerous ambiguities — to give the PLO a realistic platform and to allow Arafat — with wider powers — to continue on the path of political and diplomatic action. But almost at once the divisions resurfaced.

22. An Uncertain Future

The Failure in Amman and the Outbreak of Dissidence

10 April 1983 is another of the 'black days' that mark the history of the Palestinian people. Issam Sartawi, a member of the PNC and the leading advocate of a dialogue with the Israeli peace movement, was assassinated. He was attending the 16th Congress of the Socialist International in Portugal. Responsibility for the murder was claimed by the Abu Nidal group. On the same day, in a long press release, the Jordanian government announced the failure of negotiations between Hussein and Arafat. The talks between the two men had lasted for several days and led to the drafting of a joint communiqué.[56] This stated that 'Jordan and the PLO are responsible for finding an effective form of political action capable of breaking the current paralysis . . .' In order to build a confederal union between the two peoples there had to be political action 'on the basis of the Fez resolutions which have won the agreement of most of the Arab nation, and in conformity with Arab and international resolutions, including the initiative launched by President Reagan . . .' To this end, 'it is necessary that Jordanians and Palestinians work together in a joint delegation . . .' On 5 April, Arafat flew off to Kuwait where he put the draft before his fellow members of the Fatah Central Committee and the Executive Committee of the PLO. Their reaction was decidedly hostile, and they asked for at least three amendments: the removal of any reference to the Reagan plan, the assertion of the right of Palestinians to self-determination, and a high level of representation for the PLO in the 'joint delegation'. The King rejected these alterations; the failure was apparent. The main protagonist in the game being played out that April was the United States. By negotiating with Hussein, Arafat was seeking to secure concessions from the Republican Administration. He was prepared not to reject the process opened up by the Reagan plan, on condition that Washington make firm commitments. King Hussein himself said, 'Non-recognition of the PLO by the United States is one of the reasons that have prevented the successful conclusion of the negotiations between the Jordanians and the Palestinians.'[57] American intransigence, and the priority given to a settlement of the Lebanese question, were blocking the peace process. Thus Yasser Arafat lost the initiative. The hour had struck for the

'dissidents' in Syria.

It was in this atmosphere of setback that what was rather hastily dubbed the 'colonels' revolt' got underway. Initially it involved a small number of Fatah leaders: two members of the Central Committee, Nimr Saleh (Abu Saleh) and Samih Kuweyk (Qadri), out of 13. And none of the historic leaders were involved; ten members of the Revolutionary Council out of 75. They belonged to the group of Fatah leaders who had declared themselves against the idea of a mini-state and political solutions in 1974. Some, such as Abu Nidal, had already broken with Arafat. But others had remained within Fatah out of discipline or a desire to have some influence. They had already set themselves militarily against the majority of Fatah in 1978; the signing of the Camp David agreements had reunited the organization.

Thus, in the background there were longstanding differences. They were revived by the political situation created in the PLO after Beirut and the failure of the Jordanian–Palestinian negotiations. At the meeting of the Fatah Revolutionary Council held in January 1983, Colonel Abu Musa launched a long attack which was to become the dissidents' political platform.[58] It was, he asserted, inadmissible that the PLO should accept the Fez plan, item 7 of which meant recognition of Israel. The Reagan plan was even more unacceptable, and Abu Musa denounced those who saw 'positive aspects' in the American proposals. He went on that all contacts with Jordan, Egypt, and 'the Zionist organizations called, for the sake of convenience, the democratic peace forces in Israel', must be broken off. And the corollary of this profession of faith was the need to relaunch the armed struggle, which is Fatah's *raison d'être*. He added to this condemnation of political options an attack on the undemocratic way in which the PLO functioned and the personal nature of Yasser Arafat's power, and a condemnation of the corruption prevalent among certain leaders of Fatah and the PLO leadership. It was the transfer of a number of military personnel, decided upon by Arafat, and seen as arbitrary, that was to be the catalyst of the dissidence in May 1983.

The dissidents initially had significant advantages. The disarray among the Palestinian people and organizations in the aftermath of Beirut created a climate favourable to 'radicalization'. The PFLP and DFLP declared themselves in favour of 'a democratic reform within the personnel and institutions of the PLO and in the ranks of the Palestinian forces on the basis of national unity.'[59] Finally, Libya, and above all Syria — which controlled the Bekaa valley where the Palestinian forces were concentrated — openly supported the dissidents. But, within the space of a few weeks, the dissidents had lost all credibility. The unrealistic and chauvinist nature of their stand became very apparent. Abu Musa went so far as to declare:[60] 'The whole of Palestine must be liberated. [There will be] no reconciliation and no recognition of Israel', adding that all Jews who had settled in Israel since its establishment would have 'to return to their countries of origin'. Not since Shukairy had such language been heard from a Palestinian leader. The sectarianism of the dissidents was such — they did not hesitate to launch violent attacks on Hawatmeh whom they accused of being one of the main architects of the proposal for a 'mini-state' — that it offended even those best disposed towards them: only Jibril's PFLP–GC financed by Libya and the pro-Syrian Sa'iqa gave them wholehearted support. When they took the responsibility of transforming the political dispute within Fatah into an armed confrontation they lost all sympathy among the Palestinian masses. Finally, their total dependence on Libya, and above all on Syria, rapidly transformed them into 'agents' of the Arab capitals and precipitated a nationalist reaction in the Palestinian ranks.

Damascus versus the PLO

Of all the Arab countries involved in the Palestinian question, Syria was certainly the one most concerned by the future of the PLO. It was one of the front-line states. Moreover, for more than ten years the PLO had been a factor in the Lebanese crisis, which closely affected Damascus. Finally, the establishment of a Palestinian state would be happening in what Syria considered to be its 'sphere of influence'. Until 1976 the contradictions between Syria's interests and those of the PLO did not seem to be serious, although it might be recalled that Damascus strictly banned any military operations by Palestinians across its borders. The situation changed dramatically in the spring of 1976. In the Lebanese civil war, after a period of hesitation, the PLO came down on the side of the Lebanese National Movement led by Kamal Jumblatt. Victory seemed assured. But the prospect of the establishment of a revolutionary government in Beirut worried the Ba'athist leadership, especially as at the time they were on good terms with the United States with which they were discreetly negotiating. With the green light from Washington and Tel Aviv, allying themselves with the Phalange, Syrian troops intervened directly on 1 June 1976 and crushed the PLO and its Lebanese allies. But the evolution of the situation in the region, the failure of the negotiations between Washington and Damascus, the alliance between the Phalangists and Israel, and above all the Camp David agreements once again brought Arafat and Assad closer together. But the mistrust born of the bloody events of 1976 — the Palestinians remember Tal al Zaatar as much as they do Deir Yassin — had not disappeared. The asylum granted by Damascus to Abu Nidal, the murderer of Kalak and Sartawi, is one indication of this hostility.

On 6 June 1983, Israeli troops poured into Lebanon. On 11 June Syria signed a ceasefire, which left the PLO and the Lebanese National Movement alone to face the Israeli army. Outraged by being thus abandoned, Arafat, when he had to leave Beirut, refused to go to Syria and set up his headquarters in Tunis. The Palestinian leader, feeling himself released from any obligation towards the Arab capitals, began to develop his own political strategy, as we have seen above. But there was no way Damascus could accept an alliance between the PLO and Jordan, not only because Amman was supporting Iraq, but because such an alliance would involve Damascus being kept out of a political solution in the Middle East.

It took the Syrian leaders several months to salvage the situation. Several events helped: the failure of the negotiations between Arafat and Hussein; the Syrian rejection of the Lebanese–Israeli treaty of 17 May 1983, which enhanced the standing of the Ba'athist leaders which had been seriously undermined by their passivity in the summer of 1982. In this new situation there ensued a new trial of strength, the first round of which consisted in an attempt to destabilize Arafat within the PLO. By supporting the 'dissidents' and the groups hostile to the PLO leader, Damascus was attempting to secure Abu Ammar's removal.

Tripoli

By using the weaknesses and mistakes of his adversaries in Fatah, Yasser Arafat was able, in a few weeks, to circumvent them. First he seemed to give ground: he condemned the Reagan plan all the more harshly because the negotiations with Jordan had broken down; he agreed to the holding of the fifth General Congress of Fatah called for by the dissidents; he withdrew the military appointments that had been used as an excuse for the revolt; finally, he called for a political settlement of the dispute. The Palestinian leader did the rounds of the various units in Syria and the Bekaa valley, helping to limit the rebellion. Faced with this multi-pronged onslaught, the rebels responded by attacking the military positions of the loyalists and seizing their offices in Damascus. By taking the responsibility for causing Palestinian blood to flow, Abu Musa's men totally isolated themselves within Fatah. The Fatah Revolutionary Council met on 20 June attended by 55 members (the ten dissidents were not present) and condemned the secessionists while at the same time inviting them to take part in the preparations for the Congress. Yasser Arafat's expulsion from Syria on 24 June precipitated an outburst of national feeling; Palestinians everywhere demonstrated in support of their leader. The Executive Committee, meeting on 1 July, expressed its 'extreme regret' at the expulsion; the PFLP and DFLP were obliged to support Arafat. The dissidents responded by digging in their heels and by military escalation.

By deciding to return to Tripoli on 16 September, Arafat was not falling into a trap. Quite the reverse, it was a stroke of genius. He knew that Syria had decided to get rid of him and take control of the PLO. This was a political necessity for the leaders in Damascus, involved as they were in complicated dealings with Washington over the future of Lebanon. Abu Ammar's presence in northern Lebanon not only galvanized the Fatah fighters and once again thrust the PLO into the international limelight but also confronted the Ba'athist leaders with a difficult choice. Either they could halt their offensive against the loyalists who were being driven out of the Bekaa valley – and thus lose the advantage of a year of manoeuvring – or they could carry on and lay siege to a city with over 400,000 inhabitants. By opting for the latter course Damascus was to repeat the bitter experience of the Israelis before Beirut: it is not easy to get rid of a man like Arafat. After driving all the loyalist forces out of the Bekaa valley and the north, the Syrians — and their 'allies' — launched the attack on Tripoli and the two Palestinian camps at Nahr el Bared and Badawi at the beginning of November. The battles were very hard-fought: Nahr el Bared fell on 6 November, Badawi on 16, and the fighting reached Tripoli. In spite of the disparity of forces, the loyalists — aided by the Lebanese militias of the Islamic Unity Movement — resisted resolutely. As at the siege of Beirut, international opinion became concerned. As for the Arab countries — with the noteworthy exceptions of Algeria, Egypt and Kuwait — they stayed silent; not without some satisfaction, they watched the weakening of the PLO, 'a source of disturbance and destabilization'. But the Palestinian people made its feelings known very clearly. In the camps in Syria and Lebanon, under Israeli occupation or in exile, at the cost of dozens of dead, it demonstrated its attachment to Arafat, the 'symbol of national independence'. In a poll carried out in the West Bank and Gaza,[61] 95% of Palestinians expressed their support for Abu Ammar. This unanimity — which led the PFLP and DFLP to condemn the dissidents unambiguously — weighed heavily in the scales. Combined with the resistance of Tripoli, it forced Damascus to make its first retreats. On 24 November, a ceasefire came into effect. The UN agreed to suprevise the departure of the PLO, while Arafat scored a spectacular success by exchanging six Israeli soldiers for 4,400 Palestinian and Lebanese prisoners. The departure originally planned for the beginning of December was delayed first by the Syrians, then by Israel.

But, after lengthy negotiations — and pressure from many quarters — and under the protection of the French fleet, Arafat and 4,000 fighters left Tripoli.

The 17th PNC: Towards a Break-up

With this departure, Yasser Arafat and his supporters could claim a moral victory, but the path before them was narrower than ever. It was in order to open it up that Arafat took it upon himself to meet the Egyptian Raïs. The embrace of 22 December 1983 brought to a close the breach between the Palestinians and the Egyptians that followed the Camp David agreements. It strengthened the Palestinian hand in the negotiations with King Hussein as well as with Washington, Tel-Aviv and Damascus. But yet it provoked a wave of protest in the ranks of the PLO. Nayef Hawatmeh, in the name of the DFLP, spoke of a 'bloody blow against the revolution'. George Habash called for the removal of Yasser Arafat. The governing bodies of the PLO, notably the Executive Committee, were unable to meet. The whole of 1984 was taken up with negotiations, bargaining, haggling among the various groups involved: Fatah, which supported its leader; the Democratic Alliance formed by the PFLP, DFLP, PCP and PLF; the National Alliance — under the aegis of the Syrians — which brought together the PFLP–GC, Sa'iqa and the 'dissidents'. After six months of meetings — and many efforts at mediation by the Algerians and the South Yemenis — an agreement was signed between Fatah and the Democratic Alliance; to enable, it was felt, the 17th PNC to meet. But Damascus' veto, the tensions within the Democratic Alliance, the differing interpretations of the text given by the signatories, all combined once again to delay the holding of the PNC.

The deadlock was total, and all the more worrying in that none of the PLO's leadership bodies had met for over a year. In an unprecedented initiative, Arafat decided to force fate's hand. With complete disregard for the sacrosanct concept of a pre-existing consensus between all the organizations, he called on the PNC to meet.

In this risky venture, he held two trump cards: the Palestinians' attachment to the PLO as the symbol of their national renaissance, and the extremism and verbal excess of his opponents. Even the DFLP, which refused to attend the PNC, attacked the PFLP and the National Alliance for their part in the resulting situation.

The PNC was thus held in Amman, from 22 to 28 November 1984. Only Fatah, the pro-Iraqi ALF and one section of the PLF came. Nevertheless, thanks to the massive attendance of independents, a quorum was achieved. But no historic decisions were taken during the session, even if it did mark a significant rapprochement with Jordan.

This alliance, at first aimed chiefly against Damascus, was above all an attempt to revive the peace process in the Middle East, by trying yet again to establish contact with the United States. The pact also had the advantage that it forestalled any separate action by King Hussein and made it possible for the PLO to move back closer to the 'battlefield', with access to the occupied territories. The loss of Beirut was in part compensated for by the setting up of certain Palestinian institutions in Jordan.

But did Arafat choose the right moment to run the risk of a split? It was no longer 1982, when international public opinion was mobilized in favour of the Palestinians and thousands of Israelis were taking to the streets to call for peace. By the end of 1984, there was nothing happening in Europe; the national unity government in Israel had managed to reestablish its hold on public opinion; and on the eve of his second term, Ronald Reagan confirmed the absolute priority he gave to the alliance with Israel. Indeed the American leaders were clearly hoping to bring about a new consensus amongst the key countries of the Middle East, a consensus in which the Israeli-Arab conflict would be much lower on the agenda.

Yet Arafat held firm and reopened the negotiations with King Hussein which had failed in 1983. At the beginning of 1985, an agreement was signed, and the Jordanians published the details. This caused Fatah considerable embarrassment, since the text was vague on two crucial points: the right of the PLO to participate autonomously in negotiations; and the creation of an independent Palestinian state. The resulting ambiguity was no doubt deliberate, since the agreement was primarily aimed at the Americans, and the extent of any concessions would depend on Washington's response. But the unease within Fatah itself and amongst certain of its historical leaders (Abu Iyad, Farouk Kaddoumi) was nonetheless quite real.

In any case, the Amman agreement smashed what was left of PLO unity. On 15 March 1985, the Palestinian National Salvation Front (PNSF) was formed in Damascus. Its members included the PFLP, the PFLP-GC, Abu Musa's Fatah, Sai'qa and the Palestinian Popular Struggle Front (PPSF). The Abu Nidal group joined some time later. Its political platform was not disimilar to that of the Rejection Front between 1974 and 1977: rejection of any recognition of Israel and of any political solution; intensification of the armed struggle; condemnation of Egypt and Jordan. . . . The DFLP and the CP refused to join the Front; although they had long been in favour of a political settlement, they nevertheless reproached Arafat for his concessions to the Americans, his siding with 'Arab reaction' and his abandonment of the idea of an independent Palestinian state.[62]

Each of these three currents, Fatah and its allies, the PNSF, and the DFLP and CP, nonetheless refused to consummate a *de jure* break-up. Faced with mortal external danger, even the re-establishment of unity was possible. This happened in Lebanon in Spring 1985 during the 'battle of the camps', the assault launched by the Shi'ite militia, Amal, against the Palestinian camps of Sabra, Shatila and Bourj el Barajneh. The antagonism between Amal and the PLO goes back several years, to the days when the two movements clashed in southern Lebanon. Once it had seized power in West Beirut in February 1984, Amal sought to consolidate its hold on the capital. The camps had rearmed, and constituted an obstacle to the Shi'ite movement. Amal also, and above all, sought to satisfy its Syrian allies, who were displeased to see Arafat's faithful followers returning to the city. Amal's offensive eventually failed and even brought all the Palestinian organizations together again: on the ground the organizations had felt they were struggling for a common survival, and none of them could accept Amal's demands for disarming the PLO fighters. During 1985 and 1986 Amal repeatedly tried to attack the camps in South Beirut. Every assault failed. Although much weakened, the Palestinians, during those two years, had become once again a factor on the Lebanese scene.

The Year of Defeats

On 30 September 1985, three Israelis were assassinated in the port of Larnaca. On 1 October, the Israeli air force retaliated by bombing the head-quarters of the PLO in Tunis, killing 70 people including many civilians. The lesson sank in and a few months later the Tunisian authorities closed down most of the PLO offices, which then moved to Sanaa or Baghdad.

On 7 October, a Palestinian commando group seized the *Achille Lauro*, Abu Abbas, a leader of the PLF and a member of the executive committee of the PLO, was implicated in the action. Although some aspects of this act of piracy are still unclear, and although Yasser Arafat himself sorted matters out and promised to punish the instigators, the PLO was blamed. Arafat was even forced to drop his planned visit to the United Nations. The increase in terrorism — attacts on El Al offices in Rome and Vienna — reflected a two-fold change: the growing despair of some Palestinians and the determination of some extremists to destabilise the peace strategy sketched out by Yasser Arafat.

The signature of the agreements between Jordan and the PLO opened up the way for negotiations between the Palestinian resistance and the American administration. The PLO and the White House exchanged messages, and sought to pave the way for a meeting between US officials and PLO representatives. On 5 February 1986 the PLO made a new offer: in exchange for recognition by the United States of the Palestinians' right to self-determination, it would formally accept Security Council resolutions 242 and 338, Mr Reagan refused, the negotiations broke down and the Jordan-PLO agreement did not survive this new setback; on 19 February, the King abrogated it. Questioned by a member of the House of Representatives, the American State Department justified itself as follows: 'The explicit reference [by the PLO] to resolutions 242 and 338, and to Israel are new. . . . But in a Middle-East content the term self-determination is loaded; it could mean the creation of a Palestinian state . . . and the US is not in favour of an independent Palestinian state.'

A strange argument, this. The right of peoples to self-determination, championed by Reagan when it suits him, is not negotiable. The forms in which this right would be exercised by the Palestinians (and by the Israelis) could, on the other hand, raise difficulties, and should thus be the subject of later negotiations. By feigning to have confused a principle and its application, Washington sabotaged any prospect of peace in the short term, and increased the risk of Palestinian radicalization. The approach of the Rejection Front, that violence alone is worth pursuing, gained in conviction. A poll carried out among the inhabitants of the West Bank and Gaza, who are supposedly more moderate than their compatriots in exile, not only confirmed their unanimous support for the PLO, it also signalled growing support for terrorists. Of those questioned, 60% approved of attacks on El Al aeroplanes.

The road of separate negotiations now seems blocked, for all that Arafat reminded the delegates at the non-aligned summit in Harare of his wish to find a political solution. On 5 September 1986, he declared:

> The PLO has done everything in its power to reach a just and equit-able solution, preserving the inalienable rights of the Palestinian people as defined in international law, including their right to return, to self-determination and to build their own independent state, with Jerusalem as its capital. We demand that an international conference be held to establish peace in the region as a whole. Such a conference would bring together the five permanent members of the security council and all the parties involved in the conflict, including the PLO. It would

be based on international law and all the resolutions of the United
Nations General Assembly and Security Council resolutions dealing
with the Palestinian problem, including resolutions 242, 338, 465 and
471 . . .[63]

This was Arafat's first public endorsement, in such clear terms, of resolutions 242 and 338. Resolutions 465 and 471 concern the dismantling of the
settlements in the occupied territories. The US voted for 465, and while
they abstained on 471, they did not use their veto.

The 18th PNC: Towards a Revival of the PLO?

In late 1986, the two strategies — the one proposed by Yasser Arafat and that
advocated by the PNSF — had run into a dead-end. The long siege of the
Palestinian camps in Lebanon during the winter and the renewed mobilization of the people of the West Bank and Gaza accelerated the slow movement
which, from Prague to Moscow, from Algiers to Tripoli, had marked the
evolution of dialogue amongst Palestinians. Finally, after endless negotiations, the main elements of the resistance came together again at the 18th
PNC which opened in Algiers on 20 April 1987.

Those present included Arafat and Fatah, George Habash and the PFLP,
Nayef Hawatmeh and the DFLP, the PCP, the ALF and Abu Abbas' fraction
of the PLF. Although Habash announced that the PNSF no longer had any
reason to exist, and despite the mediation of Colonel Qadhafi, now reconciled
with Fatah, the groups most closely linked to Syria stayed away. The PFLP-GC, Sai'qa, the Fatah dissidents and the PLF did not attend the meeting.
Abu Nidal, who was also invited and who joined in the preliminary negotiations, backed out at the last moment; his participation would in any case
have seriously damaged the PLO's standing in the West and probably elsewhere as well.

To bring the Palestinian parliament together, Arafat had to consent to
abrogate the Palestinian-Jordanian accord of 11 February 1985. He thereby
acknowledged the failure of a policy based on separate negotiations and
reliance on Washington's intervention alone. But this decision was not
without risks. From 21 April 1987, the Jordanian Government let it be
known that the 11 February pact would continue to be the basis of its policy.
And Amman, which had encouraged the split in Fatah led by Colonel Abul
Zaim, still hoped to find Palestinian interlocuters more malleable than the
PLO. Nonetheless, the PNC confirmed its attachment to a confederation
between Jordan and the future independent state and the need to reinforce
the 'specific' relations between the two peoples.

Abu Ammar had to make a further concession; the text of the PNC's
political resolution reiterated the decisions of the 16th PNC on Egypt and did
not ratify the special relationship that Arafat had developed with Mubarak in
the meantime. Nobody had foreseen that the Egyptians would react to this

so violently. Cairo announced the closure of all PLO offices in Egypt and the official press savaged the Resistance. Yet despite appearances, is the gulf between the PLO and Cairo as big as it seems? The *Rais* needs the PLO more than ever to help his reintegration into the Arab world. Hence his conciliatory attitude towards Arafat and the announcement that some PLO offices at least would be allowed to stay open, notably that of the Palestinian Red Crescent. Also, even leftist organizations such as the DELP and the PCP recognize that a break between Tel Aviv and Cairo is a pipe-dream and that there can be no peace process without Egypt. But they do demand that the *Rais* unambiguously recognize the Palestinians' right to self-determination and the PLO as the only legitimate representative.

For the radical organizations, the decision to accept the holding of the Council stemmed from other calculations and reassessments. Speaking of Syria, Abu Ali Moustapha, Deputy General Secretary of the PFLP, recognized that 'those we had chosen to stand alongside as strategic allies failed and disappointed us'[64]. The long siege of the camps in Lebanon will not be quickly forgotten. The inability to overthrow Arafat or even seriously to dent his prestige have also encouraged a more flexible approach. Finally, the Soviets, with whom the DFLP, the PFLP and the PCP maintain solid links, have helped to turn these glimmers of unity into a reality.

All observers have noted the Soviet role in the Palestinian reunification. It fits into a vast redeployment of Soviet diplomacy in the Middle East, aimed at bringing an end to the USSR's exclusion from the region since the Camp David agreements. Moscow's central idea remains an international conference on peace in the Middle East, which would reestablish its role and put an end to the ten years of exclusive US hold over any process of negotiations. In this context, the reunification of the PLO is a blow to attempts to find a separate Israeli-Jordanian solution but keeps the door open for a political solution.

Three main political decisions marked the Council. The PLO fully endorsed the negotiating process by supporting 'the calling of an international conference in the framework and under the auspices of the United Nations, with the participation of the members of the Security Council and all parties concerned in the conflict, including the PLO as an equal partner with the other participants'. The Council stressed that such a conference should have 'full powers'[65]. The Council also backed the idea of a preparatory committee for this forum, as first advanced in July 1986 during François Mitterrand's visit to Moscow.

A second decision, taken despite the 'reservations' expressed by the PFLP, approved the 'development of links with democratic Israeli forces struggling against the occupation and Israeli expansionism and who recognize the inalienable rights of our people, including its right to return and to self-determination, as well as to build its own state, and who recognize the PLO as the only legitimate representative of the Palestinian people'. Arafat thereby at last saw his efforts over ten years of contacts with various Zionist forces ratified. The resolution provides him with a legal basis for much greater activity in this field.

Finally, the election to the executive Council of a delegate of the Palestinian Communist Party marked the rise to prominence of an organization whose military activity has been very limited. It is not properly speaking a fedayeen organization and yet — unprecedentedly — it is recognized as a full member of the PLO. There is more at stake here than a simple recognition of the dynamic role played by this party in the Occupied Territories; the move legitimates an organization which has not feared to call for a Palestinian State on the West Bank and in Gaza, alongside Israel, since 1974.

In organizational terms, the only major change was the election of a Central Committee of 75 members, with the same powers as a PNC and charged with supervising the work of the Executive Committee. The latter, and Arafat in particular, nevertheless retain the real power.

The 18th PNC undeniably marked the end of a very difficult stage. In the short term, it put the PLO in a better position to confront political developments and an eventual international conference on peace in the Middle East. The new unity could also pave the way for an Arab summit ratifying the political stance adopted at Algiers. Finally, the Palestinian parliament has yet again shown the organization's incredible capacity to survive, for all that it has over the years piled up dubious judgements and awkward political positions. Yet despite these undeniable successes, one cannot but wonder about the PLO's ability to bring into fruition the State-building project with which it has been entrusted.

The Future in the Balance

Five years after Yasser Arafat's departure from Beirut, the PLO is still hesitating about the great organizational and political choices it faces. 1982 was not, it seems, the great watershed one might have expected.

What does the PLO want? This simple question still has no simple answer. The Resistance has accepted the Fez plan and ratified the calling of an international conference on Middle East peace; it has come a long way since 1967. But the PLO's state-building project remains unclear; where will the Palestinian state be? In the West Bank and Gaza? Or will it cover a larger territory, including Galilee? Or all of Palestine, in the framework of a binational state, to which Arafat referred as recently as 1987? Even if it is obviously the first of these projects which is at the top of the agenda today, the ambiguity remains an important weapon in the hands of the Resistance's enemies, especially as nobody really thinks that any other goal is realistic for the next two generations at least. But the truth is that even in the occupied territories, the PLO has to face a rising young generation that is even more radical than its parents. The current deadlock can only favour the extremists and lead to an ungovernable situation, akin to Northern Ireland.

Organization is another key question. The rapport which has been established between the Palestinians and the PLO is not at the same level everywhere. Apart from during the 1967–1970 period, the PLO has never 'governed' more than a small proportion of Palestinians. From 1970 to 1982, it organized the practicalities of camp life in Lebanon and effectively managed the affairs of about 400,000 Palestinians — barely one tenth of the total population. Elsewhere in the diaspora, it was unable or did not know how to establish the kind of extensive in-depth network that the FLN, for instance, built among Algerians in France through fund-raising. And in the occupied territories, the army of occupation is everywhere and block all links with the outside world, thereby making PLO control very difficult. The Organization's leadership is so worried that an alternative leadership might develop in the West Bank and Gaza that Fatah has sought to break all attempts at setting up 'Fronts', and has even undermined trade union unity. The PLO has thus become more of a symbol — albeit a very effective one as the rallying point for the national movement — than the organization of the Palestinians in a more concrete sense. These tendencies have been accentuated since 1982, with the removal of the leadership from the 'battlefield' and an aggravation of the negative traits of the bureaucratic apparatus, which tends to perpetuate itself rather than to act.

These two factors — political and organizational — will, in the short term at least, have great bearing on the future of the PLO. Yet whatever it may be, the Palestinian national awakening has become an unavoidable fact, and, unlike in 1948, this people will not disappear from the political map of the Middle East. In the last analysis, it is partly on this people itself that the future peace of the region will depend.

Notes

1. *Al-wathaiq al-'arabiya al-filastiniya 1971* [Palestine Arab Documents], Beirut, Institute for Palestine Studies, p. 398. (Henceforth cited as *PAD* with the year of reference); *International Documents on Palestine 1971*, Beirut, Institute for Palestine Studies, p. 407. (Henceforth cited as *IDP* with the year of reference.)

2. M. Dayan, *Paix dans le désert*, Paris, Fayard, 1981.

3. *PAD 1977*, pp. 389–93.

4. Abu Iyad, *My Home, My Land: A Narrative of the Palestinian Struggle*, New York, Times Books, 1981, p. 203.

5. *PAD 1977*, pp. 434–5.

6. Ibid., p. 439.

7. See the communiqué from the main West Bank municipalities, 18 November, in ibid., p. 438, and the appeal from the mayors, associations and leading personalities in the West Bank and Gaza on 8 December, ibid., pp. 563–4.

8. Ibid., pp. 504–7.

9. *Le Monde*, 23 November 1977.

10. *PAD 1977*, pp. 508–10.

11. Letter of 30 November 1977, ibid., pp. 516–17; *IDP 1977*, pp. 453–5.

12. Abu Iyad, *My Home, My Land*, pp. 209–12.

13. *PAD 1977*, p. 530.

14. *Le Monde*, 4–5 December 1977.

15. On the negotiations see P. Rondot, *Le Proche-Orient à la recherche de la paix 1973–1982*, Paris, PUF, 1982.

16. *International Herald Tribune*, 3 May 1977.

17. *Le Matin*, 26 and 27 July 1978.

18. See the declaration by G. Habash in May 1978, *PAD 1978*, pp. 234–7.

19. *Le Monde*, 27 April, 5 May and 5 August 1978.

20. *PAD 1978*, pp. 237–9.

21. See the text and the appendices in the *Journal of Palestine Studies* (henceforth *JPS*), Beirut, no. 30, winter 1979.

22. See the text and appendices in ibid., no. 32, summer 1979.

23. For a detailed Palestinian critique of 'self-government', see F.A. Sayegh, 'The Camp David Agreements and the Palestine Problem', ibid., no. 30, winter 1979.

24. On the legal criticism of the agreements see *Les accords de Camp David: un défi au droit international*, Paris, Sycomore, 1980, 196 pp.

25. See articles in the Israeli press, in *JPS*, no. 33, autumn 1979.

26. See *Les Arabes sous l'occupation israélienne 1978*, p. 44.

27. See *Les Arabes sous l'occupation israélienne 1979*, pp. 94–102.

28. See for example *PAD 1978*, pp. 422–3 and *PAD 1979*, p. 115.

29. *PAD 1979*, pp. 36–9.

30. *Palestine*, Bulletin d'information de l'OLP, vol. 5, no. 13, 15–30 July 1979.

31. *Events*, 20 April 1979; *Club de la presse d'Europe I*, 18 May 1980; *International Herald Tribune*, 31 July 1980.

32. *Le Monde*, 27 March 1980.

33. See A.M. Lesch, *Political perceptions of the Palestinians in the West Bank and the Gaza Strip*, Washington, D.C., The Middle East Institute, 1980; and *The Arabs Under Israeli Occupation, 1978, 1979, 1980*.

34. See the Jerusalem weekly *al-Fajr*, 23 April 1982.

35. See for example the PNF's memorandum to the PLO leadership in *al-Hurriyah*, 8 October 1979.

36. See *Bulletin des amitiés franco-palestiniennes*, no. 6, 4th quarter, 1980; I. Lustick, 'Israel and the West Bank after Elon Moreh: the mechanics of de facto annexation', *Middle East Journal*, autumn 1981; J.F. Legrain, 'L'annexion de la Cisjordanie', *Revue d'études palestiniennes*, no. 4, summer 1982.

37. *Carte de l'implantation en Eretz Israël*, Jewish Agency Settlement Department, July 1982.

38. On this phenomenon see Meron Benvenisti's interview to *The Jerusalem Post*, 10 September 1982; the survey in the same newspaper, 7, 14 and 21 January 1983; and *al-Fajr*, 4 February 1983.

39. *BBC Summary of World Broadcasts*, 10 August 1981. (Henceforth cited as SWB with the date of reference).

40. *Le Monde*, 21 October 1981.

41. *Le Figaro*, 14 October 1981; *Le Monde*, 2 November 1981; *Der Spiegel*, no. 48, 1981.

42. See Kaddoumi's argument in *Monday Morning*, Beirut, 16 November 1981.

43. *Le Monde*, 24 November 1981.
44. Ibid.
45. See for example Arafat's declaration in the *International Herald Tribune*, 14 December 1981.
46. All quotations, except where otherwise mentioned, are taken from the special survey 'La guerre d'Israël au Liban', *Maghreb-Machrik,* no. 98, October 1982, especially pp. 94–7.
47. *Le Monde*, 1 October 1982.
48. *SWB*, 26 January 1983.
49. *SWB*, 2 December 1982.
50. *SWB*, 29 November 1982.
51. See, for example, the interview with Y. Arafat in *Témoignage Chrétien*, 3 January 1983.
52. *SWB*, 26 January 1983.
53. *SWB*, 7 December 1982.
54. 17 January 1983.
55. For the text of the PNC resolution, see *al-Moudjahid*, 24 February 1983, but, since the translation is not at all good, see the text in Arabic in *al-Sha'b*, 23 February 1983. For Brezhnev's proposals, see *Maghreb-Machrik*, no. 98, October 1982, pp. 109–10.
56. See text in *Afrique-Asie*, no. 269, 23 May 1983.
57. *Revue d'Etudes Palestiniennes,* no. 9, autumn 1983, p. 213.
58. See E. Rouleau, 'La mutinerie contre M. Yasser Arafat', *Le Monde Diplomatique*, August 1983, or the full text of Abu Musa's statement in *Revue d'Etudes Palestiniennes*, no. 9, autumn 1983, pp. 263–8.
59. Statement of 2 June 1983 in *Revue d'Etudes Palestiniennes*, no. 9, autumn 1983, p. 213.
60. *The Guardian*, 4 July 1983.
61. *Al Fajr*, 9 December 1983.
62. Democratic Palestine, June 1985.
63. *Filastin al-Thawra*, 20 September 1986.
64. SWB, 20 April 1987.
65. All the texts cited from the 18th PNC are taken from *Filastin al-Thawra*, 2 May, 1987.

Conclusion

If we attempt to draw up an assessment of the PLO's 'long march' towards acceptance of the idea of a state in part of Palestine, or towards what we in the West call 'realism', we cannot but be struck by a double phenomenon. On the one hand, a real advance towards acceptance of a compromise solution; on the other, the gap in relation to the requirements of a true solution (or, put differently, the inability of the PLO to lay down, and get accepted, a programme expressing its viewpoint).

First, the advance. Before 1967, for the Palestinian people, and for the political organizations, the dominant notion was one of 'return' to a mythical Palestine, one that had undergone no changes since 1948. Jews and Zionists, Israelis and settlers were all lumped together. And if every leader did not call for them to be driven into the sea, they all thought that they should go away and return to their countries of origin.

Then came the 1967 War, the political renaissance of the Palestinian people and the emergence of Fatah as the dominant force in the Resistance. The development of the armed struggle, the end of passivity, a certain degree of clear thinking among the new leaders of the PLO and an awareness of international realities, all led to the first significant change. The myth of return was replaced by the myth of a democratic Palestine in which Jews, Muslims and Christians would co-exist. The future of Israelis — at least for those who wished it — would be in Palestine; the PLO then thought that its proposals, combined with the development of the armed struggle, would enable some Jews to join its struggle and that a division would emerge within Israeli society.

While it had little real impact on the Israeli community, the slogan of a democratic state did constitute an important stage in Palestinian political thought. The decline of the armed struggle, the fact that there was little change in Israeli public opinion, and particularly the contradiction between the fact of accepting that all Jews should remain in Palestine with the same rights as other citizens, and at the same time denying their right to self-determination and a state — in short to 'separation' —raised complex problems for the PLO. But it was, above all, the PLO's growing involvement in the international political game during the 1970s, and the emergence of the Palestinians in the occupied territories — both as a political force *within* the PLO and as a force opposing the occupation — that encouraged the increasing realization on the part of the Palestinian leadership of the need for a compromise solution. The October 1973 War was, in this respect, a powerful catalyst.

The PLO then came out with the idea of a 'national authority' and then of a state 'in every liberated part' of Palestine. This was a *de facto* acceptance of the partition of Palestine decided by the UN in 1947; even if the ultimate objective remained a democratic state. Fundamentally, the PLO's stand did not greatly differ from that of wide sectors of the Zionist movement who had accepted the UN plan in 1947 while retaining their territorial claims. With one vital difference, that Zionism had the means of its policy and its ambitions.

The contradiction between acceptance of the establishment of a Palestinian state in a part of Palestine and the refusal — at least publicly — to recognize the state of Isreal, served Israeli propaganda enormously. It reduced the support of international opinion for the PLO. But would formal recognition have unfrozen the situation? Certainly one cannot but be struck — especially when one is a Western observer — by the impression of 'missed opportunities' that litter the history of the Palestinian people. Rejection of the 1947 Partition Plan, which would have made possible the establishment of a Palestinian state in territories much much larger than the West Bank and Gaza. Rejection of Resolution 242 and the Rogers plan, in 1970, which would have enabled the occupied territories to be won back. Refusal to wage a clear fight to go to the Geneva conference in 1973, at a time when the balance of forces had hever been so favourable to the Palestinian people.

But this should not lead us to a simplistic view and over-hasty assertions: 'it should have . . .', 'it only needed . . .', etc. The adoption, by all the Arab states meeting in Fez in September 1982, of a plan accepting guarantees of peace for all states in the region did not make Begin budge one inch. The idea that recognition of Israel could have increased support for the PLO in Western Europe is undeniable; but it is not these countries that decide matters in the Middle East. And it is not enough to win Western public opinion to secure a just settlement in the region. This was seen very clearly during the siege of Beirut in the summer of 1982. In preference to this way of posing the problem we would opt for the one adopted by Professor Rodinson in an introduction to a highly critical text by O. Carré on the Palestinian Resistance in 1978

> I think . . . that many decisions — or lack of decisions — of the highest Palestinian leadership have, for several years, been wrong in the sense that they create obstacles in the way of successes that this leadership could have won in the way of meeting the aspirations of the masses that it represents. However, I wonder whether these decisions or lack of decisions could have been avoided. I have long been convinced that the core PLO leadership is perfectly aware of their harmfulness. But it judges that it cannot do otherwise than take these harmful decisions

and refrain from taking useful decisions. It would be necessary to know more in detail about the life of the Palestinian organizations and the constraints operating on them to judge how far, on what point, a different line of behaviour might have been possible, given more political courage (not to be confused with physical courage) among the leaders.[1]

This study has enabled us to assess some of the constraints acting on the Resistance. First the Arab constraints. As we have said, few independence movements have been so heavily dependent on external assistance; this assitance has varied enormously with the interests of each state and the situation of the moment. The Resistance paid dearly in 1970, in 1976, and after 1982, for not having taken the proper measure of this reality. How could it have decided alone on such an important initiative for the Arab world as the recognition of the existence of Israel? But we have also shown the internal constraints on the PLO: the historic weight of rejectionist positions in Palestinian minds and the weight of rejectionist organizations. But also, and above all, the need to seek 'unity at any price', the condition for the very survival of the PLO. This is what led us to define the PLO as a 're-active' organization.

It must not be forgotten that to these factors must be added the absolute intransigence of the Israeli leaders, their rejection of every offer — veiled or otherwise — of negotiations. As we stressed, the PLO has never been confronted with the alternative of choosing between a Palestinian state and peace with Israel or the maintenance of extremist positions. And this is quite the opposite of what happened to the Zionist movement in 1947 when, confronted with the Partition Plan, it was able to choose 'realism' against its extremist sections. However that may be, after the setback suffered by the PLO in Lebanon, it seems necessary to ask oneself some questions. What were in part nothing more than intellectual debates have become bloody confrontations. The Palestinian people, despite its heroism, has once again paid a heavy tribute in dead, wounded and refugees. In short, the weapon of criticism has been replaced by the criticism of weapons. And the result could not be less satisfactory for the PLO.

Asked about his mistakes, while the siege of Beirut in 1982 was still continuing, Yasser Arafat mentioned only one:

> We failed to explain our cause to the Israelis, we did not understand the Israeli mentality. Moreover, we do not have the communication skills to transmit our ideas to the inhabitants of Israel.[2]

And he added:

> I invite the activists of the Peace Now Movement, of *New Outlook* and all those who recognize our rights to self-determination to come to Beirut and see the destruction and the sufferings of the population.

A day will come when the Israelis will be ashamed and want to forget what their present leaders have done to the Palestinian people during this summer of 1982 in Lebanon.

Here, it seems to us, we are touching the basic problem. Behind the declarations, one has the distinct impression that the PLO sees the essential problem as winning over Western Europe and the United States. The leadership of the Resistance accepts the idea that 99% of the cards are in Washington's hand. It is thus waging a campaign to win its recognition by relying on the struggle of the Palestinian people, and its resistance to the occupier. Their view of Israel in the framework of this analysis is, essentially, rather simplistic: an American pawn. But this 'pawn' has real autonomy; it can resist a considerable amount of pressure. In the first place because it has, in the Jewish community in the United States, a major means of influence on the American administration. Using the blackmail of anti-Semitism, the Israeli leaders also have a powerful means of pressure on Western opinion. And, next, because the 'national consensus', that has long existed in Israel, enables it to mobilize public opinion within the Jewish state. Finally, because the divergences between Washington and Tel Aviv, real as they are, cannot conceal a strategic convergence between the two capitals. This means that the PLO's room for manoeuvre is limited. But it does exist: it has to break the consensus in Israel; which, among other things, would facilitate an evolution in the United States. No one can be certain that this strategy will make it possible to impose a solution of the Middle East conflict; but one may observe that the other strategies have all failed.

The constaints acting on the PLO have in part diminished. Acceptance of the Fez plan, a year after the rejection of the Fahd plan, indicates this. But they have not disappeared altogether. The internal debate has resumed more fiercely and the contradictions with Syria are stronger. In addition, by leaving Beirut and the whole of Lebanon the Palestinian Resistance finds itself in a situation unprecedented since 1968; it no longer has any place where it can enjoy political and, even less, military autonomy. Finally, for the first time in the history of the liberation movement, the time factor is working against the Palestinians. The colonization of the West Bank, begun by the Israel Labour government in 1967, has taken on unprecedented dimensions. The Israeli government can thus wait tranquilly. The PLO cannot.

The PLO has its back against the wall, and any waiting for external initiatives may be fatal for it. One often hears Palestinian leaders saying: 'It is we the victims who are asked to make concessions.' That may, indeed, seem unjust, contrary to a certain moral outlook. But it happens that morality has scarcely any place in a political situation. The PLO's path is narrow, but it does have a number of strong cards: wide international recognition, major support from the Palestinians in the West Bank and Gaza, and an unprecedented peace movement in Israel. But this latter has little chance of growing and becoming a major factor in Israeli life unless the PLO 'recognizes' it, and gives it real legitimacy. To all those in Israel, who say to the Israeli people:

'there is no alternative to force', the peace forces must be able to give a convincing reply. True 'political courage' is required today for the PLO to confront the *de facto* alliance between the moderate Arab regimes and the Israeli government with the alliance of peoples, true internationalism.

After the elimination of the PLO from Beirut, after the scattering of its military forces, and after the betrayal of the Arab states, the time for outbidding is over. But is the time for the alliance between the PLO and the Israeli peace forces about to begin at last? Or will the goal of unity at any price once again take the place of a political line in the PLO? Will the organization once again opt to confine itself in a wait-and-see attitude that will avoid inflaming the contradictions? Then all the experiences will have served no useful purpose. The working 'reflexes' of the PLO will have shown themselves stronger than experience; and for many more years the Palestinian people will continue their long march marked by tragedies, martyrs and heroism. But at the end of the road will there be the promised land?

Notes

1. M. Rodinson, in *GRAPP* (Groupe de Recherches et d'Action pour le Règlement du Problème Palestinien), nos. 42, 43, 44, July 1977, March 1978.
2. Interview to *Le Monde*, 10 August 1982.

Appendixes

APPENDIX I: Members of the Central Committee of Fatah (1969–70) (derived from various sources)

Yasser Arafat (Abu Ammar)
Salah Khalaf (Abu Iyad)
Khalil al-Wazir (Abu Jihad)
Farouq Kaddoumi (Abu Lutuf)
Khalid al-Hassan (Abu Said)
Mamduh Sabri Saydam (Abu Sabri)
Walid Ahmad Nimr (Abu Ali Iyad)
Kamal Adwan
Mahmud Abbas (Abu Mazen)
Muhammad al-Najjar (Abu Yusif)

Mamduh Sabri Saydam and Walid Ahmad Nimr were both military leaders of Fatah; the former died in 1971, the latter was killed in Jordan during the events of 1970–71.

Kamal Adwan and Muhammad al-Najjar were killed in Beirut in 1973 during an Israeli commando raid.

The other six were still members of the central committee of Fatah in 1984.

APPENDIX II: Relations between the Leaders of Fatah in Gaza and Egypt before 1957

Yasser Arafat (Abu Ammar): spent his youth in Gaza; his family took refuge there after 1948. He remained there until December 1950, when he left for Cairo. When in the Egyptian army, he took part in the 1956 campaign, but in Port Said.

Salah Khalaf (Abu Iyad): his father was an official in Gaza, where his family took refuge in 1948. He remained there until 1951, then left to pursue his studies in Cairo. He took part in civil defence during the Suez war and in providing material assistance to the Resistance in Gaza in 1956–57. In 1957 he returned to Gaza as a teacher.

Khalil al-Wazir (*Abu Jihad*): his family took refuge in Gaza in 1948. He became active in politics from a very early age and was the leader of the Palestine Students' Union in Gaza. Arrested in 1954 by the Egyptian authorities after a raid against Israel, he was released. He was responsible for the biggest raid against Israel in 1955, after which the Israelis carried out the large-scale reprisal operation of 28 February 1955.

Farouq Kaddoumi (*Abu Lutuf*): after 1948, he went to Nablus, and then to Saudi Arabia. He studied in Cairo between 1954 and 1958.

Khalid al-Hassan (*Abu Said*): a refugee in Syria, he had no contact with either Gaza or Egypt. He met the other Fatah leaders in Kuwait.

Mamduh Sabri Saydam (Abu Sabri): Born in 1935, a refugee in Gaza after 1947.

Walid Ahmad Nimr (*Abu Ali Iyad*): born in the West Bank, he left to teach in Saudi Arabia for eight years until 1962, when he went to Algeria.

Kamal Adwan: born in the Gaza Strip, he organized the first cells of the Resistance against the Israeli occupation in 1956.

Mahmud Abbas (*Abu Mazen*): no information available, except that he was in Egypt in 1956–57.

Muhammad al-Najjar (*Abu Yusif*): born in 1931; he took refuge in Gaza in 1948 and was a teacher there until 1956. He became involved in political activity very early and joined the Muslim Brothers in 1951. He was imprisoned for four months in 1954. He organized a demonstration with the slogan 'The Arab regimes have signed a settlement plan in ink, we shall erase it in blood', after which he was arrested in March 1955 and spent more than a year in prison. He left Gaza in 1956 after the Suez events.

APPENDIX III: Dates and Venues of Palestine National Councils (1964–1983)

First: 28 May – 2 June 1964, Jerusalem
Second: 31 May – 4 June 1965, Cairo.
Third: 20 May – 24 May 1966, Gaza.
Fourth: 10 July – 17 July 1968, Cairo.
Fifth: 1 February – 4 February 1969, Cairo.
Sixth: 1 September – 6 September 1969, Cairo.
Seventh: 30 May – 4 June 1970, Cairo.
Extraordinary
  session: 27 August – 28 August 1970, Amman.
Eighth: 28 February – 5 March 1971, Cairo.
Ninth: 7 July – 13 July 1971, Cairo.
Tenth: 11 April – 12 April 1972, Cairo.
Eleventh: 6 January – 12 January 1973, Cairo.

Twelfth:	1 June – 9 June 1974, Cairo
Thirteenth:	12 March – 20 March 1977, Cairo.
Fourteenth:	15 January – 23 January 1979, Damascus.
Fifteenth:	11 April – 19 April 1981, Damascus.
Sixteenth:	14 February – 22 February 1983, Algiers.
Seventeenth:	22 November – 28 November 1984, Amman.
Eighteenth:	20 April – 26 April 1987, Algiers.

APPENDIX IV: The Organizations Members of the PLO (1987)

Fatah

This is the oldest of the Palestinian Resistance organizations. The idea of creating it came from Yasser Arafat and his friends who had the experience in Cairo in the 1950s of independent activism through the Palestine Students' Union. But it was in 1959, when Yasser Arafat, Salah Khalaf, Farouq Kaddoumi, Khalil al-Wazir and Khalid al-Hassan were in Kuwait, that Fatah was formed.

From its very foundation, Fatah came out against the dominant theory of the time, pan-Arabism, whether in its Nasserite or Ba'thist form. Fatah saw the first task as liberating Palestine, not waiting first for the unity of the Arab world. The victory of the Algerian revolution in 1962 confirmed for the Fatah leaders the need for armed struggle. While Nasser set up the PLO in 1964 and made it into an instrument in his hands, Fatah was preparing for people's war. The first armed action against Israel took place on 1 January 1965; this day became the anniversary of the Palestinian Resistance. But it was only after June 1967 that Fatah became prominent on the Palestinian and Arab stage; the battle of Karameh in March 1968, between the Israeli army and Fatah men based in Jordan, considerably enhanced Arafat's prestige. At the beginning of 1969 he became chairman of the executive committee of the PLO. From this date, the history of Fatah tends to merge with that of the PLO, which it controlled more and more tightly.

The emergence of a dissident movement in May 1983, led by two members of the central committee, Nimr Saleh (Abu Saleh) and Samih Kuweyk (Qadri), and by several militant cadres, notably Abu Musa, threatened the Organization's unity for a while. But the new faction's extremism and their complete alignment with Syria soon led to their isolation. By 1986, the dissidents, now divided amongst themselves, were no longer a substantial force.

Fatah has held four congresses: a constituent congress in October 1959; the second congress in 1965; the third congress in October 1968; the fourth congress in May 1980. In between congresses the organization is run by a revolutionary council of some 40 members: effective power is in the hands of the central committee which has 15 members. Its main leaders are Yasser Arafat, Khalil al-Wazir, Salah Khalaf (Abu Iyad) and Farouq Kaddoumi.

Fatah's armed wing, called al-Assifa [the Tempest], forms the bulk of the

PLO's military potential; it is headed by a 'general command' chaired by Yasser Arafat, whose deputy is Khalil al-Wazir; before the evacuation of Beirut in August 1982, Fatah was estimated to have 15–20,000 troops. In 1985–86 several thousand fighters returned to Lebanon.

The Popular Front for the Liberation of Palestine (PFLP)

The PFLP emerged from the Arab Nationalist Movement (ANM), an organization set up in the 1950s which very soon identified itself with Nasserism. The PFLP was founded in December 1967; it laid stress on people's war but also, and above all, on the Arab dimension of the struggle. It was the PFLP that advanced the slogan, 'The road to the liberation of Palestine goes through Amman' and pushed the PLO into confrontation with the Jordanian regime in 1970.

The PFLP, Fatah's main rival, has opposed the latter on most political issues: the attitude to the Arab regimes, the need for political and diplomatic action and, after October 1973, the question of a 'mini-state'. In 1974 the PFLP set up the Rejection Front, which attempted to oppose the PLO's participation in any negotiated settlement, particularly through the Geneva Conference. Opposition to the Camp David agreements reunited the PLO but profound differences still remained between the PFLP and Fatah; the PFLP, which had walked out of the executive committee of the PLO, rejoined it in 1981.

The PFLP proclaims itself a Marxist organization and seeks to create a 'revolutionary party'. It became well-known through its actions outside the occupied territories, particularly aeroplane hijackings; it was only in 1972 that it decided to suspend this form of action.

Following the signature of the agreement between Arafat and King Hussein in February 1985, the PFLP set up the Palestinian National Salvation Front (PNSF) in Damascus to denounce Fatah's 'capitulation' and to demand Arafat's resignation. The front regroups the PFLP-GC, the Fatah dissidents, the PPSF and Sai'qa. The PFLP broke with the PNSF over the holding of the 18th PNC meeting in Algeria in April 1987.

The PFLP has held four congresses: the first in August 1968, the second in February 1969, the third in March 1972 and the fourth in April 1981.

Its main leader is George Habash, who commands great respect in every Palestinian organization.

The Popular Democratic Front for the Liberation of Palestine (PDFLP) (subsequently DFLP)

This organization was born out of a leftist breakaway from the PFLP, in February 1969. It changed its name to Democratic Front for the Liberation of Palestine (DFLP) in August 1974. It proclaims itself Marxist–Leninist, denounces the petty bourgeois Arab regimes and calls for the strengthening of co-operation between the PLO and the socialist countries (especially after 1971). The DFLP became well-known as a result of a series of political initiatives, particularly towards the Israelis. It was this organization that denounced most clearly 'chauvinistic' slogans such as: 'Drive the Jews into the sea'. In 1970 it opened a dialogue with the extreme left-wing Israeli organization Matzpen. Finally, from 1973 onwards, it was, with Fatah, one of the strongest defenders of the idea of a Palestinian mini-state. Between 1973 and 1977 its alliance with Fatah and Sa'iqa made it possible to impose this slogan on the PLO. After 1977, the date of Sadat's visit to Jerusalem, the DFLP moved away from Fatah which it criticized for its compromises with 'Arab reaction'.

Since 1982, the DFLP has been in the 'centre' of the Palestinian spectrum. While condemning the Jordan-Palestinian agreement, it does not endorse the ultra-leftism of the PFLP or the latter's alignment with Damascus. The DFLP played an active part during the 18th PNC meeting.

The DFLP has held only two congresses: the first in August 1968 (before the split), the second in May 1981. This latter one came out in favour of the establishment of a Palestinian Communist Party. Its main leaders are Nayef Hawatmeh, the secretary-general, and Yasser Abd al-Rabbo, assistant secretary-general.

Sa'iqa

Sa'iqa was set up by the Ba'thist leaders in Damascus after the June 1967 war; it has quite large military forces and its influence within the PLO is closely tied to the role of Syria in the Middle East conflict. At the time of the war in Lebanon in 1975-76, it came out wholeheartedly for Damascus and against the Palestinian Resistance. Sai'qa refused to attend the 18th PNC in Algiers.

The Arab Liberation Front (ALF)

The ALF is the Iraqi counterpart of Sa'iqa. Totally under the thumb of the Ba'thist leaders in Baghdad. The ALF — formed in April 1969 — is however much less important than its Syrian counterpart. In 1987, it supported Arafat.

The Popular Front for the Liberation of Palestine-General Command (PFLP-GC)

The PFLP-GC is a small group, founded by Ahmad Jibril, which left the PFLP at the end of 1968 a few months after joining it. Although one of the oldest Palestinian organizations, it does not have much influence. It made its mark with suicide operations against Israel in 1974-75. Under Syrian and Lebanese influence, it took an ambiguous stand during the events in Lebanon in 1975-76, which led to an anti-Syrian breakaway from it, the Palestine Liberation Front (PLF). The PFLP-GC is in the vanguard of the Palestinian rejectionists. In 1987, it spearheaded the opposition to Arafat.

The Palestine Liberation Front (PLF)

The PLF, a splinter group of the PLFP-GC, has itself undergone several splits since its formation in 1977. Its main wing, led by Abu Abbas, supports

Yasser Arafat; another faction is close to the PFLP. These two factions officially reunited in 1987.

The Palestinian Popular Struggle Front (PPSF)
A little organization without any great influence started in 1968, the PPSF is part of the Palestinian National Salvation Front and refused to attend the 18th PNC in Algiers.

As well as these eight 'armed' organizations, there is the Palestinian Communist Party. Started in February 1982 as an extension of the activities of the Jordanian Communist Party, its main base is in the West Bank where it exercises considerable influence, especially over the trade union movement. During the 1984–86 PLO split, it stood in the centre of the spectrum between Arafat and the PNSF. Since the 18th PNC, it has elected members to the Executive Committee. It is the only organization which openly demands a Palestinian state in the West Bank and Gaza, alongside Israel.

APPENDIX V: Members of the Executive Committee elected at the 18th Palestine National Council

Yasser Arafat (Fatah), President
Farouq Kaddumi (Fatah)
Mahmud Abbas (Fatah)
Yasser Abd al-Rabbo (Democratic Front for the Liberation of Palestine, DFLP)
Abu Ali Mustapha (Popular Front for the Liberation of Palestine, PFLP)
Ahmad al-Rahim (Arab Liberation Front, ALF)
Suleiman al-Najjab (Palestinian Communist Party, PCP)
Muhammed Abbas (Palestinian Liberation Front, PLF)
Jamal al-Surani (Independent)
Abd al-Razzaq al-Yahya (Independent)
Ilyas Khuri (Independent)
Muhammed Milhem (Independent)
Abdallah Hurani (Independent)
Mahmud Darwish (Independent)
Jawid al-Ghisayan (Independent)

Bibliography

Bibliographical Abbreviations

ARR	Arab Report and Record
ASPQ	Annual Survey of the Palestine Question (in Arabic)
FMA	Fiches du Monde Arabe
IDP	International Documents on Palestine
JPS	Journal of Palestine Studies
MECS	Middle East Contemporary Survey
MEJ	Middle East Journal
MER	Middle East Record
PAD	Palestine Arab Documents (in Arabic)
SWB	Summary of World Broadcasts (BBC)

Primary Sources

For the bibliography the main source used is:

Khalidi, W. and J. Khaddouri, *Palestine and the Arab-Israeli Conflict: An annotated bibliography*, Beirut, Institute for Palestine Studies, 1974, xxi + 736p.

and also:

La Question de Palestine, n.p., United Nations, 1974.

For sources in the occupied territories, see:

Ghis, Hussein, *Al-bibliughrafiya al-filastiniya fil-watan 1967-1980* [Palestinian bibliography in the homeland], Jerusalem, Society of Arab Studies, 1981.

I. Documents, Collections of Documents, Memoirs and Statements by Palestinian Organizations and Leaders

Collections of documents

Al-wathaiq al'arabiya al-filastiniya [Palestine Arab Documents], Beirut, Institute for Palestine Studies. Published annually from 1965.

International Documents on Palestine, Beirut, Institute for Palestine Studies. Published annually since 1967.

Hamid, Rashid (ed.), *Muqararat al-majlis al-watani al-filastini 1964-1974*

[Resolutions of the PNCs 1964–1974], Beirut, PLO Research Centre, 1975.

Kadi, Leila S. (ed.), *Basic Political Documents of the Armed Palestinian Resistance Movement*, Beirut, PLO Research Centre, 1969.

Khader, Bichara and Naim Khader (eds.), *Textes de la révolution palestinienne 1968–1974*, Paris, Sindbad, 1975.

The Resistance of the Western Bank of Jordan to Israeli Occupation 1967, Beirut, Institute for Palestine Studies, 1967.

Fatah documents

Abu Hatem, interview with *Nouvelle Revue Socialiste*, no. 5, 1974.

Abu Iyad, *Palestinien sans patrie*, Paris, Fayolle, 1968, 361 pp. (Translated into English by L.B. Koseoglu as *My Home, My Land: A Narrative of the Palestinian Struggle*, New York, Times Books, 1981.)

Arafat, Yasser, *Khitab al-akh Abu Ammar fil-majlis al-watani al-filastini fi dawratihi al-thalitha ashr* [Speech by Yasser Afarat to the thirteenth session of the PNC], n.p., 1977.

———— Interviews: *Le Monde*, 21 February 1969, 12 November 1970, 7 January 1975, 21–22 August 1975; *L'Humanité*, 31 October 1970, 7 January 1975; *Time*, 16 July 1973.

El Fath dit non, Paris, supplement to *Fedayin*, 1970.

Fateh, English-language publication by Fatah, appearing irregularly in Damascus and later in Amman from 1969 to early 1971.

Fath, *La révolution palestinienne et les juifs*, Paris, Editions de Minuit, 1970.

Fath-Informations, published fortnightly in Paris in 1972 and 1973.

Hammami, Said, 'Making the First Step towards Peace in Palestine', *The Times*, 17 December 1973.

———— 'Une stratégie palestinienne de co-existence', *France-Palestine*, no. 51, supplement to *France-Pays Arabes*, 1975. (In English as 'A Palestinian Strategy for Co-existence', *New Outlook*, vol. 18, no. 3, March–April 1975.)

Sartawi, Issam, speech to the symposium 'Peace in the Middle East', held in Washington, 12 February 1977, mimeo.

Sha'ath, Nabil, 'Palestine of Tomorrow', *Fateh*, 23 March 1971.

PFLP documents

Al-badil al-thawri li machru' al-dawla al-filastiniya al-tasfawi [The revolutionary alternative to the plan to liquidate the Palestinian state], n.p., 1974.

'Ala tariq al-thawra al-filastiniya [On the road to the Palestinian revolution], Beirut, Dar al-Talia, 1970.

Muhimat al-marhala al-jadida [The tasks of the new phase], political report to the third congress of the PFLP (1972), n.p., 1975.

Habash, George, interview with *Le Monde*, 6 February 1975.

Issa, Mahmoud, *Je suis un fedayin*, Paris, Stock Témoigner, 1976.

Khaled, Leila, *Mon peuple vivra*, Paris, Gallimard, 1973.

PDFLP documents

Adwa' min fikr al-jabha al-dimuqratiya al-sha'biya li tahrir filastin hawla al-muhimat al-rahina lil-thawra al-filastiniya [Aspects of the thought of the PDFLP on the present tasks of the Palestinian Resistance], n.p., n.d.

Hawatmeh, Nayef, *Hawla azma haraka al-muqawana al-filastiniya* [On the crisis in the Palestinian Resistance movement], Beirut, Dar al-Talia, 1969.

———— 'Pour une solution démocratique aux problèmes palestinien et israélien', Tribune internationale of *Le Monde*, 21 January 1970.

Premier rapport sur les derniers développements de la situation dans notre région et perspectives sur l'évolution future du Moyen-Orient, Beirut, PDFLP International Relations Office, 28 January 1977, mimeo.

Programme politique du F.D.P.L.P., n.p., 1975.

PLO documents and various

al-Anwar, 8, 15 and 22 March 1970. Debate between various Palestinian Resistance leaders on the democratic state.

'Communiqué du commandement national du parti Ba'th sur la question palestinienne', 5 March 1964, *Orient*, 1st quarter, 1964.

'Communiqué publié à l'issue des travaux du Conseil Central de l'O.L.P.', 14 December 1976, *Documents d'Actualité Internationale*, no. 6, 1977.

'Letter to the Executive Committee of the P.L.O. from the Palestinian National Front in the occupied territory', 1 December 1973, *JPS*, no. 11, spring 1974.

Palestinian Leaders Discuss the New Challenges for the Resistance, Beirut, PLO Research Centre, 1974.

Communist documents

Al-maham al-matruha amam al-hizb al-shiyu'i al-urduni fil-marhala al-rahina [The tasks of the Jordanian Communist Party in the present phase], n.p., May 1974.

Ashhab, Naim, 'La crise de la résistance palestinienne', *Nouvelle Revue Internationale*, June 1972.

———— 'Le problème palestinien', *Nouvelle Revue Internationale*, April 1974.

Les communistes et la question palestinienne, n.p., n.d.

Information Bulletin, monthly bulletin of the Israeli Communist Party, Haifa, 1967–77.

Salem, A., 'Le Parti poursuit son action en Jordanie', *Nouvelle Revue Internationale*, January 1968.

Touma, Emile, 'Palestinian Arabs in Israel and Israeli Jews', *JPS*, no. 22, winter 1977.

II. Interviews

Dr Issam Sartawi, member of the PNC, assassinated in Portugal in April 1983; Paris, December 1980, and March 1981.

Dr Ahmad Hamzeh, West Bank figure; Paris, April 1981.

Aziz Shihada, lawyer in Ramallah; in the occupied territories, October 1981.

Abu Shalbaya, journalist in Jerusalem; in the occupied territories, October 1981.

Dr Emile Touma, member of the politbureau of the Israeli Communist Party; Haifa, October 1981.

Abu Ja'far (Abd al-Latif Abu Hijle), deputy head of the political department of the PLO; Paris, October 1981.

Abu Adnan (Abd al-Karim Hamad), member of the politbureau of the PDFLP; Paris, December 1981.

Abu Ali Mustapha, assistant secretary-general of the PFLP; Beirut, May 1982.

Abu Hatem (Muhammad Abu Mayzar), offical responsible for international affairs of Fatah, Beirut, May 1982.

Arabi Awad, member of the PNC; Beirut, May 1982.

Newspapers, journals, annuals

Arab Report and Record, London, fortnightly.

The Arabs under Israeli Occupation, Beirut, Institute for Palestine Studies, annually.

Fiches du Monde Arabe, Beirut.

Israël et Palestine, Paris, monthly, from 1971.

Journal of Palestine Studies, Beirut, quarterly from 1971.

Al-kitab al-sanawi lil-qadiya al-filastiniya [Annual survey of the Palestine question], Beirut, Institute for Palestine Studies, annually 1968–79.

Middle East Contemporary Survey, Tel Aviv, Shiloah, annually 1976–77.

Middle East Record, Tel Aviv, Shiloah Center, annually 1967–70.

Le Monde, Paris.

Le Monde Diplomatique, Paris.

The New Middle East, London, monthly 1968–73.

ONU Chronique, Information Department of the UN, monthly.

Palestinian Statistical Abstract, Damascus, Palestine National Fund, annually from 1979.

Les résolutions des Nations Unies sur la Palestine et le conflit israélo-arabe, Beirut, Institute for Palestine Studies. One volume for 1947–74, then annually.

Summary of World Broadcasts (BBC), London.

Secondary sources

General

Abdel-Malek, Anouar (ed.), *La pensée politique arabe contemporaine*, Paris, Seuil, 1970.

Carré, Olivier, 'Evolution de la pensée politique arabe au Proche-Orient depuis 1967', *Revue Française des Sciences Politiques*, no. 5, 1973.

Colombe, Marcel, *Orient arabe et non-engagement*, Paris, Publications Orientales de France, 1973, 2 vols.

Conférence internationale des Partis communistes et ouvriers Moscou 1969, Prague, Editions Paix et Socialisme, 1969.

Gramsci dans le texte, Paris, Editions Sociales, 1975.

Kissinger, Henry, *A la Maison Blanche 1968–1973*, Paris, Fayard, 1979, 2 vols.

———— *Les années orageuses*, Paris, Fayard, 1982, vol. I.

Lenin, V.I., *Collected Works*, vol. 20 (December 1913–August 1914), Moscow,

Progress Publishers, 1964.

Rodinson, Maxime, *peuple juif ou problème juif?*, Paris, Maspero, 1981.

The Arab–Israeli conflict

Carré, Olivier, *Proche-Orient entre le guerre et la paix*, Paris, EPI, 1970.

Le conflit israélo-arabe*, special issue of *Les Temps Modernes*, no. 253 bis, 1967.

Couland, Jacques, *Israël et le Proche Orient arabe*, Paris, Editions Sociales, 1969.

Curiel, Henri, *Pour une paix juste au Proche-Orient*, Paris, Association Henri Curiel, 1979.

————— 'Trois inédits sur le conflit israélo-arabe et le droit imprescriptible des peuples arabes et juif en Palestine à une existence nationale', *Peuples Méditerranéens*, no. 7, April–June 1979) (introduced by D. Fawzi).

Gilbert, Martin, *The Arab–Israeli Conflict: its history in maps*, 3rd edn, London, Weidenfeld and Nicolson, 1979.

Harkabi, Y., *Arab Attitudes to Israel*, London, Vallentine, Mitchell, 1972.

Kadi, Leila S., *Arab–Israeli conflict: the peaceful proposals 1948–1972*, Beirut, PLO Research Centre, 1973.

Laqueur, Walter (ed.), *The Israel–Arab Reader: a documentary history of the Middle East conflict*, London, Penguin, 1970, 591p.

Mandel, Neville J., *The Arabs and Zionism before World War I*, London, University of California Press, 1980, xxiv + 258p.

Rabinovich, I. and H. Shaker (eds), *From June to October: The Middle East between 1967 and 1973*, New Brunswick, N.J., Transaction Books, 1978 xxiii + 419p.

Rodinson, Maxime, *Israël et le refus arabe*, Paris, Seuil, 1968.

Rondot, Philippe, *Le Proche-Orient à la recherche de la paix 1973–1982*, Paris, PUF, 1982.

Rouleau, Eric, 'Israël: le ghetto des vainqueurs', *Le Monde*, 2, 3, 4, 5, 6, 7 July 1969.

Palestine in the Arab and International context

L'Afrique Noire et le Moyen-Orient*, Paris, Documentation Française, Problèmes Politiques et Sociaux, no. 139–40.

Behbehani, Hashim S.H., *China's Foreign Policy in the Arab World, 1955–1975: Three Cases Studies*, London, Kegan Paul International, 1981.

Chagnollaud, Jean-Paul, *Maghreb et Palestine*, Paris, Sinbad, 1977, 259p.

Colombe, Marcel, 'Les problèmes de "d'entité palestinienne"dans les relations interarabes', *Orient*, Paris, 1st quarter, 1964.

Confino, M. and S. Shamir, (eds.), *The USSR and the Middle East*, Jerusalem, Israel University Press, 1973, xxii + 441p.

Dawisha, Adeed I., *Syria and the Lebanese Crisis*, New York, St Martin's Press, 1980, xii + 208p.

Golan, Galia, *The Soviet Union and the PLO*, London, International Institute for Strategic Studies, Adelphi Papers no. 131, 1976.

————— *The Soviet Union and the PLO: An Uneasy Alliance*, New York, Praeger, 1980, xii + 289p.

Heikal, Mohammed, *The Sphinx and the Commissar*, New York, Harper and Row, 1978.

Kazziha, Walid W., *Palestine in the Arab Dilemma*, London, Croom Helm, 1979.

Khalidi, Walid, *Conflict and Violence in Lebanon: Confrontation in the Middle East*, Cambridge, Mass., Harvard University Center for International Affairs, 1980.

Quandt, William B., *Decade of Decisions: American Policy towards the Arab-Israeli Conflict, 1967-1976*, Berkeley and Los Angeles, University of California Press, 1977, vii + 313p.

Rubin, Barry, *The Arab States and the Palestine Conflict*, New York, Syracuse University Press, 1981, xvii + 298p.

Shadid, Mohamed K., *The United States and the Palestinians*, London, Croom Helm, 1981.

The Palestinian National Movement

Abu Lughod, I. (ed.), *The Transformation of Palestine*, Evanston, Northwestern University Press, 1971, xv + 522p.

Amos II, John W., *Palestinian Resistance: Organisation of a Nationalist Movement*, New York, Pergamon Press, 1980.

Asmar, Fouzi al, *To be an Arab in Israel*, London, Francis Pinter, 1975.

Avineri, Shlomo (ed.), *Israel and the Palestinians*, New York, St Martin's Press, 1971.

Baron, Xavier, *Les Palestiniens, un peuple*, Paris, le Sycomore, 1977.

Bertelsen, Judy, *The Palestinian Arabs: a Non-state Nation System Analysis*, London, Sage Publications, 1976.

Budeiri, Musa, *The Palestinian Communist Party 1919-1948, Arabs and Jews in the Struggle for Internationalism*, London, Ithaca Press, 1979.

Carré, Olivier, *L'idéologie palestinienne de résistance*, Paris, Armand Colin and Fondation Nationale des Sciences Politiques, 1972.

———— 'Les Palestiniens à Genève?', *Maghreb-Machrek*, no. 64, July–August 1974.

———— *Septembre Noir: refus arabe de la résistance palestinienne*, Brussels, Editions Complexes, 1980.

Chaliand, Gerard, *La résistance palestinienne*, Paris, Seuil, 1970.

———— 'Le double combat du F.P.L.P.', *Le Monde Diplomatique*, July 1970.

Cobban, Helena, *The PLO: People, Power and Politics*, London, Cambridge University Press, 1984, London xii + 305p.

Cooley, John K., *Green March, Black September: The Story of the Palestinian Arabs*, London, Frank Cass, 1973.

Curiel, Henri, 'Conférence au Grand Orient de France', 8 June 1977, mimeo.

Denoyan, Gilbert, *El Fath parle: Les Palestiniens contre Israël*, Paris, Albin Michel, 1970.

El-Rayyes, Riad and Dunia Nahas, *Guerrillas for Palestine: A Study of the Commando Organisations*, Beirut, An-Nahar Press Service, 1974.

Flores, A., 'The Arab C.P.s [Communist Parties] and the Palestine Question', *Khamsin*, no. 7.

Gresh, Alain, 'Informations sur les centres de recherches palestiniens', *Recherches Internationales*, no. 2, 3rd quarter, 1981.

———— 'Etat et société palestinienne: une deuxième vague d'études', *La Pensée*, no. 228, July–August 1982.

Harkabi, Yehoshafat, *Fedayeen action and Arab strategy*, London, International Institute for Strategic Studies, Adelphi Papers no 53, December 1968.

———— *Palestine et Israël*, Geneva, Editions de l'Avenir, 1972.

———— 'The Palestinians in the fifties and their awakening as reflected in their literature', *Palestinian Arab Politics*, Jerusalem, Academic Press, 1975.

Hudson, Michael, 'The Palestinian Arab Resistance Movement: Its significance in the Middle East Crisis', *Middle East Journal*, summer 1969.

Jureidini, Paul and William Hazen, *The Palestinian Movement in Politics*, Lexington, Mass., D.C. Heath, 1976.

Kazziha, Walid W., *Revolutionary Transformation in the Arab World*, London, Croom Helm, 1975.

Khalidi, Walid, 'Thinking the Unthinkable: a Sovereign Palestinian state', *Foreign Affairs*, July 1978.

Lentz, Jean-Jacques, 'Les Palestiniens: de la Nation à l'Etat?', *Etudes*, April 1978.

Migdal, Joel S. (ed.), *Palestinian Society and Politics*, Princeton, Princeton University Press, 1980.

Mishal, Shaul, *West Bank/East Bank: the Palestinians in Jordan, 1949-1967*, London, Yale University Press, 1978.

Mury, Gilbert, *Septembre Noir*, Paris, Sinbad, 1972, 171p.

Muslih, M.Y., 'Moderates and Rejectionists within the PLO', *Middle East Journal*, no. 30(2), Spring 1976.

Nakhleh, K. and E. Zureik (eds.), *The Sociology of the Palestinians*, London, Croom Helm, 1980, 238p.

Nissam, M., 'PLO Moderates', *The Jerusalem Quarterly*, no. 1, 1976.

O'Neill, Bard E., *Armed Struggle in Palestine: an Analysis of the Palestinian Guerilla Movement*, Boulder, Col., Westview Press, 1978, xiii + 320p.

The Palestinians: People, History, Politics, collective work, New Brunswick, N.J., Transaction Books x + 277p.

Les palestiniens et la crise israélo-arabe, collective work, Paris, Editions Sociales, 1974.

Plasciv, Avi, *The Palestinian Refugees in Jordan 1948-1957*, London, Frank Cass, 1981.

———— *A Palestinian State? Examining the Alternatives*, London, International Institute for Strategic Studies, Adelphi Papers, no. 163, 1981.

Porath, Yehoshua, *The Emergence of the Palestinian Arab National Movement 1918-1929*, London, Frank Cass, 1974, ix + 406p.

———— *The Palestinian Arab National movement 1919-1939: From Riots to Rebellion*, London, Frank Cass, 1977, xii + 474p.

Poupard, Olivier, 'La révolution palestinienne et l'Etat palestinien', *Politique Etrangère*, no. 5, 1975.

Pour la Palestine (Actes de la première conférence mondiale des Chrétiens pour la Palestine, Beyrouth 1970), Paris, Témoignage Chrétien, 1972.

Quandt, William B. *et al.*, *The Politics of Palestinian Nationalism*, University of California Press, 1973.

Rouleau, Eric, 'Le peuple palestinien: histoire d'une conscience nationale', *Le*

Monde Diplomatique, January 1975.

Said, Edward W., *The Question of Palestine*, London, Routledge and Kegan Paul, 1980.

Sayigh, Rosemary, *Palestinians: from Peasants to Revolutionaries,* London, Zed Press, 1979.

Sharabi, Hisham, 'Palestine Guerillas: their Credibility and Effectiveness', *Middle East Forum*, vol. XLVI, nos. 2 and 3, Beirut, 1970.

Yaari, Ehud, 'Al Fath's Political Thinking', *New Outlook*, November–Decem-

Yodfat, A.Y. and Y. Arnon-Ohanna, *PLO Strategy and Tactics*, London, Croom Helm, 1981, ix + 255p.

Yodfat, A.Y. and Y. Arnon-Ohanna, *Plo Strategy and Tactics*, London, Croom Helm, 1981, ix.

The West Bank and Gaza; the Israeli occupation

Brown, Neville, 'L'idée d'abandonner la rive occidentale du Jourdain gagne du terrain dans le royaume hachemite', *Le Monde Diplomatique*, September 1972.

Duclos, Louis-Jean, 'Description de l'occupation militaire israëlienne', *Politique Etrangère*, no. 4, 1972.

Hassan Bin Talal, *Palestinian Self-determination, a Study of the West Bank and the Gaza Strip*, London, Quartet Books, 1981.

Kapeliouk, Amnon, 'En Cisjordanie: les Israéliens ont misé sur les élections pour normaliser la situation', *Le Monde Diplomatique*, April 1972.

───── 'L'implantation des colonies israéliennes dans les territoires occupés crée des faits accomplis irréversibles', *Le Monde Diplomatique*, June 1972.

Khalifa, Sahar, *Chronique du figuier barbare*, Paris, Gallimard, 1978.

Langer, Felicia, *With my own Eyes: Israel and the Occupied Territories, 1967-1973*, London, Ithaca Press, 1975.

Lesch, Ann Mosley, 'Israeli Deportation of Palestinians from the West Bank and Gaza 1967–1970', *JPS*, no. 30, winter 1979.

───── *Political Perceptions of the Palestinians in the West Bank and the Gaza Strip*, Washington, D.C., The Middle East Institute, 1980.

Marsden, Eric, 'Naissance d'une nouvelle Jérusalem?', *Le Monde Diplomatique*, August 1972.

Marx, Emanuel, 'Changes in Arab Refugee Camps', *The Jerusalem Quarterly*, no. 8, summer 1978.

Sela, Abraham, 'The PLO, the West Bank and the Gaza Strip', *The Jerusalem Quarterly*, no. 8, summer 1978.

Sesser, Asher, 'Jordanian Influence in the West Bank', *The Jerusalem Quarterly*, no. 8, summer 1978.

The economic viability of a Palestinian State

Bull, Vivian A., *The West Bank: Is It Viable?*, London and Toronto, Lexington Books, 1975, xviii + 170p.

Kapeliouk, Amnon, 'Un Etat en Cisjordanie et Gaza serait-il économiquement viable?', *Le Monde*, 30 March 1977.

Khader, Bichara and Naim Khader, *Le peuple palestinien: ses potentialités humaines, économiques et scientifiques*, Louvain, Catholic University, 1980.

Nakhleh, Emile A., *The West Bank and Gaza: Towards the Making of a Palestinian State*, Washington, American Enterprise Institute, 1979.

———— (ed.), *A Palestinian Agenda for the West Bank and Gaza*, Washington, American Enterprise Institute, 1980.

Tuma, Elias H. and Haim Darin-Drabkin, *The Economic Case for Palestine*, London, Croom Helm, 1978.

Van Arkadie, Brian, *Benefit and Burdens: A Report on the West Bank and Gaza Strip Economies since 1967*, New York, Carnegie Endowment for International Peace, 1977.

Ward, R.J., Don Peretz and E.M. Wilson, *The Palestinian State: A Rational Approach*, 2nd edn, New York, Kennikot Press, 1977 (1st edn 1970).

Works in Arabic

Bsiso, Mu'in, *Dafatir Filastiniya* [Palestinian Notebooks], Beirut, Dar al-Farabi, 1978.

Hilal, Jamil, *Al-Dhaffa al-Gharbiya: al-tarkib al-ijtima'i wal-iqtisadi 1948–1967* [The West Bank: Social and Economic Structure], Beirut, PLO Research Centre, 1974.

Hourani, Faisal, *Al-fikr al-siyasi al-filastini 1964–1974* [Palestinian Political thought], Beirut, PLO Research Centre, 1981.

Namel, Hussein Aboul, *Qita' Ghaza: tatawurat iqtisadiya wa siyasiya wa ijtima'iya wa 'askariya, 1948–1967* [The Gaza Strip, economic, political, social and military development], Beirut, PLO Research Centre, 1979.

Sakhnini, I., 'Al-kiyan al-filastini 1964–1974' [The Palestinian entity], *Shu'un filastiniya*, no. 41–42, January 1975.

Shalbaya, M. Abu, *La salam bighayr dawla filastiniya hurra* [No peace without a free Palestinian state], Jerusalem, n.d. (1971?].

al-Sharif, Maher, *Al-shiyu'iya wal-mas'ala al-qawmiya al'arabiya fi filastin 1919–1948* [Communism and the Arab national question in Palestine], Beirut, PLO Research Centre, 1981.

Touma, E., *Juzur al-qadiya al-filastiniya* [The roots of the Palestinian problem], 2nd edn, Jerusalem, 1976.

Yasin, Abd al-Qadir, *Hizb shiyu'i thuhruhu ital ha'it: shihada tarikhiya 'an al-haraka al-shiyu'iya fi qita' Ghaza 1948–1967* [A Communist Party with its back to the wall: a historic eye-witness report on the Communist movement in Gaza], Beirut, Dar Ibn Khaldoun, 1978.

———— *Tajribat al-jabha al-wataniya fi qita' Ghaza* [The experience of the National Front in the Gaza Strip], Beirut, Dar Ibn Khaldoun, 1980.

Zayadin, Ya'koub, *Al-bidayat* [The beginnings], Beirut, Dar Ibn Khaldoun, 1980.

List of Abbreviations

ALF	Arab Liberation Front
ANM	Arab Nationalist Movement
CENTO	Central Treaty Organization
DFLP	Democratic Front for the Liberation of Palestine
EEC	European Economic Community
FLN	National Liberation Front (Algeria)
LCAO	Lebanese Organization for Communist Action
PDFLP	Popular Democratic Front for the Liberation of Palestine (became the DFLP in August 1974)
PDRY	People's Democratic Republic of Yemen
PFLP	Popular Front for the Liberation of Palestine
PFLP–GC	Popular Front for the Liberation of Palestine – General Command
PLA	Palestine Liberation Army
PLO	Palestine Liberation Organization
PNC	Palestine National Council
PNF	Palestine National Front
PPSF	Palestinian Popular Struggle Front
UAR	United Arab Republic (Union of Egypt and Syria, 1958–61)
UN	United Nations
UNIFIL	United Nations Interim Force in Lebanon
UNRWA	United Nations Relief Works Agency
US	United States of America
USSR	Union of Soviet Socialist Republics

Index